The Progression of the American Presidency

Bryan,

Thank you for all your support, encouragement & help during my time at E.C. The best to you & Sheila as you move forward in life

Jim

Brian,
Thank you for all
your support,
encouragement +
help during my E.C.
My time at E.C.
the best to you
Stella as you
move forward in
life

The Progression of the American Presidency

Individuals, Empire, and Change

By
Jim Twombly

palgrave
macmillan

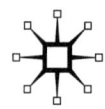

THE PROGRESSION OF THE AMERICAN PRESIDENCY
Copyright © Jim Twombly, 2013.

All rights reserved.

First published in 2013 by
PALGRAVE MACMILLAN®
in the United States—a division of St. Martin's Press LLC,
175 Fifth Avenue, New York, NY 10010.

Where this book is distributed in the UK, Europe and the rest of the world, this is by Palgrave Macmillan, a division of Macmillan Publishers Limited, registered in England, company number 785998, of Houndmills, Basingstoke, Hampshire RG21 6XS.

Palgrave Macmillan is the global academic imprint of the above companies and has companies and representatives throughout the world.

Palgrave® and Macmillan® are registered trademarks in the United States, the United Kingdom, Europe and other countries.

ISBN: 978–1–137–30053–9 (pbk); 978–1–137–30052–2

Library of Congress Cataloging-in-Publication Data is available from the Library of Congress.

A catalogue record of the book is available from the British Library.

Design by Newgen Imaging Systems (P) Ltd., Chennai, India.

First edition: February 2013

10 9 8 7 6 5 4 3 2 1

This work is dedicated to Doris and Fred, who nurtured my curiosity and my love of knowledge.

To Denise, who nurtures me every day. And to Annabelle, Henry, Kyra, Caleb, and Payton, hoping this helps to nurture the world they will inherit.

Contents

List of Illustrations ix

Acknowledgments xi

Part I Introduction and Background

1 Introduction 3
2 The Historical Context: How We View the Presidency 13

Part II Presidential Candidate Selection

3 Introduction: The Process in General 25
4 The System Changes Forever 33
5 Campaign Finance 45
6 The National Nominating Conventions: Are They Worth It and What's Next? 53
7 The General Election: So You've Got the Nomination, Now What? 67

Part III The Individual Presidency

8 You've Been Elected, Why Is This Guy Asking How You Feel All the Time? The Vice President and Succession 83
9 Presidential Character: Everybody Has One 91
10 The Presidential Advisory System: For Good or Ill, There Really Is One 105

Part IV The Presidency in Isolation

11 The President and the Bureaucracy 117
12 Presidential Decision Making 125

Part V The Presidency Interacting

13 The President and the Media — 139

14 Presidential Popularity: How Do I Approve of Thee? Let Gallup Count the Ways — 147

15 The President and Congress — 153

16 The President and the Judiciary — 167

17 The President and Policymaking: Domestic, Economic, and Foreign — 181

Part VI Conclusion

18 Hope and Change and the Future of the Presidency — 201

Notes — 211
Bibliography — 231
Index — 247

Illustrations

Figures

9.1	Barber's personality matrix	95
9.2	Sample of more recent presidents in Barber's personality matrix	97
10.1	Hub-and-spoke organizational style	107
10.2	Iron Triangle	111
10.3	Double-Sided or Folded Triangle	111

Tables

1.1	Examples of presidential powers checked by powers of other branches	6
15.1	Barbara Hinckely's veto patterns	161

Acknowledgments

While the actual writing of this work took about two and a half years, it derives from the evolved lecture material from about a quarter century of teaching the American Presidency. It is fitting then to acknowledge the many students who have sat through all of those classes over the years, whether they attended Stony Brook University, the University at Buffalo, or Elmira College. The most recent group from Elmira College in Winter Term 2012 should be acknowledged for their helpful comments on the early draft of the manuscript—sorry that you folks had to be the guinea pigs, but your patience and help have made this a better product.

I wish to thank a number of recent students more specifically for their help in shaping this manuscript. Sarah Burr, Jeremy Gray, and Kat Slye all contributed well beyond their roles as students. Sarah's skill as a writer was most helpful in keeping me honest with respect to the writing to make the text more accessible for undergraduate readers. The same is true of the help provided by Jeremy and Kat. Both of them also worked as undergraduate research assistants, not only keeping my writing from getting too out of reach, but also providing essential help in tracking down references and sometimes obscure quotes. Kat, in particular, was here for the heaviest lift as I sought to have a draft ready for use in my Winter 2012 American Presidency class. I also thank Margaret Feldman for her assistance in compiling the index for this work.

Naturally, the right environment is necessary for any such project and I must acknowledge the assistance and encouragement of the various deans of the faculty at Elmira College—Brian Reddick, Peter Viscusi, and especially Stephen Coleman. They provided the work-study money to pay Jeremy and Kat and helped arrange a large block of time to get huge chunks of writing done. The two executive secretaries from the dean's office were also great facilitators of help and encouragement—thank you Sue Carpenter and Darlene Wilson—and thank-you as well to Hollie Snyder who was always encouraging to the project. And, thanks to Andrea Rosati for her guidance on Chapter 9.

A number of my closest colleagues at Elmira College (and some from bygone days at Buffalo and Stony Brook) were most encouraging as I went along. At the risk of forgetting anyone, I'll leave it as a blanket thank-you. You all know who are you are and how much your encouragement meant as I worked to complete this project and as I awaited the always-stressful conclusion of the tenure process.

I also thank Matthew Kopel at Palgrave Macmillan who saw something in my draft that he thought was worthy. The process of trying to sell a little bit of yourself, as all writers, artists, and politicians do, is a tough one with many injuries to one's ego. Matthew was enthusiastic from the very beginning and the turnaround time still has my head spinning. His assistants and staff have been helpful with any and all questions and the two of them have been very understanding about all the concerns a first time author might have.

Last, but by no means least, I must acknowledge the encouragement, patience, and assistance of my now—gosh it seems like yesterday—longtime partner, Denise King. Denise not only sacrificed access to her partner and a social life, but she also listened patiently to all my venting; she was my first and last editor. In short, I doubt this project would have ever gotten this far without her help and encouragement—thank you Denise.

Part I

Introduction and Background

Chapter 1

Introduction

The presidency is unquestionably the central institution in the American government. The president and vice president are the only two officials elected by the nation as a whole. The media focuses attention on the office and person as well as his or her friends, family, and advisers. There is not as much attention paid to substantive activities, such as policy and governance. We as a nation look to the president for leadership.

This makes the American presidency a highly individualistic office and institution. The individuals elected to it or who ascend to the office very much determine the shape and functioning of the second branch of government. These individuals influence the parameters of the office for those who follow. The overall theme of this work will be the effects that individuals who occupy the office of president have on the institution—for both them and their successors.

Background and Constitutional Roots

The current institution of the American presidency has developed predominantly since the 1930s. The look, the duties, and the behavior we attribute to American presidents is not what one might expect from a reading of the Constitution or of the accounts of those who met in Philadelphia in 1787. The Framers were ambivalent toward the office of president and the duties and powers that should be assigned to it. Naturally, after having just fought a war for independence against what they had felt was a tyrannical monarch, the delegates to the Constitutional Convention were leery of a singular executive office with vast powers. As a result, the Constitution says little about the scope of the presidency as a key concern on the one hand, and, on the other hand, the powers for the legislative branch, while being sufficiently vague to allow room for future adaptability, are rather well laid out.

The Articles of Confederation, the first document detailing the structure, duties, and powers of the government, delineated no real executive power. The executive was viewed predominantly as a chief administrator whose responsibility was to ensure the day-to-day functioning of government. All real national governmental power rested with the Congress. Soon after the adoption of the articles, however, it became clear that the new nation would have some difficulty functioning, perhaps even surviving, if some stronger powers were not ceded to the central government. Under the Articles of Confederation, most power really was left to the states. This set of circumstances led to competing policies on interstate trade, the minting of money, and the ability to quell public disturbances (e.g., Shays's Rebellion).

This early view of federalism made arbitration between states and central coordination of activity difficult, to say the least. Many states would coin their own money and impose tariffs on goods crossing their borders from other states. Voluntary contribution of revenue by the states to the central government made national budgeting often unsteady and filled with the unexpected. Such uncertainty in the revenue process also made it difficult for the new nation to repay debts it incurred during the war against Great Britain.

The Constitutional Convention was called, in part, to resolve these weaknesses. As with the compromises that shaped the structure of the national government and the powers given to it, the powers given to the presidency were also a compromise. Specifically, this compromise was between those who sought great powers for the office and those who did not wish to see a powerful executive. The delegates did consider the possibility of an executive by committee because of their fear of monarchy, but soon discarded the concept as unworkable.

It was delegate James Wilson of Pennsylvania who delineated powers for the chief executive based on the powers granted to governors in the New York and Massachusetts State Constitutions. Those powers had been based in the philosophies of John Locke and Baron de Montesquieu, who both saw the need for a singular office to which the responsibility for the execution of the laws would go. Montesquieu, in particular, seems to have been the driving force behind the concept of separation of powers and the creation of a strong executive with limits on its powers. Much less frequently discussed are a number of philosophers who may have influenced the Framers. In his detailed intellectual and philosophical history of *The American Presidency*, Forrest McDonald (1994) wonderfully depicts many of these thinkers and their beliefs. In particular, the work of Jean-Louis De Lolme on the English Constitution is enlightening and has a familiar ring to it. De Lolme, naturally, is referring to the King when he discusses "the executive," but describes many of the powers of the central government that would emerge from the Constitutional Convention and specifically the very powers the Framers would assign to the executive. Much of the debate, however, centered around two views or models of the executive: the weak executive model and the strong executive model.

In the *weak executive model*, the executive would be chosen by the Congress for a limited term of office. He (historically speaking) would serve at the pleasure of the Congress—much like a prime minister in a parliamentary system of governance. It would be the chief task of the executive to carry out the will of the legislative branch and serve mostly an administrative function. All war and treaty powers would be reserved to the legislature and there would be no executive veto of legislative action.

In some versions of this model, the executive was conceived of as an executive by committee (Madison 1787).

The *strong executive model*, in contrast, would be independent of Congress. In this view of the executive branch, there would most certainly be a single individual to occupy the office and carry out the duties. The Congress would have only limited power to remove the president and, similarly, there would be limited ability by the legislature to control the actions of the executive. Any council (i.e., a cabinet) would be advisory in nature and would serve solely at the will of the executive.

As with most aspects and provisions of the new governing document, the end result was a compromise. In this case, however, the final structure more closely resembled the strong executive model. The difference was that the Framers had created a potentially strong institution that would share power with the other elected branch of government—the legislature. Perhaps, the single greatest achievement of the delegates at that convention was to create the system of checks and balances, or as Madison put it, "Ambition must be made to counteract ambition" (Madison 1788). Throughout our history, we have seen one branch of government check the overreaching of another or two branches working together to prevent one branch from so totally dominating the political process that democracy is frustrated entirely. The common sense of the deliberative process prevented the overtly partisan actions of some in the legislative branch from reaching fruition. In the cases of the impeachment of Andrew Johnson and William Jefferson Clinton, the more statesmanlike tone and the deliberation in the Senate thwarted the efforts of the House. In the case of Richard Nixon's abuse of power, the investigative powers of the Senate, the impeachment power of the House, and the power and prestige of the Supreme Court (and in the end, Nixon's ability to see the inevitable) saved the nation from perhaps its most grave constitutional crisis since the Civil War.

What Are the President's Duties and Powers?

Article II of the Constitution delineates not only the most basic process of selecting the president, but it also lays out the duties and powers granted to the executive. Once again, though we often use terms like "powers granted," it is *more often* the case that the powers are held in check by some limiting power held by either Congress or the courts. Naturally, there are some powers held by each of the three branches that are exclusive to that branch. See table 1.1 for a list of powers held by the president and the powers of other branches that can check those powers.

More often than not, we as a society refer to the president as "the commander-in-chief." While this is a direct quote from the constitution and seems to be a rather traditional view of the presidency, it is a somewhat misleading statement. The constitution actually states that "the president shall be Commander-in-Chief of the Army and Navy of the United States and of the Militia of the several States, when called into the actual Service of the United States." This wording must be taken in its actual context. As we will see throughout our discussion, the presidency has changed over the two hundred plus years of our nation's history. It has grown

Table 1.1 Examples of presidential powers checked by powers of other branches

	President	Congress
Powers	Appointment	Senate approval
	Commander in chief	Legislative regulation of the army, navy, and militias
	Treaty making	Senate ratification of treaties
	War making	Congress declares war
	Executive privilege	Limited by defendant's right to fair trial

in scope, relevance, and political (if not legal or constitutional) power. When the founders wrote those words in 1787, the armed forces of the United States consisted of the various state militias—the organizations we today think of as the National Guard. So, at least in the infancy of our nation and of the institution of the presidency, the president was commander in chief of very little. This is not the image we have of our contemporary president in command of millions[1] of fighting men and women and the technological marvels they use to defend our national interests.

We usually think of the legislative process as one involving only those we elect to the US House of Representatives and the Senate. The president is, in reality, a key player in the process. Some scholars have referred to the president as the nation's chief legislator (see e.g., Stephen Wayne's *Legislative Presidency* 1978). Most students of American government and politics, even if only at the high school level, are aware of the president's power to veto[2] legislation passed by both chambers of Congress. The president's legislative duties, functions, and abilities are not limited solely to the veto, however.

In addition to the more well-known power of the veto, the president has a number of other powers that relate to the legislative process. The president may recommend legislation to Congress and may "from time-to-time" address the Congress with respect to the state of the union.[3] Most presidents in the twentieth century used this vehicle to lay out their legislative agenda for the coming year. Another power exists where the two chambers cannot agree about when to adjourn; the president may adjourn the legislature. More importantly, and not used very often in recent history, is the president's power to convene extraordinary or special sessions of Congress to deal with pressing national matters. Perhaps, the most effective use of this power to achieve a political end was when Harry Truman called the Republican controlled Congress into session in August of 1948 for a two-week special session. The Republicans in the legislature refused to act on the proposals Truman sent to them and Truman then campaigned against the "do-nothing Congress."

Presidents influence public policy in a number of ways outside of the legislative arena. Obviously, as the principal foreign policy officer of the nation, the president has a great deal of influence over our relations with other countries. It is not only through personal visits or the pronouncement of policy under the scrutiny of the press or in the halls of the United Nations that he or she may do so, but also through the negotiation of treaties with foreign leaders. Such agreements must be approved or ratified by two-thirds of the US Senate.[4] With each new administration come many appointments to key positions in government, among some of the most important of these are our ambassadors to other countries. Who the president selects to represent both our nation and him- or herself affects how we interact with other players in the arena of world politics. It is rare that a presidential nominee for an ambassadorship is rejected by the Senate. Presidents also have the power to receive ambassadors from foreign powers and it is usually carried out in a rather routine fashion. New nations seek out this exchange as a measure of legitimacy among the players on the world political scene.

Similarly, the president has available the appointment of a great many positions in the executive branch. These individuals range from the White House chief of staff to cabinet secretaries to other lower-level political appointees. All of the highest-ranking appointees must be confirmed by the Senate, but the president may make sole appointments of "such inferior officers" as granted by Congress. All of these individuals have significant influence over the development and implementation of public policy of all kinds, whether it is the terms of a nuclear arms treaty or workplace safety specifications promulgated by the Occupational Safety and Health Administration. If a president selects the wrong individual for one of these posts it could spell disaster for the president's position on the policy or for the administration itself. Presidents have been placed in the position of requesting the resignation of key administration appointees or having to dismiss them outright because of an appointee's deviation from the president's position, failure to implement policy in accordance with the president's wishes, overzealousness, and other offenses.

Perhaps, the highest profile appointments any president can make, and they are such because of the potential long-term impacts on public policy and interpretation of the law, are those to the US Supreme Court. Additionally, presidents also make appointments to the lower levels of the federal court system, but none garner the level of attention, scrutiny, and potential opposition as those to the Supreme Court. All federal court appointments are for life and while this term of office makes it difficult for judges to fall victim to the whims of politics, it also means that once confirmed their impact on public policy can be quite long lasting. More youthful appointees to the federal bench can have influence on law and policy making for many decades before they retire or pass away. Presidents can use this fact to their advantage in attempting to ensure their own lasting impact on policy beyond their maximum term (for more on presidential appointment strategies and qualifications of judges see chapter 16).

Continuing in this vein, presidents have more powers of a quasi-judicial nature. Just as we are all well aware of the powers that state governors have to grant reprieves and pardons, so too does the president have similar powers. We may even recall old movies where the convicted criminal awaits the last minute phone call from the governor pardoning him for his crimes. While rarely as dramatic, the president has a similar power with respect to those convicted of federal crimes. Usually, such grants on the part of the president are not very controversial, but on occasion they do stir some conflict. The most recent example of such controversy was the last minute pardons by Bill Clinton[5] as he prepared to turn over power to George W. Bush in January of 2001. Gerald Ford's pardon of Richard Nixon was certainly controversial and served to undermine the initial public goodwill enjoyed by the Ford administration.

As many students of American government and politics are well aware, Congress has among its grant of powers something called "the elastic clause" or "the necessary and proper clause" to provide room for it to stretch its reach or expand its explicit powers.[6] Some have argued that the oath of office that all presidents must take upon their ascension contains a particular phrase that provides much the same flexibility or elasticity given to Congress. All presidents must swear that they will "faithfully execute the office of President." Some have argued that this phrase provides the "wiggle room" necessary for presidents to implement some laws in a way that the original authors of the law might not agree as their intent. Thus, a vaguely written law may give the president vast room in which to maneuver.

Limitations on Executive Power

It cannot be stressed enough that presidents, or for that matter any branch of government, cannot act alone. Presidents have little ability to act unilaterally. They need a majority of both houses of Congress to pass legislation; they need approval of the Senate to make many appointments, and they cannot raise revenues by simple executive order. Even in an era when we have conducted many significant military actions (some more the equivalent of war and others as "peacekeepers"), without a constitutional declaration of war by Congress, presidents cannot unilaterally wage war. They are constrained by congressional budgetary authority, international law, the War Powers Act, judicial review,[7] and public opinion.

So, not only is presidential action constrained by the normal system of checks and balances, which gives the power of the purse to Congress, the ability to declare war to Congress, confirmation of appointees to the Senate, and the power to impeach to Congress, but it is also constrained by the actions of other nations and by the American people. In addition, unlike parliamentary systems of government where the political executive is a member of and elected together with the legislature, the United States has a separate election of the executive. This is relevant to our discussion of limitations on executive power because a prime minister in a parliamentary system can, by definition, almost always count on the support of a majority of the legislature to support his or her programs. Here, even when the president's party is the majority in the legislative body, there is sufficient interbranch rivalry to make it impossible to count on party support in all cases. Certainly, recent presidents can attest to this fact, but more so for recent Democratic presidents. Jimmy Carter had no easy time achieving a majority for his legislative agenda and though Bill Clinton had much greater success in his first two years when he had a partisan majority, he suffered some major setbacks due to the actions of his own party in Congress.

Birthers, Qualifications, and Perquisites

The first African American president of the United States, Barack Obama, has been the subject of allegations that he did not meet the minimum qualification to serve as president because he had not, to the satisfaction of critics often called "birthers," produced a valid US birth certificate. How could this be? How could someone rise through the ranks of his or her party and through various elected offices and not have such basic credentials questioned at a much earlier stage of his career? What constitutes the minimum qualification to serve as president?

To ensure that no foreign agent might immigrate to our shores and serve in our highest elected office, the Framers included the phrase "natural born citizen" among the requisite qualifications for the office of president. What exactly does this mean? A natural born citizen is someone who was born in the United States or its territories, born of US citizens, or has one parent who is a citizen and has lived ten years as a resident of the United States (five continuously) after the age of 14 years. In all cases, the qualifying candidate must have resided in the United States for at least 14 years.

In order to make sure that the individual elected will have had sufficient real world experience before attempting to serve, the Framers included a minimum age of 35 years. One legal scholar, Akhil Reed Amar (who has written extensively on the Constitution and its bearing on governmental and criminal procedure), argues that one reason the Framers used this age was to ensure that any son of a well-known politician would have to have developed his own record and not assume a title and responsibility as William Pitt the younger did in England to become prime minister (Amar 2008). Naturally, such "inheritance"—whether by blood or election—of an office without consideration for a real record of accomplishment by the offspring in his or her own right would remind the Framers of the very monarchy, from which they had just separated. Milkis and Nelson (1999) assert two other reasons the Framers may have had. First, that political opinions of younger adults were "crude and erroneous" (51). Second, in quoting John Jay from the "Federalist Papers #64," the argument is made that the age requirements for all federal offices (representative, senator, and president) should provide time to *voters* to form judgments about political office seekers.

While George Washington set the precedent of presidents serving for only two terms, such a limit was not included in the original document. It was only after the record setting four electoral victories of Franklin Roosevelt that the Republican Congress moved quickly to amend the Constitution to limit presidents to two terms.[8] If ever challenged in a game of political or historical trivia do not fall victim, however, to the trick question: "How many years may a president serve?" More often than not, the author of the question has fallen into the trap of simply multiplying the two-term limit by the four years of each term. To be sure, this would be the usual circumstance—presidents, generally speaking, will serve no more than eight years. The trick, however, lies in the provision that a vice president may rise to fill a vacated presidency and serve two years of the prior president's term in addition to two terms in his or her own right.

Naturally, once elected or having attained the office by filling a vacancy, the president is compensated in a number of ways for his or her time and effort. The most visible symbol of this compensation is the building located at 1600 Pennsylvania Avenue, NW, Washington, DC. We, the taxpayers of the United States, provide our president with a home and a domestic staff to keep her or him (and family) comfortable for the time he or she works for us. Yet another highly visible example of the compensation we provide is the aircraft commonly known as Air Force One.[9] Why do we provide such apparently luxurious housing and travel accommodations? Aside from making these accommodations a part of a much larger package of compensation, there are security and communications concerns at work—we want the president safe and we want her or him to be able to communicate with advisers, the military leadership, and foreign leaders. Lyndon Johnson was criticized by some for his bold move to get to Air Force One as quickly as possible after the assassination of John Kennedy (it was seen by some as a callous grab for power). Yet, not knowing whether the shooting was part of a larger attack on the nation or if some power might seek to take military advantage of our moment of confusion, the plane was the location where the new president could quickly, easily, and securely communicate with the world.

It is not just a large, white house or a big, shiny plane that we use to compensate our elected leader. As of 2001, the United States of America provided the president with a salary of $400,000. At the start of the presidency with George Washington, the annual salary was set at $25,000, which was a fair sum of money in the late 1700s.[10] The amount of monetary compensation was first doubled in 1873, then increased to $75,000 in 1909, increased again in 1949 (to $100,000), and then doubled in 1969 (to $200,000). Additionally, the president receives an expense account of $50,000 (not including $19,000 for entertainment and $100,000 for travel)[11] for expenses "related to the discharge of his official duties" (3 U.S.C., Chapter 2, § 102).

As of 1958 (and updated periodically), presidents who retire from office without being removed through impeachment and conviction are entitled to a pension and retirement package (see Former Presidents Act, 3 U.S.C., Chapter 2, § 102). The pension is $193,400—equivalent to a cabinet member's salary. In addition to the pension, presidents are given funds to transition to a private office and to pay staff. Former presidents who entered the office prior to January 1st, 1997, are given continuing lifetime protection by the Secret Service. Although they and their families used to receive such protection for life, the time of taxpayer funded protection has been substantially limited. In legislation passed for Fiscal Year (FY) 1995, Congress limited Secret Service protection of former presidents and their spouses to 10 years and their children are covered for that same period or until they reach 16 years of age, whichever comes first (Stephanie Smith 2008; 18 U.S.C., § 3056).

Presidents are also provided with the ability to create lasting memorials to themselves by establishing presidential libraries and museums. Much of the money is raised through private foundations, but the primary responsibility for the safety and preservation of the documents from any president's administration is in the hands of NARA—the National Archives and Records Administration. These buildings or complexes serve as a means of securing the documents for the sake of history and for providing a lasting monument to the individual's impact on history and politics. The physical structures often reflect the personality of the president and/or the tone of the administration.[12] For example, the Kennedy Library in Boston, Massachusetts, looks out over the water much as the Kennedy family compound in Hyannis did (and still does) and provides the visitor with a sense of vision; Gerald Ford's library is a rather unassuming structure on the North Campus of the University of Michigan; Jimmy Carter's library, museum, and foundation offices are low-key structures that blend into the landscape displaying a harmony with nature; Ronald Reagan's library and museum reflect his comfort in the country life of southern California; and Bill Clinton's library and museum bring to mind his reference to a bridge to the future while at the same time seems to reflect his humble origins through the critique of its architecture—the infamous "double-wide."

Presidential Roles

Presidents play many roles in our political process. They have official roles as both the "head of state" and the "head of government." Certainly, these roles contain within them other roles as legislative leader and commander in chief. They have less official roles as spiritual or parental leaders and as the leaders of their political party. Together, these different roles lead to a highly complex and demanding job.

As head of state, the president stands as an equal to monarchs around the globe. Diplomatically speaking, this places the US president at a rank above the many heads of government (i.e., prime ministers) with whom he or she must interact. In his memoir, Jimmy Carter (1982) recalls that this matter of protocol was a bit of a stumbling block during the Camp David negotiations between himself, Egyptian president Anwar Sadat, and Israeli prime minister Menachem Begin. Where Carter and Sadat were heads of state—diplomatically the equals of kings and queens—Begin was a head of government, a functionary who according to protocol is required to walk behind heads of state. Carter recalls, that Begin was uncomfortable confronting himself or Sadat on issues raised during the discussions, resulting in differences not being fully aired and making compromise difficult.[13]

The role of head of state places the president in the position of the nation's chief diplomat and the individual charged by the Constitution with conducting our relations with foreign powers. Naturally, our ambassadors act as representatives, not just of our nation, but also of the president in particular. Presidents have also been known to appoint high-profile individuals to act as representatives—often "special envoys"—in specific circumstances. This sometimes includes former presidents with an especially high cache in particular regions or circumstances. Such envoys might also be religious leaders, or individuals with a particular expertise.

As the head of government, the president plays a role more like that of a prime minister in setting the policy agenda and leading the public debate on issues. In this role, the president also is the titular head of the bureaucracy he or she is purported to lead. Practice has demonstrated, however, that presidential leadership of the vast federal bureaucracy is irregular at best, even at times in the very areas where we might expect he would most certainly be in control—foreign and military affairs (see chapter 12).

Beyond the legal/constitutional roles of the president, there is the political need for the president to provide leadership to his or her party. In contemporary politics, presidents are expected to espouse the positions of the party from which they come. It is the president and his or her spokespersons that the media go to first for a political assessment about policy. It is also the case that, by tradition, the president gets to pick who shall serve as the chair of his or her party's national committee. It is the candidate who appears to have a party's nomination in hand who gets to determine the party's platform and the organization of its convention.

In Sum

Presidents play many parts in our political theater. They have many responsibilities and the American people place high expectations upon them. Because of the scope of the job, they cannot help but to have a large impact on the political stage both during their time in office and beyond. Further, successful, strong presidents (and even weaker ones) have a great impact on the shape of the office for those who follow them. That is why the focus of the remainder of this book is how we get the kinds of individual presidents we do and how these individuals leave a very personal mark on the institution for future historians and political scientists to analyze.

Chapter 2

The Historical Context: How We View the Presidency

The history of the American presidency can be broken down into three basic periods or eras, and our perception of the office can be categorized into a number of views. The interpretations of context, boundaries, and purpose of the office from those who have served in it or studied it provide two basic functions. First, from both former presidents and observers, we are provided with plentiful fuel for debates over the extent and proper use of presidential power. Was there justification, for example, from these perspectives on the presidency for George W. Bush's expansion of presidential power immediately after the attacks of 9/11 (and throughout his presidency)? Do such points of view allow us to be more accepting of presidents who are less active than others are? Second, the observations and reflections allow both average citizens and students of politics to see the presidency in a different light, perhaps, from the light in which it is regularly portrayed in the media.

Further, placing the presidency into historical periods or categories allows us to find similarities across presidencies of politically and personally different individuals. Finding anomalies among presidents from one time period might shed light on the similarities held by the other presidents in that era. So too, such anomalies might also allow us to see the seeds of what is yet to come. A president before his time gives us a peek into the future, to see what the presidency might look like decades in the future. By observing the patterns in personality, politics, and powers over the course of history, we can see the evolution of the presidency from one occupant of the Oval Office to the next. We get to see what effect the "mutations" have on the course of that evolution.

Views of the Presidency

A number of presidents and scholars have shared their views of the presidency and provide a glimpse of the evolution of the office. One of the first of such views that reflects on the earlier presidency comes to us from William Howard Taft. In Taft's *Strict Constructionist Presidency*, we see a similarity with the perspective on constitutional interpretation favored by some Constitutional Law scholars and occupants of the Supreme Court. Taft (1916) wrote, "The President exercise[s] no power which cannot be fairly and reasonably traced to some specific grant of power or justly implied" (139).

Teddy Roosevelt (1913), as a precursor to a very different presidency that would emerge not long after his time, postulated a *Stewardship Presidency*. Roosevelt argued that a president must be "a steward of the people bound actively and affirmatively to do all he could for the people" (357). To be sure, this is a far different view of the presidency than that of his successor—Taft. How prescient Roosevelt was. This was most certainly the view held by his cousin Franklin D. Roosevelt who came to the office about two and a half decades later. As we will see later, this "Rooseveltian" approach to the presidency sets the tone for all future presidents and establishes the character of the modern presidency.

In a similar view of the office, Abraham Lincoln (1864) established the concept of the *Prerogative Presidency* in which the Constitution and its seemingly limited grant of power to the president is seen as "organic law" (66). As Taft saw the presidency as more closely tied to the literal constitutional grants of power—"specific" or "justly implied," Lincoln preferred to think of the powers of the president as based on some prior grant of power. In this view, a president challenged with a national crisis like the Civil War or the Great Depression could make great strides in stretching the powers of the office by finding a precedent and expanding its applicability. During the Civil War, Lincoln did just this to wage a war for the preservation of the Union. So too, during the Depression and World War II, Franklin Roosevelt sought ways to stretch the powers of the office using precedent or a broad interpretation of the Constitution. To be sure, Roosevelt was often rebuffed by the Supreme Court, especially early on, and it took the unpopular threat of "packing the Court" with the switch of key votes on the Court to get a more agreeable interpretation of the powers, not just of the presidency, but of the national government as a whole.

While Woodrow Wilson's (1908) view is perhaps both more constrained and a bit naive, it is nonetheless prophetic. In referring to the president, Wilson said, "When he speaks his true character he speaks for no special interest" (68). He went on to say, "If he lead the nation, his party can hardly resist him" (69). In today's political environment, we wish for such idealism in our leaders, and might scoff cynically at the notion that an elected official at any level, in any office might be so unaffected by the interests of those who helped to elect him (or her). But, in this *Public Presidency* lies more indication of the institution yet to emerge. Wilson notes that the office varies with the individual who occupies it and that the president's duties will increase "as it must with the growth and widening activities of the nation itself" (81). Not only is the first assertion the focus of this treatment of the institution, but it would be about a dozen years after Wilson leaves office that latter assertion about growth would come to fruition under Franklin Roosevelt.

Three Historical Periods

We can also think of the presidency in terms of consecutive periods of time during which the office shares many common characteristics. The first of these, often referred to as the *premodern Presidency*, could also be viewed as the *Impaired Presidency*. Why impaired? Beginning with the Constitutional Convention, it could be said that with the Framers' fear of a powerful executive office occupied by a powerful individual such that the office was impaired by other leaders skeptical of its value, impaired by vague wording in the Constitution, and impaired by its secondary placement to the legislative branch in the Constitution.

With but a few notable exceptions, this period, with its characteristic weak presidents and a dominant Congress, lasts well into our nation's second century. Presidents like Jefferson, Jackson, Lincoln, Teddy Roosevelt, and Wilson stand out more as harbingers of the more aggressive nature of the office that will emerge and dominate American politics from the 1930s onward, with little exception. Andrew Jackson, for example, vetoed a total of 12 bills—more than all of his predecessors put together—including the controversial bill to create a national bank. It is alleged that Jackson was the first to employ the veto, not because he viewed those bills as unconstitutional but because he opposed the policy (Milkis and Nelson 1994).[1]

It is not so much that presidents in this period were all ineffective or failures. Rather, presidents in this period *start* from a position of impairment. While Washington had the advantage of being seen as the first true American hero, he was also cognizant of establishing precedents for all of his successors. Though the legislature would often defer to Washington as a result of his hero status, partisan divisions began to emerge in Congress between supporters of Alexander Hamilton and Thomas Jefferson. This was yet another factor in conducting the business of the nation that the Framers had not accounted for in the Constitution.

Jefferson took office after an election that tested the very process designed by the Framers. Ending in an Electoral College tie with his own vice president—Aaron Burr—Jefferson was faced with a government, the judiciary in particular, filled with last minute appointments by the opposing Federalists. Being an advocate of smaller government, even Jefferson recognized the need for great presidential capability. Milkis and Nelson (1994) argue that Jefferson was aware of the office's shortcomings, but he "altered the tone and manner of executive authority to make it consistent with the essence of popular rule, as he and the Democratic-Republicans understood it" (109). It was this mechanism of party leadership that Milkis and Nelson cite as Jefferson's legacy. In other words, Jefferson was able to make use of the fledgling party structure to influence public opinion and get things done in government.

This work is far from a comprehensive history of the presidents and the office they have occupied, but the important point here is that like Washington and Jefferson, all presidents—especially those in this transition period—have had to find ways to make the institution work so as to accomplish their goals and in the collective interests of the nation. The Constitution provides little guidance and vague wording. The Founders and Framers feared a return to the tyranny of unitary leadership and sought to create an executive with limited power. This creation made functioning in office a more difficult task for each occupant, more so for the earliest occupants. Most found a way to make it work for them, while some had more difficulty overcoming this impairment left by the Framers. We can ponder, for example, how history may have been different, how perhaps we might have avoided Civil War with a stronger executive institution. Naturally, once a strong executive did come to the office, it was almost too late.

Certainly, Abraham Lincoln was also both an exception to the period and yet another example of the impaired presidency. In order to meet the challenges posed by the Civil War, Lincoln had to "stretch" the powers of an office apparently not designed to handle a crisis of the magnitude Lincoln faced. However, with a combination of creativity and political and personal character, Lincoln succeeded in putting down the rebellion and expanding the scope and powers of the office of president.

The *Imperial Presidency*, so named by Arthur Schlesinger (1973) for its isolation and royalty-like organization and style, is also known as the modern presidency. What distinguishes the institution during this time—beginning with Franklin Roosevelt and continuing at least until Richard Nixon—is the overall activism of the individuals in the office, the expansion of the power of the office, and the much greater and more consistent role of the office in everyday life and politics. Just as Wilson had predicted in his *public presidency*, the institution and its duties and powers expanded with the growth of the nation and with the role of government. So too, the notion of finding the cracks through which new or newly expanded powers could emerge as postulated by Lincoln's *prerogative presidency* took hold, and the very first modern president—Franklin Roosevelt—sought those cracks and welcomed the expansion of presidential and governmental power.

Taking over the presidency following the administration of Herbert Hoover, Franklin Roosevelt, like Lincoln before him, came into office facing a serious crisis that threatened the very foundations of our way of life. In Lincoln's case it was the slide into civil war. In Roosevelt's case it was whether or not the government could (or should) take steps to right the sinking economic ship. Hoover had governed from a philosophical viewpoint that the role of the federal government in the economy should be minimal and that relief efforts were the job of state and local governments or charitable organizations. In the view of Hoover and other conservatives of the time, the market should be allowed to work and to correct itself.

Roosevelt's response was a series of massive public works and relief efforts coupled with large-scale government regulation of economic activity in order to prevent such a crisis from occurring again. These efforts, though met by resistance in political and legal circles, eventually led to dramatic growth in the size, scope, and power of the presidency. The veritable "alphabet soup" of new government agencies created for the purposes of providing relief and regulation grew to what even Roosevelt saw as unmanageable proportions. The appointment of the Brownlow Commission[2] was his attempt to find a solution to the problem of governability of this unwieldy bureaucracy. This alone, could be sufficient reason to trace the modern or imperial presidency back to the administration of Franklin Roosevelt. The recommendations of the commission that were implemented give us the structure and appearance of the contemporary presidency. The Executive Office of the President (EOP) with its elevation above the cabinet, and its assumption of the budget function through the Bureau of the Budget (today's Office of Management and Budget—OMB), owes its existence to the commission's recommendations.

Certainly, Roosevelt was stopped at the outset by a Supreme Court laden with jurists holding the Taft-like view of the presidency that stayed closer to those more explicit grants of power contained in the words of the Constitution. Roosevelt's attempts to use a broader conception of the powers of his office, and of the government more generally, met with stiff opposition from the Court. Attempts to use government power to regulate the economy, to provide jobs, and to alleviate economic suffering were met by the Court with the argument that Franklin Roosevelt and the Democratic Congress had overreached and had manufactured constitutional authority where none existed. Stifled in this way, Roosevelt proposed yet another expansion of presidential prerogative—his "pack the Court scheme"—which would allow him to appoint sufficient new justices to change the majority on the Court to one that would be more likely to support the initiatives of the president and Congress. Before the unpopular plan could gain any momentum, we saw the "switch in time that saved nine." Justice Owen Roberts—one of two swing votes on the Court—had been voting consistently with four justices often referred to as "the Four Horsemen," who opposed much of the New Deal agenda and struck down initiative after initiative including those from more progressive states like New York in regulating economic activity like working conditions and minimum wage laws. In *West Coast Hotel v. Parrish* (300 U.S. 379, 1937), Justice Roberts joined the more liberal justices—Chief Justice Charles Evans Hughes, Justices Brandeis, Cardozo, and Stone—on the Court to uphold a state of Washington minimum wage law. Thus, the Court struck down an earlier decision in *Adkins v. Children's Hospital* (261 U.S. 525, 1923) that had overturned a New York minimum wage law (Epstein and Walker 2012).[3]

Whether Justice Roberts acted in a politically strategic manner to save the honor of the Supreme Court or had a true change of heart on the issue matters less than the fact that his vote in the *West Coast Hotel* case is an important consideration in the growth of the modern presidency. Authors of fiction who dabble in the what ifs of history can speculate about whether or not Roosevelt would have moved forward with his plan, whether it would have succeeded or failed, and if it failed whether it would have damaged Roosevelt enough politically to thwart the emergence of the imperial presidency. Instead, the EOP has grown to include just under 1,900 employees with a requested budget of $393 million in Fiscal Year 2011.[4]

Franklin Roosevelt's successors did little to change the overall trajectory of the EOP. Certainly, with the new role for the United States in world military and diplomatic affairs brought about as a result of World War II, there would be no rapid return to an older, leaner presidency. Truman picked up where Roosevelt left off in conducting the war and appeared not to look back with respect to the new government role in economic activity. The advent of the Cold War, to be sure, contributed to further growth in the presidency as international security became paramount. So, the presidencies of Dwight Eisenhower and John Kennedy saw no let up in the growth of size and power of the institution. Lyndon Johnson's Great Society and his expansion of our role in the Vietnam conflict created more government bureaucracy and led to a more difficult relationship with other nations, respectively. Though Nixon made attempts to reorganize the bureaucracy, his efforts also included centralization of power in the White House and the creation of a "super cabinet" to which other departments would report.[5] For the most part his efforts failed, but his restructuring of the Bureau of the Budget resulted in the creation of what we now know as the OMB. It was also under Nixon that the presidency appears to come into greater conflict with Congress (where Congress had often deferred to the president since FDR) and comes under greater scrutiny of the press. This, coupled with a diminished image resulting from Vietnam, could be seen as the seeds of a newer, more troubled era of the presidency.

Political scientist Richard Rose (1991) has postulated a postmodern presidency in which a president may have too much expected of him or her. The demands of world leadership, partisan leadership, image maintenance, and policy achievement make presidential success difficult at best and impossible at worst. Further, with such high expectations, whether set by the media or by the presidents themselves, presidents become easy targets. Add to the political recipe a media emboldened by its role in Watergate, a resurgent Congress, a highly partisan atmosphere, and a digital universe where nearly everyone can weigh in on the political debate and it is not simply a postmodern presidency, but an *Imperiled Presidency*.

In the imperiled presidency, not only is a president's success in the polls at stake, but so also is his/her legislative and diplomatic success. More to the point, it is not just about public approval ratings, but also about the president's very political survival. Certainly, over the course of the decades since 1960 we can see that even those presidents who have survived for what might be considered a "normal two-term presidency" have done so just barely. Even the most popular of these two-term presidents—Reagan and Clinton—barely escaped political disaster. Reagan's problems with the Iran-Contra Scandal and Clinton's impeachment over the Lewinsky Scandal are symptomatic of this era and this environment.

Scandal is not the only symptom of the imperiled presidency, but also certainly of a news media and blogosphere with the tenaciousness of a bulldog that would never let go of a substantiated scandal. Going back to the presidency of John Kennedy, we can see a well-established imperial institution. In fact, given his appearance, his wife's beauty and stature, and his large wealthy family, all coupled with the new hope brought to American politics by his youth, energy, rhetoric, it was dubbed "Camelot." This was a reference to the mythical reign of King Arthur, where according to the musical version of the story, "The rain may never fall till after sundown / By eight, the morning fog must disappear / In short, there's simply not a more congenial spot for happily-ever-aftering than here in Camelot" (AllMusicals.com n.d.). At the same time, however, we can see the beginning of the imperiled presidency. Just as in the myth, the true utopia of Camelot was struck by tragedy and did not last very long. Kennedy became the first president since McKinley to be assassinated, shot by Lee Harvey Oswald in Dallas on November 22nd, 1963.

Kennedy was succeeded by his vice president, Lyndon Johnson, elected in his own right by a huge margin in 1964. Johnson, though not endowed with the Kennedy charisma and not the subject of modern American myth making, attempted to continue Camelot in his own way with the introduction and passage of his Great Society programs. It was under Johnson that major legislation such as the Civil Rights Act, the Voting Rights Act, Medicare, and Medicaid were passed. From that record of legislative success alone, future observers should have been led to a highly positive assessment of his tenure. Johnson's policies with respect to US involvement in Vietnam served to overwhelm his reputation. Instead of being remembered for his accomplishments in the area of social legislation, Johnson has been more easily remembered for the chants of college students and other antiwar protesters, "Hey, hey, LBJ, how many kids did you kill today?" (see, e.g., PBS 2008). As a result, he was challenged for his own party's nomination by antiwar candidate Senator Eugene McCarthy whose unexpectedly strong finish as a write-in candidate in the New Hampshire primary brought New York Senator Bobby Kennedy into the race. In a national TV address, Johnson announced not just a change in US military policy in Vietnam, but also that he was withdrawing from the race for his party's nomination.

Following Bobby Kennedy's assassination immediately after his victory in the California primary, the subsequent tumultuous Democratic National Convention in Chicago in the summer of 1968 nominated Vice President Hubert Humphrey—who never contested a single primary. Humphrey, saddled with Johnson's Vietnam War record, lost a very close race to former vice president Richard Nixon. Nixon conducted himself well enough to get reelected by landslide proportions in 1972. With Franklin Roosevelt's expansion of the office and John Kennedy's mythical stature as foundation, it was Nixon's presidency that cemented the notion of the imperial presidency and inspired Schlesinger to write his book critical of this type of presidency. To Schlesinger and other critics, Nixon's administration was the epitome of the imperial presidency—the president insulated from the day-to-day politics and isolated from many of his advisers through a rather steep hierarchy. To make the point, some argued that Nixon was surrounded by "German Shepherds" or a "Berlin Wall." These references were also due to the proliferation of Germanic sounding surnames among his staff—Haldeman, Ehrlichman, Kissinger, Kleindeinst, and Klein (Spoehr 2007).

The seeds of Nixon's undoing, however, were already sown by the time of his reelection. In June of 1972 a group of burglars, all with previous connections to the Central Intelligence Agency (CIA), broke into the Democratic National Headquarters (and not for the first time) to conduct eavesdropping and other surveillance activities (there are many accounts of the break-ins and the cover-up, but one early one is Sussman [1974]). The cover-up of that incident led to the eventual investigations by *The Washington Post*, the Senate Select Committee on Presidential Campaign Practices, and the House Judiciary Committee that resulted in Nixon's resignation in August of 1974. The entire affair emboldened both the media and Congress. A generation of reporters seeking to emulate the success, if not the practice, of Bob Woodward and Carl Bernstein, the two reporters acknowledged to be those who brought down Nixon, was spawned. A resurgent Congress began taking steps to reign in what to them was a runaway institution; they passed legislation to limit the president's discretion in budgetary matters, they passed legislation to limit the president's ability to conduct war without consulting or involving Congress. Even the judiciary exercised its function as a check on the powers of the other branches; a trial court subpoenaed documents from the president and the Supreme Court while recognizing a legitimate presidential claim to executive privilege, strictly limited that privilege to matters of national security.

It is Nixon's undoing, I would argue, that truly began the era of the imperiled presidency. His successor, Gerald Ford, could not gain a term in his own right (CBS News 2009). Jimmy Carter could not sufficiently navigate international political waters to gain the release of the hostages held in the US Embassy in Iran. Ronald Reagan, while known for his overall higher levels of public approval was also not immune from the effects of the imperiled presidency. In his first term, Reagan struggled with approval ratings that followed the weak performance of the economy and struggled with his management of foreign and military affairs. In his second term, Reagan endured the scrutiny brought on by the Iran-Contra scandal and his approval ratings dipped once again. While he was personally popular throughout his term, his positions and policies were less so.

For Reagan's successor, George H. W. Bush, it was his inability to capitalize on his high approval following the victory in the Gulf War and his failure to keep his promise not to raise taxes. Bush's imperilment cost him reelection in 1992. While riding high at one point in his presidency with a near 90 percent approval rating (at the end of hostilities in the Gulf War), he failed to break the 40 percent mark in votes.

The winner of that campaign in 1992—Bill Clinton—survived a presidency under constant scrutiny for scandal and ultimately had to endure a trial on impeachment in the US Senate, the only second time in history a president has been impeached. It seemed as though conspiracy theorists had a field day during the Clinton administration and with the advent of the Internet, some scandals and allegations just wouldn't die. Clinton was investigated for his family's involvement in the Whitewater Real Estate Development in which they lost money. He and his wife Hillary were alleged to have been involved in the death of White House aide and longtime friend Vince Foster. His adviser, Dick Morris, was involved with revealing national security information in front of a prostitute. And, Clinton was regularly accused of some sort of sexual indiscretion (what Republican strategist Mary Matalin once referred to as "bimbo eruptions"—See, Matalin and Carville [1994]), one of which involved an affair with White House intern Monica Lewinsky and was the direct cause of his impeachment.

Bush's son, George W. Bush, though a winner of two terms as a wartime president, was not immune to the imperiled nature of the presidency. His administration also seemed to be adrift in a sea of controversy, from allegations of padding the wallets of corporate friends to accusations of manipulation of intelligence data for political purposes and accusations of illegality in the outing of CIA operative Valerie Plame—not to mention Vice President Cheney's shooting of a hunting companion. And, just like his father, he not only squandered high levels of public approval, but in his case also became one of the least popular presidents in history.

The contrast between the two Bush presidencies in some ways highlights the difference between the imperial (modern) presidency and the imperiled (postmodern) presidency. While it would be easy to argue (as I have here) that the elder Bush was a victim of the imperiled presidency, it is also easy to see the remnants of the imperial presidency. In preparing for the US response to the Iraqi invasion of Kuwait, the elder Bush was masterful at lining up international support and cooperation in the effort. It would seem that under the right circumstances a US president could still dominate international politics. His son, however, was roundly and regularly chastised for his inability to gain much more than British cooperation with his policy toward Iraq.

In the case of George W. Bush, we can also see evidence of Rose's (1991) claim that in the postmodern or imperiled presidency there is too much to do. Bush had to deal with the US response to the 9/11 attacks (a war in Afghanistan), a war in Iraq, and toward the end of his administration a rapidly and dramatically failing economy. This theme continued into the administration of Bush's successor, Barack Obama. Obama came into office inheriting the failing economy, and the two wars. He very quickly faced domestic political difficulty in attempting to pass major health insurance reform legislation followed by a major environmental disaster brought about by the explosion and sinking of British Petroleum's oilrig in the Gulf of Mexico.

Putting the Views and Eras Together

In an era when we have come to expect that presidents will be active and may seek to expand the scope and powers of the office or in a time when we have the historical examples of Lincoln, Franklin Roosevelt, and others to call upon, should we be surprised when presidents attempt to expand their power? No doubt, there are those citizens who might welcome a time when presidents behave as Taft laid out in his strict constructionist presidency. Yet, actions by presidents to expand their powers seem not to know partisan boundaries—both liberal presidents and conservative presidents have sought to exert powers not explicitly stated in the constitution. Similarly, there have been Congresses controlled by both parties (at different times) that have supported and opposed those presidential efforts. Republicans in Congress under George W. Bush seemed to support attempts by him to expand the powers of the president and many of the same Republicans under Barack Obama opposed similar efforts by Obama.

Recent history has shown us that Taft's view of the presidency is outdated. Cynics would likely argue that Wilson's *public presidency* is a hopeful but impractical view. During the period of the imperial and imperiled presidency, we have observed presidents' behavior consistent with either Lincoln's *prerogative presidency* or Teddy Roosevelt's *stewardship presidency*. More recently, George W. Bush, following the arguments presented by Terry Eastland in his work *Energy in the Executive* (1993), has pushed the prerogative presidency to higher levels of power.

Part II

Presidential Candidate Selection

Chapter 3

Introduction: The Process in General

Any examination of the presidency as an institution, especially one that focuses on the role and impact of the individual on the institution, must pay attention to the manner by which the individuals are selected. In the United States, it is essentially a two-stage process. The selection of candidates by political parties is the first stage, the second being the electoral contest between those candidates and any others who have made it to the ballot by some other means.

The process of electing a president in the United States is a long and arduous one, both for the candidates and the public (voting or simply observing). More recently, it often begins many years in advance, not out of legal necessity, but out of the need to organize in many individual state contests and, most importantly, to raise money. For example, less than a week after the 2004 general election in which President George W. Bush had narrowly won reelection, two members of the US Senate thought to be the front runners for their respective parties' nomination for 2008 appeared together on the NBC Sunday morning talk show—*Meet the Press*. Hillary Clinton and John McCain were asked questions about many topics, but also about the prospects of running against one another come the fall of 2008. In booking those two guests, host Tim Russert was half-prescient—John McCain did end up as the Republican nominee in 2008.

The example above is important not so much as it reflects Tim Russert's ability as a seer of the political future, but because the 2008 campaign was already underway and the person elected in 2004 had not yet been certified the winner in most states and was still more than two months away from being sworn in. McCain had just won reelection to the Senate from Arizona, and Clinton had to clear the hurdle of getting reelected from New York in 2006. Both had a great deal to accomplish and precious little time in which to do it, even though the election they both sought was still four years away.

The process they were soon to enter has been designed, not by choice but by evolution, to narrow the field of presidential candidates to 2 or sometimes 3 individuals.[1] In 2008, each party had enough potential candidates to play a series of basketball games against each other. That is, the Democrats had 8 candidates who sought the party nomination and the Republicans had 11.[2] That field of 19 presidential aspirants was eventually narrowed to 2—Barack Obama and John McCain. In 2008, it was not a process for a shy, retiring individual or a candidate who thought that his/her party should seek them out, and it hasn't been that way for many decades. During the nation's first one hundred years and on, well into the twentieth century, some candidates could expect that their stature and prior service would lead their party to pick them. How and why did that change?

The short answer is that it evolved with the changes in the institution, with the growth of the nation, and with advances in technology. The longer answer reveals an interesting history and the development of traditions and their later abandonment. Here, I will seek a middle course sufficient for our understanding of what kinds of people get to be president and later how that affects the office itself.

Despite the apparent lack of organization and squabbles over what the public might view as incomprehensible rules (e.g., when states may hold intraparty contests or why the apparent winner of a contest for delegates might not get to go to a convention), the process is rational. The overall goal is simple—narrow the field. Each political party has a goal of nominating the candidate (and his/her running mate) best suited to win the election for it in the fall. Sometimes, the process yields a candidate who is the popular choice of those who came out to vote in the primaries and caucuses, but is just far enough out of the ideological mainstream to be too weak an opponent for the other party's more centrist candidate.

Because it is the parties that dominate the rule making for this process, those rules tend to favor candidates from the two major parties—the Democratic Party and the Republican Party. It is also the case that because early leaders of the quadrennial contests tend to be more establishment candidates—those who have held office for a significant time and/or have been among the party leaders in the national legislature or among the state governors—the rules often seem to provide an advantage to these more easily recognizable names. It is not surprising therefore that *Meet the Press* guest John McCain from 2004 became the Republican Party candidate for president in 2008. What is surprising given these rules is that Hillary Clinton was not the Democratic Party candidate in 2008 and that Barack Obama was. At the time of the airing of that *Meet the Press* Barack Obama had just been elected to the US Senate from Illinois for the first time.

Why might it be that Barack Obama, Jimmy Carter, or some other less "established" candidate could come from, seemingly, out of nowhere to capture a major party nomination? There are other considerations besides front-runner or establishment status that can be a factor. Candidates can have an appeal to a particularly energetic constituent group or they may generally project a more pleasing image to voters. They may be more "telegenic," which is a bit like being photogenic but is not just about physical appearance. It is significantly more than physical appearance and we have moved sufficiently beyond the old technologies of radio and TV that some refer to it as being "mediagenic."

Two Stages of Selection Process

As stated earlier, there are two stages to the process by which presidents are selected. The first stage is the nomination stage, which includes the primaries and caucuses and the national nominating conventions. The second stage is the general election. Each stage has a slightly different emphasis, especially for the candidates and their strategies.

In the nomination stage of the process, the focus for candidates in both parties is the accumulation of delegates to their respective party nominating conventions. With two different mechanisms and a spread out calendar of contests, there are multiple strategies candidates may pursue to achieve their goal. In order to understand the possible strategies, we need to understand what these mechanisms are.

The *primary*, first adopted for use in presidential selection by Florida in 1904 and by a total of 15 states by 1912, traditionally is an election held within the party, and is limited to members of that party. More recently, changes to primaries have moved away from the traditional role or definition. Initially, primaries were tools used by reformers in areas of single party domination to break through the control of political machines. For example, if the Democratic Party had an advantage in enrollment such that it consistently won elections and the Republicans, because of this domination could not attract viable candidates, the only way to accomplish electoral change would be to impact the process by which candidates were selected. Reformers then sought changes in state laws and party rules in areas of single party domination to be able to choose their party's candidates and thus accomplish larger reform of state and local policy.

Today's primaries, depending on state and party rules may allow for a range of possible participants. The *closed primary* is the more traditional primary where only enrolled party members may cast votes to determine the party's candidate(s) in the general election. Of course, who gets to vote in such a primary is a function of how state rules define "enrolled party member." In some states, it is a choice a voter makes at the time he or she registers to vote. In other states, it may be a choice the voter makes in that given electoral cycle. The *semiclosed primary* is one where party members and independent voters may participate. In some states, an independent voter must notify election officials at some point prior to the day of polling if he or she is choosing to vote in one party's primary or another's (e.g., New Hampshire). This provision allows campaign workers access to the lists of likely voters from outside the party to make the case for their candidate. An *open primary* is a primary where anyone may vote in any party's primary regardless of how they may be enrolled. This is a generic term that not only describes a more benign case where the state might not provide for official enrollment in a party, but it also covers what is sometimes referred to as a *crossover primary* where a voter may choose to vote in the opposing party's primary. Some view this as a dangerous practice that could lead to political mischief where voters from Party A vote for the weakest candidate in Party B's primary to give themselves and Party A an unfair advantage in the general election.

A *caucus* is an event quite unlike a primary. While the same issue of who gets to vote is present, the manner of voting is quite different. Most voters are familiar with the conduct of a primary, except for the fact that the choices are limited to candidates only from one party.[3] It is usually the same process—machine, paper ballot, or electronic device—as the state uses for the general election and is the familiar secret ballot. In a caucus, there is a public declaration of support for the candidate of the voter's choice. Party workers sometimes see a benefit from this process because they can clearly identify potential new volunteers and campaign workers can easily tell which voters lived up to their promises.

There are also *hybrid contests*. In 2008, the Texas combination was humorously (and somewhat derisively) referred to as "The Texas Two-Step" (Feibel 2008). This was a contest where voters would go to the polls during the day and vote in a more traditional primary. In the evening, once the polls closed, there would then be a caucus to select the delegates based on the vote in the primary. The catch was that a voter could not participate in the caucus unless they had voted in the primary earlier in the day. Similarly, if you voted in the primary and didn't show up for the caucus—as was the case with many who worked on shifts or had issues with child or elder care—you were, essentially, throwing away a significant portion of your vote.

In both types of contests, voters may be doing at least one thing and often two. First, they may simply be expressing a preference for a particular presidential candidate. Sometimes, the outcome of this expression is used by state party organizations to allocate delegates on an at-large basis to attend the party's national nominating convention. Second, voters may be directly choosing delegates to conventions at a higher level within the state or directly to the national nominating convention of their party. They may, in fact, be doing both, in which case the vote for delegate is not necessarily tied to their preference for president. They may have a friend or relative they would like to send to the convention even though that friend or relative supports a different presidential candidate than the voter.

While many states may in some way make use of a state convention to finalize the state party's delegation to the *national nominating convention*, that is not the convention of major interest here. The national nominating convention is a gathering of party delegates selected in primaries, caucuses, or state conventions to select the party's presidential and vice-presidential candidates, to establish rules, and the party's platform (a document detailing the party's positions on major issues). That's the traditional definition, but with the intraparty battle usually settled before the convention is ever brought to order, the convention is sometimes seen more as a rubber stamp of the outcome of the primary and caucus process. Then why have conventions? Conventions still do play an important role in launching the campaign and unifying the party. Cities all over the country vie for the right to host the party conventions, traditionally for the huge sums of money spent by delegates, candidates, the party, and interest groups that generate an economic boost for the city's businesses and that generate tax revenue from nonresidents. One Ohio political blog, in discussing the possibility that Cleveland might get one of the 2012 conventions, put it this way, "A presidential nominating convention brings millions of dollars and intense attention to its host city as well as political good will for the party itself" (Shoemaker 2010). In more recent years, the reason may be more about prestige than money because with the added cost of security since the 9/11 attacks conventions can now be a financial drain rather than an income generator (for a comparison of differences in cost see O'Brien [2004]). A more detailed discussion of conventions will follow in chapter 6.

Three Historical Periods of Presidential Selection

Once again, in order to gain an understanding of how the process of selection has evolved to what it is today, a bit of history is helpful. Broadly speaking, we can break down the history of presidential selection into three commonly recognized periods: the *Legislative Caucus Period* (1800–1832), the *Brokered Convention Period* (1836–1968), and the *Popular Choice Period* (1972 to present).[4] The earliest period (legislative caucus) is also sometimes referred to as "King" Caucus and should not be confused with the caucuses in use today. We can also see much of the structure of the brokered convention period even today, more than 30 years into the popular choice period.

In the earliest years of the nation's existence, there was little need to select presidential candidates as there was near unanimous agreement that George Washington should be president in both the 1788 and 1792 elections. Nor were there yet political parties to generate candidates to compete against one another. Due to partisan conflicts that developed in the legislature during Washington's two terms and the ensuing evolution of party structures outside the legislature, in 1800, the two parties of the time—the Federalists and the Democratic-Republicans—were ready to offer clear partisan choices in the election. It fell to the political partisans in Congress to select candidates to represent their interests when time finally came for the members of the Electoral College to make their pick. The problem was that the manner of choosing the president, as first defined in the Constitution, required electors to vote for two presidential candidates with the majority vote winner becoming president and the runner-up becoming vice president. Once the fledgling political parties began naming a team for president and vice president, there was no way to assure that one elector would cast his second ballot for someone else. In the election of 1800, this created a tie between Jefferson and his intended vice president, Aaron Burr, and sent the election into the House of Representatives for multiple ballots.

There were two factors that contributed to the change from having partisan members of the national legislature pick party presidential candidates. First, the growth of the American population and the expansion of its physical size made it compelling to find a more directly representative way to pick the candidates. Second, Andrew Jackson's loss to John Quincy Adams spurred Jackson to take his case to the people, particularly those who had migrated to the west. Expanding the physical size of the nation, these voters now lived on the grasslands of the west. Though the expression was not coined until much later (during the reform era of the early 1900s),[5] it could be argued that Jackson's efforts between 1824 and 1828 constituted the first true grassroots campaign in American history.

Yet another factor contributing to the onset of the brokered convention was the rise of political parties that may or may not have gained representation in Congress. How could a party that had not yet enjoyed electoral success sufficient to get more than a handful of candidates elected to Congress, or any at all for that matter, make use of the legislative caucus to select its presidential and vice-presidential candidates? So, it became a practical matter for smaller and somewhat less successful parties to find an alternate method of candidate selection. And, in keeping with this particular factor, it was the Anti-Mason Party that held the first nominating convention in Baltimore in September of 1831 for the 1832 election. The Democrats and the National Republicans also held their first conventions in Baltimore.

The name "brokered convention" actually comes into play a bit later, but describes how many state party leaders viewed themselves and how they acted. As political machines rose to prominence and as the ability to hand out jobs through the spoils system[6] grew, local and state party leaders could actually control the votes of most if not all the delegates within their jurisdiction. Often this would lead to the rise of "favorite son" campaigns where a local favorite would run for president with no real expectation of even coming close to the party's nomination. The leaders or "bosses" would use the delegate votes committed to these favorite sons to broker deals, sometimes an assurance that the favorite son would get a job in the administration or some other office holder would get a judicial appointment in return for the boss giving one candidate all the votes he controlled.

From its inception in the 1832 election cycle, the brokered convention remained pretty much intact until 1968 and we even have its structural remnants with us today. That is, the national nominating conventions of the two major parties look pretty much like they did prior to 1968. Why would we change from a system that gave us presidents like Franklin Roosevelt, John Kennedy, and Teddy Roosevelt? The answer lies once again, in part, in the growth of the nation. With national nominating convention delegates chosen in state and local conventions and their selection controlled by political bosses, the entire system was still mired in the prereform-era politics of the nineteenth century.

In addition to the continued growth of the nation—adding many states and tens of millions of citizens—the latter portion of the brokered convention period saw the advent of electronic media, particularly radio and TV. These new means for bringing the conventions into the homes of millions of Americans shed new light on the process and demonstrated the lack of diversity among the delegates. TV also played a crucial role in 1968 in bringing about the changes that democratized and popularized the process of candidate selection.

The 1968 race for the Democratic nomination for president was both grueling and tragic. It began with the incumbent president—Lyndon Johnson—as the seemingly unquestioned nominee of his party. The Tet Offensive in Vietnam in early 1968 brought the brutality and reality of the Vietnam War home to any American who had yet to realize it. Certainly, the news coverage of the lengthy North Vietnamese effort and the casualties suffered by all parties, especially the casualties for the North and its allies, were particularly high for so little gain. In March, however, when the real political battles back home began, it was not quite so clear that the offensive would ultimately be beaten back and there was a perception created by vivid imagery on TV that the American and allied fortunes were worse than they actually were (FitzGerald 1972; Herring 1979).[7]

Soon after the first phase of the Tet Offensive, the first contest in the 1968 presidential race was held. New Hampshire traditionally holds the first primary in the nation and though we have come to expect it much earlier in each presidential election year, in 1968 it was in March. President Johnson was virtually unopposed in this first in the nation contest, but a peace candidate, Senator Eugene McCarthy, was running a write-in campaign against the incumbent. With the backdrop of the bloody fighting half way around the globe, McCarthy polled 42 percent and Johnson failed to gain a majority of the vote in the primary. This outcome, like blood in the water to sharks, lured into the race the one person Johnson most feared and disliked among any potential opponents—New York Senator Bobby Kennedy. Johnson and Bobby Kennedy's dislike for each other went back at least as far as John Kennedy's successful run for the Democratic nomination in 1960 in which Bobby served as his brother's campaign manager. Bobby Kennedy entered the race not long after McCarthy's *perceived* victory over Johnson—one could only imagine what the outcome might have been if McCarthy had actually been on the ballot (White 1969). Shocking the nation and allegedly his advisers, in a televised address to the nation on March 31st, in which he detailed a rather large US de-escalation of the war, Johnson added, "I shall not seek, and I will not accept, the nomination of my party for another term as your President" (Johnson 1968).

Very soon after Johnson's withdrawal came the assassination of Martin Luther King, unleashing racial violence across the country. With the smoke of fires in Northeast Washington, DC, the Congress passed major legislation prohibiting discrimination on the basis of race in housing.[8] During the rest of April and May, Kennedy and McCarthy crisscrossed the nation with Kennedy continuing the family tradition of never losing an election, until the Oregon primary where McCarthy finally broke through with a victory. All the while Vice President Hubert Humphrey was playing a more traditional game and working with Johnson's help to secure delegates through state party leaders. The three candidates continued with Kennedy and McCarthy in a major face-off in the California primary in early June. Having secured an apparent victory in the California contest, Kennedy addressed his supporters and encouraged them for the next step with his final public words, "and it's on to Chicago and let's win there!"[9] (White 1969, 183). Moments later, Kennedy was shot in the head by Sirhan Sirhan, felled by an assassin's bullet—as his brother before him. It seemed that with Kennedy's death the next day (June 6th), all the momentum was taken out of the antiwar campaigns.

With Bobby Kennedy dead and McCarthy's campaign lacking momentum, Humphrey was able to garner enough delegates to secure the party's nomination. In late August 1968, not just the delegates arrived for the Democratic Convention, but so did an estimated ten thousand young antiwar protesters (Kusch 2004). Once the protests escalated and violence broke out, with network TV cameras nearby to cover the convention, technology became a factor. In one of the earliest uses of "split-screen" technology, some broadcasts of the convention also showed tape delayed coverage of the events taking place in the streets of Chicago. Regardless of whether the protesters or the police were responsible, the nation saw the side-by-side image of the business as usual convention, nominating the vice president of the administration that was the very subject of the protests to be its presidential candidate, and the image of the bloody battle in the streets. This was certainly not the way any political party would want to kick off its general election campaign.

So, in the fall of 1968, the Democrats moved into the general election campaign against Richard Nixon with a candidate who was nominated at a convention where there was violence in the streets between student protesters and the police. All of it was seen on TV by the national viewing audience. To the casual viewer, Humphrey may have seemed to have stolen the nomination without ever having competed in a primary against the other contenders. In addition, their nominee was the vice president for the administration that most people blamed for the Vietnam War. Humphrey did distance himself from administration policy later in the campaign, but it was perhaps too little too late. Further, some more socially conservative and often Southern Democrats felt left behind by their party when its standard-bearer had been one of the chief supporters of civil rights legislation, especially the Civil Rights Act of 1964.[10] As a result, Alabama governor George Wallace ran as an independent, further muddying the electoral waters.

Where Did All This Lead?

In the end, Humphrey lost to Nixon in one of the closest popular vote contests to that point in the nation's history. Some in the Democratic Party began to wonder about the appropriateness of selecting presidential candidates the way they did. "Luckily," the turmoil of their convention had already led them to appoint a commission for their next convention in 1972 to examine their selection process and make recommendations to the party for change. The McGovern-Fraser Commission and its recommended changes would forever change the process by which the two parties select their presidential candidates.

So far, in this chapter, we have set the stage for the changes that were about to happen to the long-standing process of selection. Chapter 4 lays out, in detail, what the changes were and hints at what might still come.

Chapter 4

The System Changes Forever

The 1960s was a time of upheaval and just as Americans were learning to be more accepting of one another in society and African Americans and women were asserting their rights, politics was also changing. Some of the political change was directly related to the civil rights movement and the protests against the war, but some political change came about from a more generic need for reform and an opening up of the political process. Two campaigns, the 1960 John Kennedy campaign and the 1964 Barry Goldwater campaign, had profound impact on the internal politics of political parties. These two campaigns, one from the left and one from the right, attracted new political amateurs to party politics. Regardless of party, these reformers were individuals with high hopes and high ideals who were perhaps taken aback by what they observed as they worked for their candidates (Wilson 1966). Most assuredly, the Democratic amateurs must have been horrified at the idea that a candidate (Vice President Hubert Humphrey) who hadn't entered a single primary and who, at least symbolically, represented Lyndon Johnson's position on the war in Vietnam would get their party's nomination for president. They, and even their Republican counterparts, must have been further horrified by the events in the streets of Chicago during the Democratic Convention.

The Next Step

Technically established by the 1968 Democratic Convention, perhaps as a way of recognizing that their selection process that year was flawed, the McGovern-Fraser Commission[1] worked to examine the selection process and make recommendations for change in an environment tainted by the antiwar protests in the streets of Chicago during the convention and Humphrey's loss in a very close race. The commission's work would be important not just for its impact on the 1972 race for president, but also for how it changed the Democratic Party's process of selection to this day and for its ripple effect on the Republican Party's selection process.

First chaired by George McGovern, who was the stand-in candidate for Bobby Kennedy at the 1968 Democratic Convention and who later stepped down as chair to seek the party's 1972 nomination, the commission was charged with developing the rules for the 1972 convention. The commission was established by vote at the 1968 convention, but its members were appointed afterward by Democratic National Committee (DNC) chair, Senator Fred Harris of Oklahoma. Harris steered clear of appointing old school party officials and packed the commission with members of the party known for their reform agenda. Picking McGovern, who was known for his antiwar positions and being somewhat antiestablishment, certainly was a key signal about the direction the commission's work would take. The commission began its work in 1969 with hearings in Washington and around the country listening to party rank and file members who felt slighted by the 1968 process. By 1971, McGovern was set to move on to announce his candidacy for the 1972 Democratic nomination for president and was replaced as chair by Congressman Don Fraser from Minnesota.

The recommendations made by the commission were fairly broad in scope. Tinkering with these initial changes resulted in both further democratizing, as well as later retrenchment of democratization. The letter and spirit of the recommendations have had a lasting impact on the process by which *both* political parties select their presidential candidates. The recommendations, couched as "guidelines," first made it clear that the process used by state party organizations must be clear and specific. Further, any rules used by state parties should include that all meetings related to the selection of delegates (caucuses and conventions) be advertised in advance and "open."[2] Additionally, these meetings must be held in *the same calendar year* as the presidential election. This rule would rear its head in the 2008 contest as Iowa and New Hampshire, the first in the nation caucus and primary respectively, moved their contests closer and closer to January 1st in order to maintain their status when threatened by other states moving their contests much earlier in the year.

Regardless of the mechanism any state party would employ to select delegates—caucus, convention, or primary—there were goals for the achievement of proportional representation of certain groups within the state's delegation to the national convention. These initial groups included blacks, women, and voters under the age of 30. The "unit rule," which was a mechanism to turn any contest into a winner-take-all outcome, was banned. No longer would a simple plurality of the state's delegation get to force the rest of the delegation to vote for the plurality's candidate. Other guidelines were aimed at correcting what these reformers felt were defects in state election laws that overly limited ballot access (e.g., petitioning), discriminated against minorities (e.g., literacy tests), and made it difficult for more mobile voters to get involved (e.g., students).

Not all of the guidelines were adopted and many created controversy. The guidelines urging proportional representation certainly stirred debate and still do today. The arguments raised are quite similar to those made by opponents of affirmative action programs when the charge is made that such policies are nothing but racial quotas that create reverse discrimination, or in the case of voting limit, the rights of voters to select the individuals they wish to represent them. Other recommendations would reduce dramatically the role of party officials by eliminating the ex officio appointment of certain party officers to be delegates (later reversed with the creation of the so-called super delegates). Soon after this recommendation was made, critics charged that it was a rule specifically designed to help George McGovern's army of amateurs (White 1973).

The controversy over rules designed specifically to help McGovern aside, a good many of the recommendations were adopted and praised for their democratization of the selection process. The 1972 campaign and those that followed would be more fair and create more energy. One easy way that most state parties found to meet the new requirements was to employ primaries as opposed to caucuses or conventions. As a result, the number of primaries doubled from 1968 to 1972, from 15 to 30 (Stricherz 2003). The number of first time attendees was up considerably (a trend that continued through 1984) and though the proportion of minorities was also much higher, the delegates were still from a much higher-income level than the rest of the party or the electorate (Jackson and Crotty 2001; Stanley and Niemi 2000). While the McGovern-Fraser reforms did accomplish a great deal for opening up the process, by making it more evenhanded and including more people, there were problems and some have argued that they went too far too fast. The history of candidate selection and its reform was far from over.

Other Reform Efforts

In 1972, while things were a bit quieter for the Democrats, there were problems nonetheless. Debates over controversial issues such as the war in Vietnam, abortion, gay rights, and more took place on the floor of the convention and sometimes continued well past midnight. The convention, while far more civil than the 1968 Chicago debacle, appeared disorganized, and presented the American viewer/voter with a negative image of the Democratic candidate. In fact, presidential candidate George McGovern did not get to give his acceptance speech—a crucial moment for all contenders to make their first truly national pitch—until the wee hours of the morning. An activity that is usually scheduled to reach a prime time viewing audience for most of the nation was on in prime time for viewers of network TV in Hawaii.[3] The confusion and disarray didn't end with the banging of the gavel to adjourn the convention either. It soon came out that McGovern's handpicked running mate—Senator Tom Eagleton of Missouri—had undergone electroshock therapy for depression. At first, McGovern was behind Eagleton "one thousand per cent" (White 1973, 213), but within days, McGovern dumped Eagleton and replaced him with Sargent Shriver, who had headed up the Peace Corps for brother-in-law John Kennedy.

The 1972 Democratic Convention delegates, having seen both the good and the bad of the McGovern-Fraser reforms, sought to tinker further with the rules for delegate selection and the process of choosing their candidate for president. The *Mikulski Commission*, or more formally known as the Commission on Delegate

Selection and Party Structure, was established to streamline the convention and avoid counterproductive squabbling, but even that effort ran into squabbles of its own with party old-timers wanting to do away with the mandates that led to law suits over credentials at the 1972 convention (*Time* 1974). Mikulski's Commission backtracked just a bit from the diversity goals of McGovern-Fraser by eliminating mandatory quotas, but instead mandating state party organizations adopt plans for their respective delegate selection processes that ensured an affirmative action approach to participation (Witcover 1977). The Mikulski Commission also proposed the rule that eventually became the subject of the lawsuit brought by the DNC against the state of Wisconsin, the rule that mandated that delegate selection contests be limited solely to members of the Democratic Party.

Between 1976 and 1980, the *Winograd Commission*, more formally known as the Commission on Presidential Nomination and Party Structure (DNC 2005) worked to eliminate the so-called *loophole primary*, which was a winner-take-all arrangement at the congressional district level (the primary jurisdiction used in most states for delegate selection). While states had done away with the statewide winner-take-all primary, they were a bit more lax when it came to ensuring proportionality at the congressional district level. Further, this commission, headed by Michigan Democratic Party Chair Morley Winograd, urged state parties to fill at-large seats with state party officials and elected officials. This was the first step toward creating the category of delegates known as *Super Delegates* (CNN.com 1996). Most significantly, the Winograd Commission proposed a much shorter timeframe—a window—of 13 weeks from early March through early June. This attempt to shorten the process would later become a major battle for control over the selection process between the DNC and a number of states.

Following the argument made by Senator Ted Kennedy of Massachusetts (in his failed effort to defeat incumbent President Jimmy Carter in 1980) to keep convention delegates free of any legal obligation to vote for a particular candidate, the *Hunt Commission*[4] was established to make that change and to set new rules for the 1984 race. Ted Kennedy's argument to the convention centered on the impact on Carter's popularity of the lingering hostage crisis. Early in the contest for the party's nomination Carter won nearly everything in sight, but as the hostages remained in custody and Americans watched the coverage of the failed rescue mission in April, Carter's candidacy began to lose some steam. Kennedy launched a fight over the convention rules to try to free the delegates elected early on in the process from their obligation to vote for a now wounded candidate. He lost the battle over the rules and then lost the nomination by about the same margin. The Hunt Commission's recommendations included eliminating the commitment of the delegates and changed the definition to make them simply "pledged." At the same time, the Hunt Commission retrenched a bit with respect to proportional allocation of delegates and recommended a return to the *loophole primary* (Polsby and Wildavsky 2000).

For the first time, the Democratic Party examined the critique that perhaps the reforms begun by McGovern-Fraser had gone too far in removing party and elected officials. Their response was to create what has become known generically as *Super Delegates*. Technically, there were super delegates and party elected officials (PEOs).

The super delegates were members of Congress (and later other elected officials like mayors, for example) and the PEOs were individuals who held positions like state party chair or vice chair, National Committee Members, or other state party offices. These delegates would make up 14 percent of the delegates to the 1984 convention (the original proposal was for 30%). In addition, the Hunt Commission, while bringing back the loophole primary, pushed for strict adherence to proportional representation among the delegates based on the performance of presidential candidates in the state's primary or caucus. The commission, however, did include the loophole of the "minimum threshold" that candidates receive 20 percent of the vote in caucuses and 25 percent in primaries in order to qualify for a delegate. The recommendations also included a shorter primary calendar since the schedule of contests was growing as states realized the disadvantages of going later in the season—less impact on the outcome and thus much lower turnout (DNC 2005).

The 1984 campaign for the nomination was originally thought to be a contest between Ted Kennedy and Senator John Glenn—the former astronaut—and possibly former Vice President Walter Mondale. Kennedy never got in and Glenn never caught on. The race turned into a fight to the finish between Mondale and Senator Gary Hart—McGovern's former campaign manager—with Reverend Jesse Jackson running a strong third. It was Jackson's campaign that demonstrated the inherent unfairness of the threshold requirements, with many contests where Jackson had a reasonably strong showing but came away with no delegates for the effort because he didn't reach the 20 percent in a caucus or 25 percent in a primary.

The *Fowler Commission* (the Commission on Democratic Participation), 1984 to 1988, and sometimes referred to as the Fairness Commission, would address this concern and others (Polsby and Wildavsky 2000). First and foremost, the Fowler Commission addressed the minimum threshold issue and lowered the requirement to 15 percent in both primaries and caucuses. This was seen as lowering an enormous barrier for less well-known and less well-resourced candidates. They eliminated the loophole primary and mandated that even results at the lowest level had to reflect proportionality. The primary season was further shortened and PEOs were given a greater role in the process (DNC 2005). Yet, the issue of states seeking to go early, ahead of the traditional first primary in New Hampshire or the first caucus in Iowa, continued to plague the party.[5]

For the period of the 1990s, the dominant concern for the Democrats and the commissions they used to alter their rules seemed to be the schedule of the primaries and caucuses. The opening contests during this time period were held in February and states like Arizona and Delaware would write laws that threatened the sanctity of the party's rules regarding which states were allowed to go first and when. There was some expansion of the role of super delegates

By 2000, however, many within the party began to embrace the idea of rewarding states choosing to hold their contests later in the process with extra delegates. Naturally, this would only entice the state party organization and not necessarily the state legislature if it was controlled by the Republicans, especially if the media attention and influx of money could be seen as necessary to help an ailing economy. For the 2004 convention, the Democrats continued moving the opening of the window to an earlier and earlier date.

The 2008 process moved the official start of the primary season to February 5th and added two other states to the exemptions given to Iowa and New Hampshire—Nevada and South Carolina—to answer critics who felt that Iowa and New Hampshire were not truly representative of voters in the rest of the country. Still, as soon as the early start to the window was announced, many states moved their contests to February 5th creating a rather large Super Tuesday event—a "Super Duper Tuesday."[6] In addition, at least two states—Florida and Michigan—seeking "relevance" for their contests vowed to move outside the window to an earlier date. This began a cascading effect of the exempted states of Iowa, New Hampshire, Nevada, and South Carolina—all jockeying to maintain their special status and creating a scenario where some felt that Iowa might try to move its caucuses to a point in late 2007. Naturally, this would violate another DNC rule dating back to the McGovern-Fraser reforms that required all delegate selection contests to be in the same calendar year as the presidential election itself.

In keeping with its history of using commissions to set the delegate selection process for the coming cycle, the DNC appointed another commission just after the Obama administration took office. This commission, headed by Senator Claire McCaskill (MO) and Representative James Clyburn (SC), was authorized by the 2008 convention and the appointments were made by the new DNC Chair Tim Kaine of Virginia. "In announcing the commission, Mr. Kaine outlined three goals: changing the window for primaries and caucuses, reducing the number of super delegates and improving the caucus system" (Zeleny 2009). The overriding goal was to allow greater participation of voters and to make the process appear less complex. At the same time, the intention was to construct rules such that no state, including Iowa and New Hampshire, would conduct their contest earlier than February 1st.

One of the results of all these reforms was that a number of states switched back from primaries to caucuses. The larger states still tend to use primaries and smaller states use caucuses. This is just an effect of size, since it is easier to organize smaller populations than larger ones—just imagine the Iowa style caucus in Brooklyn, New York, and you can understand the distinction. The effects of front-loading increased over time—this is the process where states compete to go early on the calendar. Originally, it was an attempt by the party leadership to favor front-runner candidates, to give them a chance to knock out "insurgent" competition quickly. In part, this worked in 2000 and 2004, but seemed to backfire in the earliest years of the practice and in 2008, the leadership lost control of the competition and had to use threats against both Florida and Michigan, to no avail, in an attempt to gain compliance with the rules.[7]

Concern grew in Democratic Party circles that George W. Bush's appeal to moderate and independent voters would cause their base to shrink and that they would be at a distinct disadvantage in the 2008 elections. To counter this, some within the party argued that the National Party should go in the direction of Wisconsin many years before and allow an open primary for delegate selection. While many in the party could not accept the idea of Republicans voting in their primaries and perhaps causing mischief, there seemed to be some sense that it would be a good idea to allow independents (sometimes referred to as nonenrolleds) to vote in delegate selection contests. The National Committee felt it couldn't force such a change on state parties—especially since it fought to preserve the partisan nature of the contests in court (see the discussion of court cases later in this chapter)—so it allowed state parties to choose the option if they wished. Overall, throughout the course of these reform efforts, turnout in Democratic primaries has increased.

Republican Reforms

Much of what the Republicans did was by ripple effect. That is, in many states where primaries were chosen by the Democrats, the Republicans sometimes chose that form of selection rather than confusing voters by having two processes. That is not to say, however, that the delegate selection processes are the same in every state. There are some states where the parties pay for any primary or caucus and sometimes the two parties will then choose different mechanisms and/or dates.

The Republicans never adopted any requirement of proportional representation of demographic groups as the Democrats did. They never had to create super delegates because their process never sought to exclude party and elected officials. The party never adopted a mandate for proportionality of outcomes—the allocation of delegates based on the proportion of the vote. While the Republicans did not formally adopt a "window" of time within which all selection contests were to be held until 2000, when they chose or the state mandated a contest on the same day as the Democratic contest, naturally, they would have most of their contests occurring within the Democratic Party's window. Though the delegation seated at Republican conventions is not nearly as demographically diverse as the Democrats' is, it has become a bit more demographically diverse than in the past.

Perhaps, two other factors are most significant in terms of the difference between the two parties. First, the Republicans tend to be organized more like a federal system[8] where the Democrats have tended to be more unitary[9] (though with limited success). As a result, the Republicans have been less likely to mandate changes upon their state party organizations. Second, where the Democrats have created a special commission to review their process in each cycle, the Republican rules made such practices far more difficult in the past, but the 2012 Republican Convention passed a rules change to allow for midcycle changes similar to what the Democrats do.

How Can Political Parties Force States to Alter Election Law?

As "associations," political parties have rights under the First and Fourteenth Amendments to the Constitution. As a key mechanism in the electoral process, political parties often also have a responsibility as agents of the state. The latitude parties have is often a question of where on the "Constitutionally protected association" to "agent of the state" spectrum a legal question falls. On a fairly consistent basis courts have ruled that as associations, political parties have the right to define who gets to be a member, who gets to make use of their "brand" by running on their line, and how their candidates are chosen. Many would argue this is the key component of being a political party (*California Democratic Party et al. v. Jones*, U.S. 567; 120, 2000). On the other hand, since the passage of the Civil Rights and Voting Rights Acts in the mid-1960s, the courts have also recognized that political parties have a duty to ensure nondiscrimination. Similarly, while the courts have said that states may not force parties to accept an electoral system that violates those protected actions, the courts have also indicated that under a compelling reason states have a duty to intervene.

For example, if a political party sought to limit its membership or participation in its primaries to only those voters who were left-handed courts would likely rule that there was no rational basis for that particular discrimination and that a state could pass a law prohibiting such a party rule. This was very much the case with regard to a practice used by the Democratic Party in southern states when it attempted to block participation by African Americans by employing the so-called whites only primary. In this case, the actions of the party went beyond simply limiting who could vote in its primary, but effectively disenfranchised black voters in the general election because in many areas of the south at that time there was, in effect, only one party—the Democratic Party—and a candidate's victory in the primary was tantamount to election.

The first of these court cases that established the precedent of the protection of party rights as associations under the First and Fourteenth Amendments was *Cousins et al. v. Wigoda et al.* (419 U.S. 477, 1975). Some of the issues in this case might seem familiar to those who watched the debate in 2008 over whether or not the DNC would seat delegations from Michigan and Florida who had been elected in contests outside of the established window and thus were elected in violation of the DNC's rules. In 1972, the McGovern-Fraser recommendations discussed earlier were to have their first impact. Paul Wigoda[10] was an operative with the old-style Cook County Democratic Committee—the Daley Machine in Chicago. He headed a slate of 59 delegates elected in accordance with Illinois State Election Law, but contrary to the provisions of the new DNC rules that mandated proportional representation of women, minorities, and young people. William Cousins was but one of the 59 delegates selected in accordance with the party's new rules. Just days before the convention was to begin in July of 1972, the Wigoda group obtained an injunction from the Cook County Circuit Court ordering the Cousins delegates to not take their seats as delegates or to perform as such. The DNC Credentials Committee ruled differently and the Cousins group was seated (*Cousins*).

One might think that the issue would now be over; the DNC had enforced its rules and denied access to the convention to delegates elected in a manner contrary to their rules. There was a larger issue at stake than just who would get to sit at the 1972 Democratic National Convention—could political party rules prevail over state election law? With this larger question still unresolved, the case made its way through the Illinois courts where, not surprisingly state election law was upheld. With the denial of appeal by the Illinois Supreme Court, the decision of the Illinois Appellate Court to uphold the injunction against Cousins stood. The US Supreme Court granted certiorari[11] and heard arguments in the case. In the opinion of the

Court, Justice William Brennan stated clearly that political parties are, in fact, protected associations under the First and Fourteenth Amendments to the Constitution. Since "the States themselves have no constitutionally mandated role in the great task of the selection of Presidential and Vice-Presidential candidates" (*Cousins*), the state needed a compelling reason to interject its authority. Brennan further asserted that given the importance of the task undertaken by political parties at these conventions, individual states should not be given the authority to determine the qualifications of delegates to such conventions without some reliance on the wishes of the party. He argued, "Such a regime could seriously undercut or indeed destroy the effectiveness of the National Party Convention as a concerted enterprise engaged in the vital process of choosing Presidential and Vice-Presidential candidates—a process which usually involves coalitions cutting across state lines" (*Cousins*).

The overall issue of state law versus party rules was addressed once again in *Democratic Party of the United States et al. v. Wisconsin et al.* (450 U.S. 107, 1981). In this case, a more recent rule, that of eliminating voting by nonparty members in primaries, introduced by the recommendations of the Mikulski Commission was in dispute. Wisconsin used a two-step process where voters of any affiliation could vote in a presidential preference primary and only party members could participate in caucuses to select delegates. The problem was that the caucuses were bound by the results of the preference primary. The DNC argued that the binding of the caucus participants to select a slate of delegates reflecting a vote of nonparty voters violated their requirement that delegates be selected in contests limited to party members only. As in the Illinois case, the state courts ruled that the DNC could not refuse to seat the delegates. Once the case got to the US Supreme Court, however, the Court disagreed just as it did with the state court in Illinois in *Cousins*. Here is where the Court uses the language "the interests advanced by the State do not justify its substantial intrusion into the associational freedom of members of the National Party" (*Democratic Party of the United States*). In other words, in absence of a compelling reason, the state could not violate the First Amendment rights of a political party.

In an ironic twist of the law, these cases were turned to favor the Republican Party in the case of *Tashjian, Secretary of State of Connecticut v. Republican Party of Connecticut et al.* (U.S. 1043, 1986). Since 1955, the state of Connecticut employed the traditional definition of a primary and required that only party members could vote in such contests. By 1984, the Republicans in Connecticut had decided to try something different.[12] So, in arguing against the position of Julia Tashjian, Connecticut Secretary of State,[13] the state Republican Party cited the US Supreme Court decisions in *Cousins* and *Democratic Party of the United States*. In doing so, it asserted that if it chooses to go in the opposite direction of the Democratic Party in those cases that was also protected behavior under its rights of association under the First and Fourteenth Amendments. The Court agreed with the Connecticut Republicans and rejected Tashjian's argument that the two different processes would be difficult to administer.

While the parties have these rights and the Court has consistently supported them in their assertion of these rights, the reality is far different. As the Democratic Party did in 2008 when asserting these rights against the states of Michigan and Florida,[14] it backed down in the *Wisconsin* case and has often backed down when confronted by states that wanted to pursue a different course. With Wisconsin and Montana (there was a similar circumstance of an open primary) the party granted the states an exemption. When the party could well have asserted its rights and taken New Hampshire and Iowa to court over their desire to hold first in the nation contests outside of the window described in party rules, it backed down and granted an exemption.

The Process in General

The process we are left with after all the reforms and legal battles looks pretty much the same as it has over the years. While the schedule changes from presidential election to presidential election and delegates are now simply pledged as opposed to committed to a candidate (for the Democrats), the first two contests have not yet changed. Additionally, the overall strategy remains much as it did in 1968 when Senator Eugene McCarthy upended everything with his surprise strong finish in the New Hampshire primary.

You may be asking why it is that Iowa and New Hampshire work so hard to keep their status as first in the nation contests. For these two states, the prestige and media attention they receive is well worth it. Each time a presidential election cycle begins, the fact that these two states go first on the schedule means that the candidates, their staffs, and the media all descend upon the state. They rent hotel rooms and cars, they buy food, they spend money on advertising, and they engage in other activities that help the economies of these states. In Iowa, it is the slower economic season with little agricultural activity in the winter. In New Hampshire, a presidential primary might be a great boon in a winter with little snow, where the state relies on the ski industry for much of its economic activity in the winter months.

Once these two states have their contests, there is no particular order to when each state (and party within that state) holds its contest. At one time, there was a rough adherence to a schedule from one cycle to another. For example, it was once the case that the California primary was almost always in early June and the New York primary would follow it by two weeks or so. With the practice of intentional front-loading by party leaders to thwart the campaigns of weaker candidates leading to many nomination battles ending before larger states like California, New York, and Pennsylvania could have an impact on the outcome, these states began moving their contests earlier within the window. Theoretically, their voters would have some reason to participate in the primaries (Wayne 2009).

As noted earlier, in 2008, for example, many states employed a strategy of going first creating what some called a "Super Duper Tuesday." As far back as the early 1980s, the Democrats, particularly southern conservative Democrats in the Democratic Leadership Council (DLC), adopted a strategy of trying to have a significant number of contests held on the same day in the South (Stanley and Hadley 1987). With the more moderate Democratic voters of the South, the DLC felt that they might slow the momentum of a more liberal candidate and give a fighting chance to a more moderate one. This strategy became known as Super Tuesday, playing off the name given to the day on which football's Super Bowl is played—Super Sunday. Eventually, the strategy got away from them and by 2008, New York and California both jumped to the head of the line and held their contests on February 5th—the first day of the window.[15]

In an earlier discussion of the history of the process, I mentioned that in 1968 the New Hampshire primary was first in the nation, but that it was in March. In 2008, the New Hampshire primary was January 5th, completing a journey backwards on the calendar through February where the contest moved a bit earlier just about every presidential election cycle. Of course, in 2008, there was competition from many other states to go early and two states—Michigan and Florida—ignored the calendar created by the DNC and went sufficiently early to push Iowa and New Hampshire back to nearly New Year's Day.

Throughout the history of primaries and caucuses, turnout by voters has generally been much lower than that for general elections. True, there have been occasions when hotly contested races have drawn voters to the polls and contests that last longer maintain voter interest from the beginning (whether March, February, or January) all the way through the last contest in June. In 2008, in fact, turnout in later contests in May and June remained higher than usual. In the Democratic Primary in Montana, the raw number of voters turning out set a record for the state in primaries (*Billings Gazette* 2010). The point of the popular choice period has been to create higher levels of turnout and greater participation of voters in selecting party candidates for the general election. In many ways, the Democratic Party's intentions have been met, yet its lack of success throughout the period has led them to constantly tinker with the process. Since this reform era began in 1968 and through the 2012 election, there have been 12 presidential elections and the Republicans have won 7 of them.[16]

There are two keys to winning in this new environment—organization and money. Vice President Hubert Humphrey was the last major party presidential candidate selected the old-fashioned way, with the support of state party chairs and not having tested himself before voters in primaries or caucuses. His organization could be small and not have to worry about advertising or get out the vote (GOTV) efforts. In the more contemporary model, organizations in the primaries and caucuses have to be large and effective. It is much tougher after the reforms for a candidate to take time to catch on gradually after winning or outperforming expectations in a few early contests. The outsider candidate now has to win two types of contests and his/her organization must be aimed at both—the invisible or money primary and the usual primary or caucus. Barack Obama's success was built on the creation of a grassroots and netroots organization that could raise record sums of money from many small dollar donors and make use of enthusiasm generated by personal charisma to build large crowds and bring supporters out to vote.

In spite of many attempts by the Democratic Party to bring party leaders back into the process, the real kingmakers are now in the media. The pundits, reporters, and anchors (though it is sometimes hard to tell the difference) who make pronouncements about the viability of candidates now often have more to do with who has the potential to be successful than does the candidate's actual viability or message. Before a single vote had been cast in 2008, the front-runner in each party had changed at least once.

Because of the length of the process and the need for money and organization, candidates must start early and have sufficient time to give to the campaign. It would be ideal if the candidate was one who had voluntarily left office (had not lost) or had been term limited. From this perspective, a recent former vice president would make a good potential candidate. In the last cycle in 2008, there were a number of different candidates from different offices, some still in office, and others out. In the end, the contest had two sitting senators running against another sitting senator and a governor.

So, we are left with a selection process where media pundits—Chris Matthews, Wolf Blitzer, and Bill O'Reilly in the 2004 to 2008 cycles—have more say over who gets to be the nominees of the two major parties than do the leaders of those parties. Do the voters have much say? Many would argue that yes, they do. If, however, voters are following the judgments of the punditry, is that any better than if we followed the judgments of party leaders and elected officials? This intersection recalls that age-old conundrum raised in the movie *Mr. Smith Goes to Washington*. James Stewart as Senator Jefferson Smith asks a group of Washington reporters what gives them the right to make judgments about government officials because after all no one elected them. One of the reporters responds, "We're the only ones who can afford to be honest. We don't have to be re-elected." During the time between the 2008 and 2012 elections, the two major parties began having discussions, together and separately, about the very questions raised by the process we have just reviewed. Questions like, who should vote in an internal party process? Or, what role is appropriate for party and elected officials in the process? And, what should the schedule of contests look like?

Chapter 5

Campaign Finance

Without money, campaigns go nowhere. In fact, the last chapter alluded to an "invisible primary" in which there is no voting and there is no public campaigning. Campaigning goes on all the time in the invisible primary but the real contest is among contributors for cash. Many critics and cynics of the campaign process, whether at the level of president or city council, talk about the undue influence of money on politics. They usually refer to the ability of the donors to get access to the elected official or they talk about the way elected officials behave in order to be rewarded by interest groups for their prior votes. Candidates make a sour face when confronted with the reality of "call time" or "dialing for dollars" and lament about the time spent doing something other than talking to voters or, in the case of an incumbent, doing the people's business.[1]

At the heart of the issue is whether or not campaign spending is speech. If spending is considered a form of political speech, it is thus protected by the First Amendment. So far, this has been the position of the Supreme Court, as in the case of *Buckley et al. v. Valeo* (424 U.S. 1, 1976) where the Court equated spending with speech. Naturally, this decision has made it impossible for Congress to tackle the real substance of campaign finance and pushed its efforts to regulate to the margins. While they can regulate what candidates can accept when also seeking federal matching funds, putting an end to the influence of money in politics has not been easy. The law that prompted *Buckley*, the Federal Election Campaign Act of 1971 and its later amendments was not the first time Congress had regulated campaign finance. One of the earliest attempts was the Tillman Act in 1907 that banned bank and corporate contributions to federal candidates. The Tillman Act stood as law for over one hundred years until the Supreme Court overturned it in January of 2010 in the case of *Citizens United v. Federal Elections Commission* (558 U.S. 310, 2010). This is the decision that prompted President Obama to admonish the Court with many of its members seated directly in front of him at the 2010 State of the Union Address for undoing over one hundred years of campaign finance regulation aimed at keeping banks and corporations out of political campaigns (in a direct way). Associate Justice Samuel Alito rather obviously shook his head and it was obvious he was saying, "That's not true" in response to Obama's comment about foreign companies influencing American elections (Barnes 2010). Critics on both sides of the issue railed on for days about the appropriateness of Obama's comments (and their timing) and the reaction of Justice Samuel Alito to those comments (see Liptak 2010 for just one example of the media coverage following the incident).

There are those who take a "purist" view and believe that perhaps the only legitimate regulation on campaign finance is public disclosure. There are others who go to the other extreme and advocate for public financing of campaigns. In the middle lies a complexity understood by few.

The History of Campaign Finance

As mentioned previously, one of the earliest attempts at regulating the manner in which federal campaigns were financed was the Tillman Act of 1907. Earlier attempts focused on solicitations from federal employees (e.g., the Naval Appropriations Bill in 1867 and the Civil Service Reform Act of 1883) (FEC n.d.; Corrado et al. 1997). In 1905, President Teddy Roosevelt, the progressive reformer who was known for his antimonopoly policies, emphasized the need to ban corporate contributions and to provide for public financing of presidential campaigns. The Tillman Act of 1907 appears to be an attempt at addressing Roosevelt's concerns, but as with much legislation, it was more symbol than substance. The Act banned contributions from corporations and nationally chartered banks, but not contributions from their officers or employees, and it lacked any significant enforcement mechanism.

The first effort to have public disclosure of campaign contributions was in the Federal Corrupt Practices Act of 1910. This law applied to candidates for election to the US House of Representatives. A year later, Congress extended the disclosure policy to Senate candidates. In both cases, however, there was little in the way of sanction provided. The intent of the law was to limit spending by parties and to require disclosure. One can imagine, however, that the limits of technology at that time would constrain the ability to share the information quickly and would work against the actual intent of the legislation. It would only be much later that technological advances such as the photocopy machine and the Internet would make disclosure requirements practical and truly enforceable.

By 1925, Congress was to make revisions to the Federal Corrupt Practices Act to enforce expenditure limits and disclosure requirements. As with many other areas, Congress was often reluctant to enforce laws against its own members since so many candidates simply disregarded the law. Even with this disregard of the law, it was the primary law in campaign finance until the passage of the Federal Elections Campaign Act (FECA) in 1971. The 1940 amendments to the Hatch Act extended rules that applied to general election campaigns to primaries and prohibited contributions by federal employees and from employees of any company doing business with the federal government. In response to the use by labor unions of money from dues to make contributions to political campaigns, in 1943 the Smith-Connally Act included unions in the prohibition against corporate and bank contributions. This law would prompt the formation of the first political action committee (PAC) in 1944. In 1947, Congress made the bans on contributions from corporations, banks, and unions permanent.

In 1971, Congress passed the FECA and the Revenue Act that established the foundations of our current campaign finance system, created the Federal Elections Commission (FEC), and set up the presidential campaign fund to provide public funding for the general election through a check off on tax returns. The legislation also included a minimal tax deduction or optional tax credit for political contributions.[2] After the revelations of abuse of campaign finances associated with the break-in at and cover-up of Watergate, Congress passed more stringent restrictions as amendments to the FECA in 1974. President Gerald Ford vetoed the amendments to the FECA and Congress overrode the veto.[3] These new regulations included strict limits on contributions and expenditures and gave the newly created FEC the authority to enforce the laws. It was the strict contribution limits and the manner of appointing the members of the FEC that led to the filing of a lawsuit by New York Senator James Buckley and others[4] to challenge a number of provisions of the new law. In the end, the Supreme Court upheld much of the law. The only parts of the law struck down as unconstitutional were the joint appointments of commissioners by both political branches[5] and the limits on independent expenditures.[6] In the years following the Court's decision in *Buckley*, Congress brought the law into compliance with the ruling and in the amendments of 1979 essentially created the category of money that came to be known as "soft money." Such contributions were virtually unlimited since they came from state and local parties and could be spent on party building activities (Whitaker 2004).[7]

This history of campaign finance reveals various stops and starts and demonstrates that the concept of public financing of campaigns can be dated back at least as far as the presidency of Teddy Roosevelt. More importantly, careful examination of the history shows where the problems lie. You may have noted that the first PAC was formed in the 1940s in reaction to the elimination of direct contributions to campaigns by labor unions. What we didn't cover was that in the late 1970s following the 1974 FECA amendments, *Buckley*, and the 1976 and 1979 additional amendments to FECA, there was an explosion of PAC formation. It is the influence of PAC money and the creation of what was essentially legalized money laundering[8] through soft money that concerned good government groups and some elected officials. It would take until the first decade of the twenty-first century for Congress to pass meaningful change, but even that change would bring new problems.

Bipartisan Campaign Reform Act (BCRA)

The BCRA (P.L. 107–155), commonly known as McCain-Feingold for its two sponsors in the Senate—Senator John McCain (R-AZ) and Russ Feingold (D-WI)—was an attempt to regulate soft money and issue advocacy advertising. As things often go in the nation's capitol, the bill that actually became law was not McCain-Feingold, but Shays-Meehan—the House version of the bill. The new law, which further amends the 1971 FECA, is perhaps best known for its requirement that the candidate appear in an ad and say, "I'm Jane Smith and I approve this message."

Among partisan political activists there was initial concern over the strict limitations placed on local party organizations and the extent to which they could employ their party's federal candidates in ads for state, county, and local campaigns. Often part of this difficulty is removed if the local party is paid by the federal candidate for his or her portion of the expenditure. While some may still see this as a problem in need of reform, it does eliminate the sometimes shoddy reporting of contributions to state and local organizations. When money is flowing from a federal campaign to state organization, it is all hard money and subject to federal regulation and disclosure requirements. According to the Cornell University Law School Legal Information Institute (2003), these provisions of the law have been upheld by the Supreme Court. State and local parties may still raise and spend money for generic party building activity such as voter registration, voter identification, get out the vote drives, and other generic activity provided no federal candidate's name is mentioned (Whitaker 2004).

The BCRA also clearly defined so-called issue ads that parties and interest groups would often run just prior to elections (primary or general) to promote a position on an issue or to highlight aspects of a candidate's record (positive or negative). Any issue ad (on broadcast TV or radio, cable, or satellite TV or radio) that mentions a clearly identified candidate for federal office within a specified time before an election[9] and is aimed at an audience that might vote in that election is defined as "electioneering communication" (Cornell 2003). As with all the previous legislation, the BCRA banned corporations, banks, and labor unions from using money from their treasuries to pay for such ads. They could, however, still form PACs to pay for the ads. Certain not-for-profit organizations were exempted.

With all the good intentions of the supporters of the law, there were those who opposed it, or at least certain provisions of it. As with *Buckley*, it was a fairly broad coalition of individuals and organizations that brought suit against its enforcement by the FEC. The group was headed by then Senate Majority Leader Mitch McConnell, but included the California Democratic Party, the National Rifle Association, and the American Civil Liberties Union to name just a few. Most of the law was upheld as were the majority of the arguments raised by McConnell and his allies about infringement of First Amendment rights, particularly those protected in *Buckley*. Only two aspects of the law were rejected by the Court. The part of the law that banned contributions by minors (intended to prevent parents from circumventing contribution limits) was struck down as was a limitation on party expenditures that were not connected to specific candidates (*Buckley*).

The BCRA would not enjoy such support from the Court for long, however. In 2007, the Court, in a decision written by Chief Justice John Roberts, said, "Enough is enough" (*Federal Election Commission v. Wisconsin Right to Life*, 551 U.S. 449). Roberts went on to say, "When it comes to defining what speech qualifies as the functional equivalent of express advocacy subject to such a ban—the issue we do have to decide—we give the benefit of the doubt to speech, not censorship." This was strong language, but still did not completely throw out BCRA. More specifically, the definition of "express advocacy" was further clarified and ads such as those run by Wisconsin Right to Life because they advocated a position on an issue—preventing filibusters of judicial nominees—were not express advocacy for or against a particular federal candidate.

Citizens United v. FEC

Still further fine-tuning of FECA and BCRA would come with the Supreme Court's decision in *Citizens United*, but it would come in the form of a landmark decision that rocked the very foundations of campaign finance regulation. So far, we have seen that campaign finance regulation is built on three legs: (1) banning of corporate, bank, and union contributions; (2) disclosure of contributors; and (3) limits on contributions and expenditures. The Court's ruling in *Citizens United* took out one of those legs—the ban on corporate, bank, and union contributions. While the Court has slowly but surely limited congressional ability to regulate campaign finance, this decision came as a bit of surprise to many, not because of the limits on regulation but because of its sweeping application of a legal doctrine that had been around at least since 1886. The doctrine was established in the case of *Santa Clara County v. Southern Pacific Railroad Co.* (118 U.S. 394, 1886) and affirmed in *Covington and Lexington Turnpike Railroad Co. v. Sandford* (164 U.S. 578, 1896)—the notion that corporations have the same constitutional protections as individuals.

According to their website, Citizens United is an organization dedicated to the restoration of "citizen control" of government. "Citizens United seeks to reassert the traditional American values of limited government, freedom of enterprise, strong families, and national sovereignty and security. Citizens United's goal is to restore the founding fathers' vision of a free nation, guided by the honesty, common sense, and good will of its citizens" (Citizens United n.d.). In pursuit of this goal, Citizens United produced a video entitled *Hillary: The Movie*, a negative treatment of her record and "about the Clinton scandals of the past and present" (hillarythemovie.com). Citizens United feared the FEC would ban the broadcast of the movie within 30 days of a primary in accordance with the BCRA definition of an "electioneering communication" and that they would be subject to civil and criminal penalties. Citizens United sued, claiming that the ban and the actions Congress took to create the ban were a violation of their First Amendment right to free speech.

Initially a three-judge panel ruled in favor of the FEC and Citizens United appealed. In his opinion for the majority, Justice Kennedy cast aside all laws banning campaign contributions by corporations, banks, and unions, thus undoing one hundred years of regulatory practice. As a result of Kennedy's opinion, such organizations may now contribute money to political campaigns and make direct independent expenditures out of their regular treasuries. However, the Court upheld the requirements of disclosure and disclaimer stating that such requirements do not place an undue burden on the corporation in exercising its right to protected speech (*Citizens United*). It was this ruling that prompted the incident between Obama and Alito mentioned earlier.

Since the *Citizens United* ruling, Congress has been attempting to craft legislation that would restore some of the restrictions on corporate, bank, and union contributions. These have been primarily Democratic attempts and it remains to be seen if they could craft any legislation that would meet the constitutional demands of *Citizens United* or the agenda of their Republican colleagues.

Whither Campaign Finance Reform?

At the very least, we are left with a system of campaign finance regulations that limit individual contributions and require public disclosure of contributions and disclaimers on independent advertisements. We are also left with the opposing questions of "is that enough?" or "is that too much?" It is doubtful that in the short term Congress will devise anything to plug what, to many, appears to be a hole in campaign finance laws created by *Citizens United*. For good or ill, money will continue to play a major role in political campaigns, forcing candidates to play dialing for dollars and spend a significant portion of their campaign day on call time.

The system as it stands still has a public financing component. Many candidates in recent election cycles have found the limits imposed by the public financing system to be too restrictive. While the tradition has been that Republicans have been more successful at raising money than Democrats to fund presidential campaigns, the Internet and targeted appeals have sometimes made the reverse true. Certainly, George W. Bush proved the stereotype to be true, but Democratic candidates, starting with Howard Dean in 2004 and culminating in a political role reversal in 2008. Barack Obama raised enormous sums of money from small donors, primarily on the Internet, and John McCain was left to use whatever public funds were available. Stereotypes have been proven wrong and technology has changed the game. It remains to be seen what impact *Citizens United* will have on this recent trend.

The public financing aspect of our current campaign finance system works in two ways. First, candidates for their party's nomination may qualify for matching funds for the primaries and caucuses. Second, once nominated at their party's convention, candidates may then choose to accept a lump sum payment from the FEC to cover the costs of the fall campaign.

To qualify for matching funds in the primary season, candidates must raise at least $100,000, but a minimum of at least $5,000 in each of at least 20 states. These contributions must be from individuals and not PACs or other organizations. No more than $250 counts toward these qualifying amounts and the FEC will match contributions up to that $250.[10] So, if John Smith gives presidential candidate Barb Jones a contribution of $500, it is legal, and Jones can keep the whole $500, but the FEC will match only the first $250 of the contribution.[11]

The 1974 amendments to the FECA established the Presidential Election Campaign Fund through the use of a checkoff on individuals' tax returns that contributes $3 to the fund.[12] The fund is used to provide the matching grants detailed above and to provide the money given to candidates who choose to accept it for the fall election. In 1976, the amount of money distributed to both incumbent President

Gerald Ford and challenger Jimmy Carter was $21,820,000 each. By 2008, John McCain was provided with $84,103,800 (Barack Obama chose to opt out of public funds). Additionally, the parties receive federal funds to help defray the costs of operating their conventions. According to the FEC's website, there have been three elections where public funds have been dispersed to third-party candidates: 1980, 1996, and 2000.

It is likely that we will be left with a legal quandary over the legitimacy of campaign finance regulation for some time to come. In the wake of *Citizens United* and *Buckley*, Congress is left with little constitutional ground on which to base any regulations. This, of course, presumes we want to regulate campaign finance. As indicated before, there are some who believe the only legitimate regulation should be limited to disclosure, and there are others, no doubt, who believe that a right to privacy might prohibit even a disclosure requirement. Certainly, if one supported some form of regulation of campaign finance beyond a disclosure requirement it will be necessary to amend the Constitution to do so.

Chapter 6

The National Nominating Conventions: Are They Worth It and What's Next?

In recent history, national party nominating conventions have not been very significant in determining the party nominees, relevant platforms, and hard and fast rules that last very long. To many observers national nominating conventions have become a mere ratification of the primary and caucus process. This begs the question, "Are national party nominating conventions worth the effort?" Certainly, the reforms discussed in chapter 4 seem to have accomplished at least one thing across the two parties—the delegations to the conventions do appear to *look* more like the general electorate. Both sets of delegates are more diverse than in the 1960s, though the Democrats are perhaps more diverse, partly due to their more stringent representational requirements and the makeup of the Democratic constituency. What does this diversity, in both parties, really mean if the delegates are left with nothing to decide?

Before answering that question, it is perhaps best if we examine the more traditional view of national nominating conventions. We have already seen from an earlier discussion (see chapter 2) that conventions reflected the nation's physical and political expansion. In this respect, conventions were an early democratizing force in American politics; more people were involved in the process of selecting presidential candidates. As such, the introduction of conventions played a role similar to that of the reforms urged by the McGovern-Fraser Commission.

Four Traditional Functions of National Nominating Conventions

The first traditional function of the national nominating conventions is to set the party rules and regulations. The Republicans have tended to be more stringent in adhering to this particular function in that they generally decide their rules for upcoming contests at their conventions. The Democrats have tended to authorize the appointment of special commissions to recommend rules to the National Committee for adoption at some meeting prior to the quadrennial convention. Still, both party conventions have the right to alter the rules for the time they are sitting to do the party's business. For example, in 1976 Ronald Reagan attempted to force Gerald Ford to reveal his vice-presidential pick prior to the vote on the presidential nomination. This attempt took the form of a motion to change the rules for the convention to require presidential candidates to announce their running mate selections prior to the vote on their own nomination[1] (Witcover 1977). Similarly, in 1980 Ted Kennedy sought to change the rules at the Democratic Convention to release delegates from their commitment to vote for Jimmy Carter. Both Reagan and Kennedy lost these rules fights and subsequently lost their party's nomination.

The second function of nominating conventions is to set the party's platform. The platform is a document that sets forth the party's positions on issues of relevance to voters in the upcoming election and beyond. The idea, of course, is to provide a basis of comparison of the two parties' positions on a wide range of issues and to allow voters to differentiate between their candidates for president, congress, state offices, and so on. In more recent years, some would argue that party platforms have little real meaning. The wording often obfuscates the true positions on issues and it is rare that candidates at all levels of office are held to the positions or wording in the platform.

Third, and perhaps most significant, is the selection of the parties' presidential and vice-presidential candidates. With the advent of committed and then merely pledged delegates, all selected in the rather public settings of primaries and caucuses, there has been no real question about who the nominees would be once the conventions were held. In fact, it is usually weeks or months before the conventions that the leading candidates for each party nomination have accumulated sufficient votes to win on the first ballot. Since Reagan's selection of Schweiker and Carter's selection of Mondale, both in 1976, the most mystery surrounded John McCain's pick of Sarah Palin in 2008—one made in the week prior to the convention and announced the day after the closing of the Democratic convention that year.[2] The more traditional route was for the presidential nominee to wait until he had secured the votes on the floor of the convention during the roll call and then to make a vice-presidential pick. In many ways, it was considered unseemly to pick the vice-presidential candidate when you, yourself, had not yet officially sown up the presidential nomination. Of course, these hurried selections might cause some difficulty—as in the case of McGovern's pick of Senator Tom Eagleton of Missouri in 1972. On the night of McGovern winning the nomination, when asked by a McGovern staffer if he had any skeletons in the closet, Eagleton assured him there were none.[3] Days later, the nation found out that Eagleton had been in therapy for depression and had, in fact, undergone the radical treatment of electroshock therapy. Without sufficient time to vet such choices these kinds of errors can be made. Many argue that McCain's choice of Palin was more a gesture to "stick it to" party leaders who supposedly wouldn't let him have his first choice—Independent Senator Joe Lieberman (CT), a former Democrat. As a result, the McCain camp was allegedly unaware that Palin's unmarried, teenage daughter was pregnant (Heilemann and Halperin 2010).

Last, and certainly not of least importance, is the function of uniting the party and launching the fall campaign. Often, the convention has been the culmination of a brutal primary battle, and can be a vehicle to heal the wounds inflicted and the rifts opened between personalities and factions within the party. Prime time speaking opportunities or other important duties given to the vanquished opponents can help the healing process. Concessions on rules or platform, seeking advice on running mates, and so forth, can go a long way toward bridging any gaps created by the recently concluded fight. In 2008, many Obama supporters took umbrage that Hillary Clinton did not formally release her delegates until the convention. Clinton supporters wanted the opportunity to show their pride in their candidate and perhaps to cast a vote for her as cathartic and necessary for them to eventually come around to support Obama (Kornblut 2009; Traister 2010).

Some critics, and even some supporters, of contemporary conventions have noted that this last function has become the real overall purpose of the national nominating conventions. Delegates, many of whom are party loyalists and workers, come to the conventions for a four to five day long party. They often will pay their own way—airfare and hotel stay—but will be wined and dined by the host committee, interest groups, causes, and candidates such that if they do it right they can eat and drink for minimal cost during their stay.[4] In some cases, if a delegate is a member of an interest group, transportation and housing will be covered by the interest group or perhaps he or she will receive a stipend to cover expenses. It would be easy for a delegate to turn a convention stay into a vacation, given that the conventions are often held in venues that are tourist attractions or are close to them. The 2004 and 2008 Democratic Conventions were in Boston and Denver, respectively, and offered many opportunities for extension of the visit. The same could be said of the Republican convention of 2004 in New York City.

The Staging and Schedule of the Convention

Both major parties have learned well the lessons of the 1968 and 1972 Democratic Conventions. Especially since 9/11, security has been a major concern at convention sites—after all, with so many political leaders and elected officials gathered in one place, a convention would be an inviting terrorist target (this is the same reason why protesters find the conventions tempting—exposure). So, there is a rather low likelihood of anything approaching the mayhem of the 1968 Democratic Convention in Chicago occurring in the foreseeable future.

The lack of organization provided by the 1972 Democratic Convention moved both parties to attempt better management of the image they project with their four nightlong opportunity to reach out to the American public. Such image management, however, has worked against them to a certain degree. All of the most controversial activity has been moved out of TV's prime time and given TV nothing of interest to cover during the time of its widest viewing audience. Some of this was begun at the request of the broadcasters, who suggested that lengthy speeches and routine procedure did not suit the live medium of TV. Over time the parties complied, and ironically, as a result, the broadcast networks give little coverage to the activities on the floor and use a "highlight show" format at best. The cable news outlets resort to "talking head" coverage where little of the action—if it can be called that—on the floor is covered, but provides an opportunity for these networks to promote their political team of reporters, pundits, and commentators. C-SPAN provides fairly unfiltered coverage, but given that most of the more "interesting" activity has been scheduled for nonprime time, there isn't much to watch. So, while the parties have manipulated the conventions to provide a four nightlong infomercial about their product—their candidates and platform—they have made the infomercial so dull that few people watch. Yet, according to Howard Kurtz, media critic with the *Washington Post* (and later also CNN and The Daily Beast), even though it had been somewhat their idea to trim back the importance of what conventions did, the broadcast media "could not quite relinquish the prestige of covering this quadrennial ritual" (Kurtz 1992).

Items of business that might cause controversy (rules and credentials fights and debates over platform positions) have been moved to the afternoon sessions of the conventions. Lengthy, so-called spontaneous demonstrations of support for candidates, whose names get mentioned, complete with hired local high school or college bands, balloons, confetti, and delegates parading up and down the aisles with placards have become a thing of the past. Certainly, there are still planned demonstrations of support, but with the contest all but settled prior to the convention the support is for one candidate, one team. In 2008, the Democrats even pushed the ceremonial roll call of the states into the afternoon to provide more time for speakers during prime-time coverage of the convention.[5]

Traditionally, the conventions followed a fairly set routine of business. Day one was almost always set aside for the welcoming speeches from the hosts—elected officials from the party local to the convention venue. Day two would normally be taken up with committee reports, credentials; rules; and platform. This is the work that the parties generally consider to be either too mundane or too potentially inflammatory to expose to the prime-time viewing audience. Day three would normally be the day of presidential nominating speeches and the call of the roll of the state delegations. Day four would be the day of the vice-presidential nomination and the acceptance speeches by the running mates.

Instead, more recent conventions attempt to highlight very popular members of the party. More senior elected officials or those retired (through their own choice or the choice of the voters) may return to speak to the delegates. In particular, past presidents are often invited to come and speak to rally the troops. Or, an aging legislator or governor may be given an opportunity essentially to say good-bye (as the Democrats provided Senator Ted Kennedy in 2008). At the other end of the spectrum would be the opportunity for a rising star who could use the boost of a national audience. Barack Obama in 2004, as an Illinois state senator running for the US Senate, got the opportunity to address the Democratic Convention as its keynote speaker giving his US Senate bid a shot in the arm (and giving him a leg up for four years later).

In the end, however, whatever rancor or hurt feelings that grew out of a bitter primary battle must be put aside as the delegates leave the convention and head back to their homes to conduct the fall campaign against the opposition. Did the ill will between Ted Kennedy and Jimmy Carter doom Carter's reelection effort in 1980? Did the lengthy battle for the Republican nomination and McCain's possible anger at the party inner circle make his difficult task nearly impossible in 2008? Would any convention in 1980 have helped the Democrats heal their wounds? Would a 2008 Republican convention not disrupted by Hurricane Gustav have given them the boost they needed to overcome the movement-like quality of the Obama campaign?

The other aspect of convention reorganization has been the shortening of speeches and trying to get speakers to "stick to the script." Long rambling speeches, while a staple of pre-TV politics and in that era considered a form of entertainment, usually don't make for good prime-time TV. Since 1972, most convention speakers have been given rather strict guidelines about how much time they may use. One of the most infamous violations of this more recent practice was then Governor Bill Clinton's speech to nominate Massachusetts Governor Michael Dukakis at the 1988 Democratic National Convention. Clinton ran long, cementing in the minds of the viewing audience his tendency to give long speeches—something he was noted for when delivering televised addresses to the nation while he was president. He ran so long, in fact, that when he uttered the phrase "and in conclusion" the delegates began to applaud and cheer. In his autobiography, *My Life* (2004), Clinton argues that his speech was much shorter, but when he sent it to the Dukakis campaign for vetting, they added a great deal to the speech. When he ultimately won his party's nomination in 1992, Clinton joked about his long-windedness as he began his acceptance speech with the words, "Well, I ran for President this year for one reason and one reason only: I wanted to come back to this convention center and finish that speech I started four years ago" (Clinton 1992).

Two things have impacted internal struggles over rules and credentials[6]—early victories by relatively wide margins and moving such conflicts out of the bright lights of prime-time TV. With early and decisive victories by candidates in both parties there is usually sufficient time before the convention to iron out disagreements. Even in the most drawn out contest in recent history—the 2008 race between Barack Obama and Hillary Clinton—the Democratic Party was still able to agree to a compromise on the one glaring issue that could have caused great difficulty on the floor. As noted earlier, the states of Florida and Michigan both held their primaries earlier than the "window" set by party rules would normally allow and were in danger of having their delegations not seated. The contest between Obama and Clinton was winding down as the Democratic National Committee's (DNC's) Rules and By-Laws Committee was able to work out a mechanism by which the two delegations would be seated.[7]

It was the loss of a battle over which delegates should be seated that ultimately lost Teddy Roosevelt his attempted comeback in 1912. In the few primaries that were held at that time, Roosevelt won all but one—Massachusetts—while a great many delegates from the West were in question. It would be up to the convention to decide, but with the Republican organization behind the incumbent president the outcome was inevitable—the vast majority of the questionable delegates were awarded to William Howard Taft leaving Roosevelt to challenge a total of 248 delegates at the convention (Gould 2008).[8]

Similarly, a battle over credentials at the 1952 Republican Convention led to the victory of Dwight Eisenhower for the party's nomination. Eisenhower and his supporters accused Robert Taft of "stealing delegates," particularly in southern states.[9] In a credentials battle that involved a "Fair Play" proposal, Eisenhower defeated Taft and his supporters, stripping Taft of many of the disputed delegates. Once again, it is here in 1952 that TV plays an early pivotal role. In the debate over "Fair Play," Taft's supporters wanted to keep the dispute out of the public eye and Eisenhower's supporters wanted it covered on live TV. "Eisenhower's camp was able to use television to force open the proceedings to their advantage" (Karabell 1998, 5). Quoting an unnamed commentator, Karabell asserts, that to oppose the Eisenhower Fair Play proposal "on television was like trying to commit grand larceny in broad daylight" (1998, 5). Eisenhower was able to win the nomination and go on to defeat Democratic candidate Adlai Stevenson in the fall.

As part of the ongoing efforts to reform the process by which they selected delegates to their conventions, the Democrats had a rules fight instigated by Senator Ted Kennedy in his 1980 challenge to incumbent President Jimmy Carter. As mentioned earlier, Kennedy's argument was that since the failed hostage rescue mission of late April, Carter was having difficulty winning contests and looked less and less viable for the fall. Since most of the delegates, especially those supporting Carter, had been selected much earlier in the process, when Carter was still more popular both with the party and in the general electorate, Kennedy argued that all delegates should be freed from their commitment to vote for Carter. This would allow the delegates to vote for him as the most viable candidate for the fall. Kennedy lost this battle and Carter went on to lose his reelection bid to Ronald Reagan.

Important philosophical battles have taken place over the wording of party platforms. In 1948, in perhaps the most famous disagreement, a number of Southern delegates walked out of the Democratic Convention in protest of a plank in the party platform supporting civil rights for minorities, a plank that was supported by then Mayor Hubert Humphrey. Among the leaders of the walkout was Strom Thurmond (then governor of South Carolina), who later that year was the standard-bearer for the States' Rights Party, otherwise known as the "Dixiecrats." Ironically, in 1964 as a US Senator from South Carolina, Thurmond defected to the Republican Party in protest against the Democratic Party's support of the Civil Rights Act of 1964 and once again it was Hubert Humphrey (US Senator from Minnesota in 1964) who played a key role in the passage of the law (Gittinger and Fisher 2004).

The issue of abortion has been a central issue in platform disputes in both parties since the 1970s. For the Democrats, it has not been as contentious an issue as for the Republicans, who have virtually eliminated all references to a woman's right to choose from their platforms. The major battle for the Republicans at more recent conventions has been with regard to other so-called social issues such as stem cell research and gay rights. In 2008, more conservative delegates to the Republican convention were prepared to contest what they perceived to be McCain's less than conservative positions on issues such as global warming, stem cell research, and immigration (Shear 2008).

Traditionally, as mentioned earlier, the pick for the vice-presidential candidate was not made (or at least not announced) until the presidential candidate had officially locked up the nomination by the *actual* vote of the delegates. This would sometimes lead to some seemingly odd choices, especially when viewed in hindsight. John Kennedy's pick of Lyndon Johnson, while having its advantages, did have some in the political world scratching their heads given the well-known animosity between the two men. Some have argued that Kennedy was merely doing the polite thing and offering Johnson the right of first refusal and Johnson shocked him by accepting. McGovern's selection of Tom Eagleton has already been addressed in this discussion, but bears mentioning for its demonstration of the impacts of insufficient vetting. This lesson about vetting, some claim, was apparently lost on McCain in 2008, when he selected Alaska Governor Sarah Palin to be his running mate.

Most presidential candidates seem to have learned the lessons of a weak vetting process or a shortened decision calendar and taken steps to ensure that their pick for vice president meets the necessary criteria. What the necessary criteria are varies from candidate to candidate, party to party, and election to election. In the more traditional manner, presidential candidates would pick their running mates based on three political criteria: party unity, geographic balance, and ideological balance. Since the 1970s, there has also sometimes been the insider/outsider balance.

The argument could be made that Kennedy's selection of Johnson was to achieve party unity, to bring Johnson's supporters in the preconvention contest back into the party fold. It could also be argued that it was geographic balance with Kennedy from the northeast and Johnson's southern roots that would help. In 1968, Richard Nixon's selection of Maryland Governor Spiro Agnew was clearly a way to balance Nixon's west coast presence.

In 1976, the newer strategy of insider/outsider balance was demonstrated in Carter's pick of Senator Walter Mondale of Minnesota. Much of the criticism of Carter throughout the primaries was that he was too much of an outsider and wouldn't know enough about Washington and how it worked to be able to get anything done. Many of those fears were quieted with his pick of the long serving senator. The pick of Mondale also appealed in two other more traditional ways—a north/south geographic balance and a moderate/liberal balance.

With 1988 and George H. W. Bush's pick of Indiana Senator Dan Quayle political analysts were once again scratching their heads. Because Bush had vast governmental and political experience, some argued in a joking manner that he could balance the ticket geographically all by himself.[10] Bush mentioned Quayle's youth and that he was trying to reach out to younger voters, so perhaps this was generational balancing. Just four years later, Bill Clinton's pick of Al Gore was again puzzling in terms of these more traditional criteria. Certainly, there was the insider/outsider aspect, but in all other respects it was hard to see where the balance was. Clinton and Gore were from the same region of the country, about the same age, and were both relatively moderate though Gore was much more liberal on the environment.

As earth shattering to the old order as McGovern-Fraser was, so too was the method by which Jimmy Carter went about selecting his running mate in 1976. The way Carter chose Mondale would forever change how most presidential candidates would select their running mates. With the contest ended by early June of 1976 and Carter sufficiently ahead in the delegate count to win, attention could be turned to the selection of a running mate. In his memoir, *Keeping Faith: Memoirs of a President* (1982), Carter notes that he had made "only one early decision about the Vice President—that it was important for me to choose a member of Congress as my running mate in order to provide some balance of experience to our ticket" (35). If he had pressed for a quick decision, Carter notes he likely would have selected one of two opponents from the primaries, either Senator Henry Jackson of Washington or Senator Frank Church of Idaho. The only reason he gives is that he was familiar with them and their positions on issues from the campaign just fought. Carter also saw that with all this time available to him he should take advantage of it and get to know some others as well. Carter insiders reviewed the entire roster of Democratic members of Congress, weighed their strengths and weaknesses, and the ever analytical campaign manager Hamilton Jordan devised a weighted point system to further filter the list. The process yielded seven names,[11] all of whom eventually would interview with Carter either at the peanut farm[12] in Plains, Georgia, or just prior to the convention in New York. Carter had been impressed with Mondale and the two established a relationship that changed not only how vice-presidential running mates would be selected, but also how presidents and vice presidents would interact.

Whither the Brokered Convention?

Naturally, from the discussion here and in chapter 4 it is plain to see that we have moved, in a rather substantial way, away from the old brokered convention model but that its facade still remains. The inability of the delegates to decide anything of real importance, and the shunting of controversy out of the spotlight, has certainly drained the meaning of the convention. With this being the case, are national nominating conventions worth the money and effort?

Recall the other function of conventions, that of providing a launch for the fall campaign and unifying the party. This function still remains, while with the others it appears more as though the parties go through the motions. Even in this era of nonstop campaigning, reliance on the media and interest groups, and a focus on a much broader array of voters than in the past—with the opening of so many primaries and caucuses to nonparty members—the conventions, for all their lack of choice, still provide an opportunity to heal wounds inflicted by the preconvention race. And, this sends the standard-bearers off on the right foot. Take the 2008 Democratic convention as an example, there was a great deal of rancor between the supporters of Obama and Clinton and a great deal of pent up emotion on the part of the Clinton supporters that needed an outlet. Though Obama supporters saw Clinton's decision to hold on to her delegates and to have her name placed in nomination as an affront, it may have been necessary for many of Clinton's supporters to get a sense of closure (see Traister 2010, especially page 216, for example). In the end, highly supportive speeches by both Clintons at the convention and Hillary being the one to ask for Obama's nomination by acclamation went a long way toward bridging the gap between the two camps. This was further cemented by the energy expended by both Bill and Hillary Clinton on the campaign trail in the fall.[13]

Similarly, in 2000 after a bruising primary battle between eventual nominee Texas Governor George W. Bush and Arizona Senator John McCain, the Republicans sought to use their convention to restore the image of party unity. Among the strategies they employed to transmit this image was to spread the traditional roll call of the states over several nights, feature speakers who would demonstrate the diverse nature of support for Bush, and include speakers who were more representative of average Americans. National Public Radio host and commentator, Scott Simon, wrote just after the convention, "A convention used to be planned to give precious prime time exposure to the party's rising political stars. But this convention has had more singers, star wrestlers, and sit-com stars" (Simon 2000). Simon went on to lament the absence of a number of stars and rising stars of the party who might have been expected to advocate for controversial positions on controversial issues. Certainly, by employing this scheduling of speakers, the party could avoid much of the turmoil that could continue the differences and disagreements of the primary season into the fall and the general election. By doing so, the party makes it less likely that those who weren't in complete agreement with the Bush agenda would sit on their hands during the campaign and not help the party. Further cementing of the bonds and healing of the wounds naturally took place with McCain's appearance on the campaign trail on behalf of the Republican ticket.

For any number of reasons the parties are not likely to surrender the convention as an anachronism. They perform, what to them are, much needed functions. Not the least of these is to provide their ticket with the so-called convention bounce. This is an uptick in the poll performance for the candidates due to all of the reasons already delineated—party unity, four nights of advertising, and so on. According to Stephen Wayne (2009), this bounce averages about 6 percent in the polls. Since this is the time by which most voters have made up their minds, this bounce is often significant in determining the outcome of the election to come. Success usually depends on what candidates do with their bounce. If they are unable to convert the bounce into a sustainable lead or into momentum with which they can catch the opponent, the bounce becomes nothing more than a short-lived news story. Wayne argues that George H. W. Bush's 1992 bounce of about five points was short lived, perhaps due to continued focus on the tone of the Republican Convention at which Pat Buchanan and others seemed to push the party far to the right.[14]

Still, we are left with the question of whether there could ever be another truly brokered convention. Not since 1952 has one of the major parties taken the balloting at their convention beyond a first ballot. Naturally, with the older, brokered system still in place for the next four convention cycles, it is somewhat surprising that in *that* time frame there were no additional ballots necessary. Beginning with 1972 and the changes made by the Democrats that rippled into the Republican process, namely the widespread use of primaries to select delegates, delegates were no longer under the direct control of party leaders (just a decade earlier they more properly were called "bosses"), and often were committed or pledged to vote for a particular candidate. The wheeling and dealing of the past just was not possible. That being said, in a multicandidate field where more than two remain viable beyond the primary season (or only two are viable with one or two others still controlling delegates) it might still be possible, but the brokers are not likely to be party leaders, but political consultants. In addition, it is safe to say that with the rules as they are just following the 2008 cycle, it is more likely that such brokering would occur in the Democratic Party than in the Republican Party. This is due to the Republican's continued use of winner-take-all rules in many states, rules that tend to shorten the contest and move it to a clear winner more quickly than on the Democratic side.

What's Next? Where Will Reforms of the Process Take Us?

Many have argued that still further reform is necessary to get the kinks out of the current system of candidate selection. Smith and Springer (2009) doubt that it really could be defined as a system with two different sets of party rules intertwined with 50 sets of state election rules (more if you count the various territories allowed to participate in the process). Gerald Wright (2009) describes it as "the result of layers of reform over the years" (26). Republicans were worried about the potential problems of front-loading in 2000, and Democrats have long been concerned about the interaction of a long, drawn out contest with their more traditional disadvantage in fund raising. That is, Democrats were concerned about the advantage their opposition might have in securing the Republican nomination fairly early and then be able to focus solely on raising funds for the general election, while they would still be fighting to survive until the fall. Certainly, recent changes in the Democrats' ability to make use of new technology have mitigated that particular danger, but many candidates and party leaders would much prefer to turn their sights on the Republicans as early as April or May than to still be sniping at one another—one of the main concerns about the lengthy battle in 2008. The Republicans would no doubt have a similar concern, but their rules make an earlier victory much more within the realm of the possible. Still others, outside of the two major parties, are concerned that the stakes in candidate selection are much too high to be left solely to partisans, while many within the parties fear the danger of being too open in what is after all the selection of *party* representatives.

So, then, what are the key issues that significant critics have argued need to be addressed if we are to proceed further with reform of the process? First, front-loading and scheduling were obviously a problem for both parties in 2008, though the Democrats' problems gained significantly more attention. How can the parties effectively impose a rigorous schedule on the states? Certainly, they have the legal authority to do so, but seem to lack the political will. For various reasons states may seek to create mischief in the opposing party process, as some have suggested was the case in 2008 with the state legislature and governor in Republican hands in Florida. Or, the state may simply be trying to be relevant in the process, as may have been the case with Michigan.

A second issue is the extent to which each party might want to fully represent the electoral outcome of the contests around the country on the floor of the convention. That is, to what extent does a party want to employ proportional representation of candidate performance within a state's delegation? Since the Democrats adopted a policy that took them in the direction of proportionality, with the exception of adjusting the threshold level for representation, they have never looked back. The Republicans, however, have never significantly considered proportionality as a *national party policy*, but have left such determinations up to the state parties. The advantage of proportionality is that you can say that all candidates have a fair chance of continuing to accumulate delegates even with a second- or third-place finish and thus have a role at the convention—in determining platform, rules, input on running mates, and so forth. The disadvantage of an adherence to proportionality is that it tends to draw the process out and nonviable candidates can continue to raise issues that could haunt the eventual nominee in the fall. What the Republicans have found is that their rules that allow for the state parties to choose winner-take-all contests, also allow for a strong candidate to quickly vanquish less viable opponents. It could be argued that this is another manifestation of the more federal culture of the Republican Party structure and atmosphere.

A third issue, raised primarily by independent voters and others with a sense that the process should be more open, is that of open versus closed contests. As defined earlier (see chapter 4), a closed primary is one in which only voters enrolled in a party may vote in the party's primary. An open primary is one where anyone, regardless of enrollment may participate in the primary. In between the two extremes is what is referred to as a semiopen primary in which only independents may vote with the partisans in a primary. This form of contest prevents the political mischief of opposing partisans participating and perhaps choosing the weaker candidate.

A number of proposals have been made by reform-minded individuals, whether political activists or scholars, with respect to scheduling.[15] A national preprimary convention, working much like the way state conventions work (in many states), would narrow the field or would select the candidates outright if there were enough support. This plan, first proposed by Cronin and Loevy (1983),[16] still would involve a process of delegate selection (a single day of closed caucuses to select delegates to county conventions. These conventions would then select delegates to state conventions, which would select delegates to the national convention) and a primary (in September) *after* the convention (in July), which could still make the convention even more irrelevant. In the early 1990s, Loevy also proposed the Small States First Plan on which the Delaware Plan was based. First proposed to the Republican National Committee's (RNC) Advisory Commission on the Presidential Nominating Process by Delaware State Republican Chairman Basil Battaglia, the Delaware Plan was endorsed by the RNC's Rules Committee in 2000.[17] According to Smith and Springer, the plan was "unceremoniously dropped when the leaders of the party and George W. Bush's campaign team realized it would be controversial on the floor of the convention" (2009, 16), and thus upset the attempt to create an image of the unified party described above. The plan would reverse the front-loading of the primary schedule and place the states with the largest populations in the last round of primaries. While the plan would do away with the first in the nation separate contests in Iowa and New Hampshire, its proponents argue that it would preserve the value of retail politics.[18] It would replace the more haphazard schedule with a series of "pods" or groupings of states based on population, the first including more than a dozen states and territories, from Maine to Hawaii (Fairvote.org n.d.). It is difficult to imagine, however, how the same level of retail politics could be achieved by candidates trying to make their case one day in Puerto Rico and the next in Alaska (see also OPS-Alaska and Fairvote at pweb.jps.net n.d.). The pods would hold their contests about 30 days apart from early March through early June.

An alternative known as the Rotating Regional Plan builds on the basic idea of grouped primaries by dividing the country into four regions: East, South, Midwest, and West. Originally formulated by the National Association of Secretaries of State (NASS),[19] the plan can trace its roots back to the original conception of Super Tuesday by the Southern oriented Democratic Leadership Council in the 1980s. The Rotating Regional Plan would employ a schedule somewhat like the one proposed in the Delaware Plan with each region beginning its voting about 30 days apart.[20] The biggest difference is that in each four-year cycle the regions would rotate their start dates so that if the East had gone first in 2004, followed by the South, then the Midwest, and the West only to have the South go first in 2008 and the East go last. The biggest advantage, perhaps, is the reduction of jealousy among the states for the media attention, given the states that now go earliest, and the sense some states may have that if they stick with a later schedule, the efforts of their voters may be without value.

The American Plan, devised by Thomas Gangale (2007), also known as the Graduated Random Presidential Primary System is a bit complex, but has two major components. First, the schedule of each state's contest would be randomized, but within groups by size. The first interval would include states where the number of congressional districts totals no more than 8. Gangale argues that this preserves the true retail politics quality that is advantageous of our current system of Iowa and New Hampshire going first. Second, large states would not be allowed to go until much later in the process as the two-week intervals would increase the size requirement by 8 congressional districts. So, any voting day could include a single state if that state fit the size requirement or it could include multiple states where the total number of districts does not exceed the limit. For example, round one could include Iowa and New Hampshire (and one other state with a single seat in the House of Representatives). Or, it could include two states with 4 seats or a single state with 8 seats, or any combination of states so long as the total number of seats does not exceed 8. The same would hold true for round two—two weeks later—except that the number of seats would be 16.

A Way to a Solution?

Whatever is done to reform the process is going to take the cooperation of the two major national parties. Smith and Springer (2009) have suggested that the two parties create "a joint commission" to develop a coherent plan. The commission, they argue, should be authorized by both conventions to serve for ten years to allow for careful study and the phasing in of the recommendations. They note that governmental action is of questionable constitutionality, at best, and if reform of the process were to be left to the states or state parties, the interests of the national parties or the nation might not be at the forefront of reform efforts. Given the two different philosophical outlooks of the two parties, and the reflection of those outlooks in their organizational and operational styles,[21] the only real issue that they could effectively address would be scheduling of the delegate selection contests. Even here, there is a logistical problem because of the way the parties differ with regard to changing their rules—Democrats use short-term commissions to change the rules for the current cycle and Republicans might use commissions to make suggestions to the convention to make changes for the *next* cycle.

Smith and Springer may be on to something as a solution. If we are to achieve the goal of the popular choice period, in balance with input from party leadership, turnout would have to be a key component of any reform proposal. Thomas Patterson (2009) has demonstrated the impact of a Super Tuesday-like event that shuts down the selection process and, while yielding an early choice, reduces subsequent turnout considerably. If either party is to make the claim that their nominee is truly the choice of their rank and file membership, wouldn't it behoove them to ensure as high a level of turnout from among as many party members[22] as possible? Among his observations, Patterson notes that clustered primaries (in terms of time), particularly those on the same day, *tend* to have lower turnout than primaries held separately. While he notes that turnout is often dependent on the vagaries of a particular election (e.g., the historical runs of both the first viable woman and first viable African American candidates *in the same contest*), steps ought to be taken to maintain turnout at as high a level as possible. Perhaps then, the Smith and Springer commission should recommend minimal clustering of primaries and allow sufficient time for candidates to develop more retail campaigns in states where retail politics is practical (the same kind of campaign that works in Iowa and New Hampshire is not likely to work in New York or California). If Patterson is correct, the single best thing such a commission, or the parties, could do is to revert to back loading (the reverse of front-loading) and enforce the schedule against states that jump to the head of the line. It requires that the two parties agree and that they stand together in using their constitutional rights.

Chapter 7

The General Election: So You've Got the Nomination, Now What?

The general election phase of the campaign for president has many similarities to, and differences from, the nomination phase. While the emphasis is still quite heavily on *states*, the particular states and their characteristics change dramatically. In the nomination phase, candidates focused on exceeding expectations and adding delegates, even if they didn't win a particular contest. In the general election, nearly all the contests are winner-take-all and all of them are at the same time—momentum is of a different kind. During the effort to gain the party nomination, candidates had to make their cases to party activists—the voters most likely to turn out to vote in primaries and caucuses and thus are more ideological. In the general election, the appeal must be to independent and middle-of-the-road voters who will decide the election, while at the same time keeping one's base[1] sufficiently motivated to work and vote. Lastly, time is even more of the essence. Where during the primaries and caucuses the campaign was at work for months and may still have had months to go before the party contest was settled, in the general election time is measured in weeks and days.

The Electoral College

After a rather close presidential election, a seemingly more frequent occurrence in recent history, a debate resurfaces about the fairness of the Electoral College and whether or not it should be reformed or abolished. The math of amending the Constitution makes its abolition unlikely[2] in the near term. Many Americans don't realize that they never, in fact, get to vote directly for a presidential candidate. Even in states that employ "preference primaries" the vote outcome is usually used to allocate delegates. When it comes to electing the nation's chief executive officer, American democracy is indirect.

While some view the Electoral College as a bit arcane, it is not an overly complex institution. Quite simply, the Electoral College contains one elector for each member of the US House of Representatives and US Senate from a state. Since the early 1960s, the District of Columbia has been represented in the Electoral College as though it were the smallest state (3 votes). So, the math then is easy: 435 votes based on the total number of members of the House, plus 100 based on the membership of the Senate, and 3 for the District of Columbia for a total of 538 votes. The candidate who wins the presidency is that candidate who wins a clear majority of the electoral votes. Dividing 538 in half gives us 269, but that is only 50 percent, so we add 1 and the magic number to win the presidency is 270 electoral votes. If no candidate achieves that number, the election is decided by the House of Representatives and the Senate decides who will be vice president. The first time a presidential contest was decided by this "contingent election" was in the 1800 election between John Adams and Thomas Jefferson. The last time it happened was 24 years later involving John Q. Adams defeating Andrew Jackson.[3] It is also possible for the candidate who wins the popular vote to lose the election. This has happened four times in our history with the most recent occasion being the 2000 election in which George W. Bush was the winner over Al Gore. The previous occasions were 1824, J. Q. Adams beat Jackson; 1876, Hayes beat Tilden; and 1888, Harrison beat Cleveland.

With this strategic backdrop, candidates must crisscross the country with a strategy designed to get them to the 270 votes in an efficient manner. This often plays out such that there are certain states that are "locks" for a particular candidate and others that are locks for the other candidate. These are the so-called Red and Blue states—Red states being those locked up for the Republicans and the Blue states being those locked up for the Democrats.[4] The result is a group of states often referred to as "the battleground"—states where the difference between the two major party candidates is narrow enough as to cast doubt on the outcome. It is in these states that, despite public claims of 50 state strategies or counting every vote, the two parties spend most of their time, money, and effort. Certainly, the math of the Electoral College would tend to favor effort being put into large states like New York, California, or Texas where the largest vote totals reside, but because those states are often not on the battleground, effort is often placed in small states—even some with as few as 4 electoral votes. To demonstrate how important small states can be, for example, in 2000 with all the controversy surrounding the recount in Florida, it has been argued that if Green Party[5] candidate Ralph Nader had not been on the ballot in New Hampshire, its 4 votes would have resulted in a different outcome with Al Gore winning. If that had been the case very few people would have even cared about what happened in Florida.[6]

The Electoral College was established by the Framers as yet another stopgap measure to mitigate mob rule and the tyranny of the majority. That is to say, as much as the Framers feared the tyrannical rule of a single individual, they also feared what a mob could do to the rights of those in the minority. In an attempt to prevent this from occurring, they placed insulation in the system they created. While giving the people "popular representation" in the House of Representatives, the Framers made the election of the upper house—the Senate—indirect by appointment of the state legislatures. Similarly, they envisioned a system where popular election of a president was at least one-step removed, and more likely four steps removed. It is argued that the Framers saw the Electoral College more as a filtering device that would narrow the field of candidates (much as parties do today), and that most contests for president would be resolved in the House of Representatives (see, e.g., Longley and Peirce 1996). That meant that voters would elect representatives to the House, but also would elect representatives to the state legislature who would in turn decide the mechanism for the selection of electors (it took some time before the popular election of electors became common practice). The electors would vote for presidential candidates, but would not arrive at a final decision and narrow the field to two candidates. At this point, the House would decide the presidency and the Senate would decide the vice presidency.

According to Lawrence Longley and Neal Peirce (1996), one of the greatest fears held by the Framers was that a popularly (directly) elected president "would consolidate too much power and influence in one person" (18). At the other end of the spectrum, they argue, were Framers who felt that congressional election of the president would remove the office's independence from and coequality with the legislative branch. So, much like the Connecticut Compromise and the Three-Fifths Compromise, the construction of the Electoral College was yet another of the compromises that allowed the discussion and adoption of the Constitution to go forward. Originally, the brainchild of James Wilson of Pennsylvania, who was opposed to the Virginia Plan's suggested election of the executive by the legislature, the Electoral College was Wilson's compromise proposal between the Virginia Plan and his original notion of popular election of the president (Milkis and Nelson 1999). Some might argue that this was a less significant compromise than the others, designed particularly to allow the delegates to move on. Adkins and Kirwan (2002) argue that the Electoral College embodies all of the basic principles espoused by the Framers—"republicanism, separation of powers, checks and balances, and federalism" (72). This dispute, embodied in the works of economic determinists like Charles Beard (1913) and J. Allen Smith (1907) and antideterminists like John P. Roche (1961), argues Shlomo Slonim (1986) is best resolved by looking at what the delegates to the convention and others at the time said of this elaborate mechanism. Slonim concludes his argument by stating that it was a practical solution to a very real problem. With an eye toward what needed to be done to choose presidents and another eye toward what needed to be done to end a lengthy debate and move forward, the Electoral College was, as Goldilocks might say, "just right."

As adopted by the Constitutional Convention, the Electoral College would have its members—electors—selected by the state legislatures (or at least their method of selection left up to the state legislatures). Each elector would cast two votes for president and at least one of those candidates could not be from the same state as the elector casting the vote. Why two votes? The executive was established with a back up plan with a vice president who the Framers felt should be the second most qualified individual to serve as president. So, with electors casting votes for two candidates, the one with the second most votes would, logically, be the second most qualified person to be president. This worked well as long as George Washington was the clear choice of everyone (and Washington was willing) to be president. In 1796 with the election of John Adams, while it might not have been as clear as the choice of Washington in the last two elections, it may have seemed logical to elevate the incumbent vice president to the office of president. It was the election of 1800, the first one where the new fledgling political parties would emerge and truly assert themselves for the first time that would create the need for modification of the Electoral College. Jefferson and his running mate—Aaron Burr—ended up in a dead heat, a tie for the presidency. In the end, it took 36 ballots with the outcome in doubt until February 17th, 1801 (Ferling 2005).[7] It became clear to lawmakers that the balloting arrangement for presidential voting needed to be changed. With the adoption of the Twelfth Amendment, electors now cast one ballot for president and a second separate ballot for vice president.

Who are these people who elect the US president? In answer to that question, Alexander Hamilton wrote, "The immediate election should be made by men most capable of analyzing the qualities adapted to the station, and acting under circumstances favorable to deliberation, and to a judicious combination of all the reasons and inducements which were proper to govern their choice" (Hamilton 1788). Hamilton saw this body, transient in nature, and none of them members of the Congress, as an elite group of "men chosen by the people for the special purpose, and at the particular conjuncture" (1788) who would use their wise judgment and be unencumbered by an ambition for the office themselves (supposedly). One could assume that the Framers hoped that the states would choose the political elite to come together to perform this winnowing process. To be sure, the Framers could not envision how the process would mutate with the advent of political parties.

Today, the electors perform neither the same role envisioned by the Framers, nor even the role electors may have played in our earliest presidential elections. As states have adopted popular election of electors and political parties have developed, the selection of the electors has been left to the parties. Not that it couldn't be the case that a set of political nobility couldn't be elected to pick the next president, but since an elector owes his or her seat to the party they represent, it is not likely that they will deviate from the party's choice. The individuals chosen by the parties are indeed chosen for their loyalty and as a reward for their longtime service to the party. Longley and Peirce (1996) have noted that an examination of the group photos of various state Electoral College gatherings revealed (unscientifically) that there tended to be high numbers of women and the elderly among the electors. They are contributors, workers, interest group allies; in short, individuals who can be counted on to abide by the party's wishes and vote for the party's ticket. In most states, the days of using well-known names for the purpose of drawing voters to the party line are over—many states no longer list the names of the electors on the actual ballot (Longley and Peirce 1996).

It is this selection process that works as well as any other measure to bind the electors to the party's nominee. Still, there are some states that find it necessary to bind the electors by law to vote for the person they were elected to vote for. Such laws are the subject of debate among constitutional scholars and provide for interesting hypothetical scenarios. For example, what if the nominee of the winning party were to die before the Electoral College met a bit more than a month after the actual

Election Day? Would those electors be bound to vote for a dead person?[8] "The preponderance of legal opinion seems to be that statutes binding electors, or pledges that they may give, are unenforceable" (Longley and Peirce 1996, 109). So, statutory restrictions imposed on electors may be unconstitutional, but nothing can prevent good old-fashioned guilt or party loyalty. In the end, what binds the electors is that they have a stake in the outcome—a financial investment via a contribution, time or effort, or their reputation.

Still, the possibility that an elector may vote in some different way from what voters might have expected when they cast their ballot for the elector (often blindly) disturbs many. When electors do this, it is referred to as the problem of the faithless elector. Through the 2008 election, electors have defected 158 times out of a total of 22,875 votes cast since 1789, a mere 0.7 percent of the time.[9] Additionally, no faithless elector's vote has ever affected the outcome of an election.

Critiques of the Electoral College

We have already seen that the faithless elector is one issue that critics of the Electoral College have raised. Among the other problems critics point to is the potential for the popular vote winner to lose the election, as happened when Al Gore lost to George W. Bush in 2000 (and on 3 other occasions). It should also be noted that on an additional 12 occasions a president has been elected who did not receive a majority of the popular vote (Fon 2004). Critics also point to the undemocratic nature of not having a direct election of the nation's chief executive. The manner by which the popular votes are aggregated can greatly exaggerate the outcome, such that elections that might be relatively close appear to be blowouts from the Electoral College result. In 1980, Ronald Reagan is often credited with a landslide victory yet he received about 51 percent of the popular vote.[10] It was his better than 90 percent showing in the Electoral College that contributes to the image of a landslide victory (Wayne 2009).

There are a number of criticisms of the Electoral College based on the biases it introduces into the election outcome, and not just that it exaggerates the margin of victory for the winner (which many see as a positive). The most often mentioned bias is the small-state bias. This critique stems from the disproportionate votes given to voters of small states.[11] That is because every state is awarded at least two of its Electoral College votes as a result of equal representation of the states in the Senate. Voters in smaller states have a much greater impact on the electoral outcome than voters in large states, whose impact on the electoral outcome is diminished by their state's larger delegation in the House. The other bias that is often referenced is that of the larger states. In this critique it is argued that by winning the largest states (a number sufficient to reach 270 electoral votes) by a single vote the candidates could end up spending little to no time in the smaller states and thus we could elect a president with limited knowledge of issues of importance to smaller states.[12] There are other scholars who argue that it is no longer states that get the attention of presidential candidates, but interests and demographic groups *within* states.

There are a number of proposals for the reform of the Electoral College and even variations on what it might be replaced with. First, if we accept that the faithless elector is indeed a threat to democratic processes, then we would look to one set of proposals that eliminate that threat. In an *automatic plan*, the electors themselves would be taken out of the equation and the votes would be awarded in the same fashion as points in a game or sport. There would be no need for the electors to meet in the state capitols—where there are elaborate ceremonies and lunches paid for at taxpayer expense—saving money as well as eliminating the human factor. If we add the further reform that the "points" are awarded to the party (or independent body), then the Greenfield-like scenario[13] of the candidate dying before the meeting of the Electoral College is eliminated, and the points simply go to whomever the party would designate. In presenting this plan, political scientist Stephen J. Wayne notes that the role of the electors "as partisan agents is not and has not been consistent with their exercising an independent judgment" (2009, 361), as Hamilton argued they would in "Federalist #68."

Second, if it is the undemocratic nature of the winner-take-all rules that is of concern there are a number of variations of reform proposals that could solve the problem. Two states already allot their electors on a congressional district basis. Maine and Nebraska use what is often referred to as the *district plan*, in which a presidential candidate who wins the popular vote in a congressional district would receive the vote of the elector for that district. This would leave the two votes derived from the state's representation in the Senate to be determined. Quite simply, they would serve as "bonus electors" and be awarded to that candidate receiving a plurality of the vote in the state.

Another way to remedy the concern over the undemocratic nature of the winner-take-all rule is to award the electoral votes within each state according to the proportion of the popular vote received by the candidate. Some *proportional plans*[14] include various threshold levels that would work in the same way as the thresholds in the primaries and caucuses did—in order for a candidate to be eligible to receive an electoral vote he or she would have to attain, say, 15 percent of the vote. Including a threshold level helps to maintain one of the advantages of the Electoral College, the creation of at least an appearance of majoritarianism if the winner has less than 50 percent of the vote. Bill Clinton did not get above 50 percent of the popular vote in either of his runs for the White House, but his substantial margins in the popular vote, and having the majority of the votes in the Electoral College, lent legitimacy to his presidency.

In the case of both of these more proportional plans, statistical analysis of recent elections demonstrates that they could create more occasions where the popular vote winner loses the election. Wayne (2009) has noted that in neither 1992 nor 1996 would Bill Clinton have received a majority of the electoral vote under the simple proportional plan. Under the district plan, Nixon would have defeated Kennedy in 1960, and Carter and Ford would have tied at 269 in 1976.

Third, we could move to a *direct popular vote* for president. Some see philosophical issues with such a system, in that it would further undermine the federalist structure of our government, taking away the separate roles for the states in the election of the president. Certainly, such a switch would require a constitutional amendment to eliminate the Electoral College, so the debate would center on to what extent we wish to limit the role of the states. Others argue that such an electoral system could also weaken the two party system (though some might see that as an advantage), and lead to a multitude of relatively strong candidates, making the likelihood of nonmajority presidents much greater. An easy fix to this problem is also available through a run off or automatic run off election. In a regular run off, the two top vote getters would face each other in another round of balloting to take place a few weeks following the first election. Many see difficulties with this regular run off scenario in that it is often difficult to get Americans to the polls once and would be that much harder to get them to go back just weeks later. An alternative would be to allow voters to cast a second ballot for the next choice candidate so that those votes could be used to calculate a winner if no candidate received a majority of the vote.[15]

Whenever the American electorate has faced the prospect of a close electoral outcome or the possibility (or actuality in 2000) of the popular vote winner losing the election, there are outcries to reform the system. In November of 2000, *The Washington Post* reported:

> The idea of abolishing or changing the electoral college has been around virtually since it was created. The Congressional Research Service has counted 1,028 proposals for changing the system, dating back to the 1st Congress, according to an aide to [Representative Jim] Leach [R-Iowa]. That total accounts for almost one out of every 10 constitutional amendments ever proposed in Congress. (Vitta and Dewar 2000, A20)

Just a week earlier in the same paper, George Will referred to these reformers as "political hypochondriacs" who seemed to be "offended" by the Electoral College (Will 2002, A29). Will, like Adkins and Kirwan, goes on to argue that the Electoral College is a reflection of the federal nature of our government and that critics who are concerned about the overrepresentation of smaller states perhaps think that the Senate should be abolished as well.

Will the system ever be reformed? There is one effort known as the "National Popular Vote Compact" (Lublin 2008). This plan has actually been circulating among state legislatures and has some support. The plan, if written into state law, would circumvent the need to amend the constitution by having the electoral votes of those states allocated to the winner of the national popular vote. The difference here is that rather than needing three-quarters of all the states to ratify an amendment, it would only require the cooperation of the minimum number of states to achieve the 270-vote majority in the Electoral College.[16] While the Constitution specifically delegates the mechanism for assigning electoral votes to the states, it is not clear if the courts would see the attempt by these states as undermining the amending process[17] and keep the smaller states from participating in a change that would affect them at least as much as it would the larger states.

The Campaign and the American Voter

In this strategic environment established by the Electoral College, even with all its ensuing controversy, candidates still must campaign out among the voters to win.

Certainly, the particular strategy and what states they might target is driven by the magic number of 270, but they still must get out and campaign—make speeches, attend rallies, shake hands, buy advertisements, identify supporters, and get out the vote (GOTV). In this day and age, it may be that these efforts are limited to a relatively small number of so-called battleground states where they at least have a chance of winning the popular vote, but nonetheless campaigns happen.

The strategy selected by the candidate is highly dependent on which of the two major parties she or he represents, or if he or she is running as a third party or independent candidate. First, we'll deal with candidates from the two major parties and treat third party or independent candidates separately. To begin with, historically the Democrats have had an advantage in terms of enrollment or affiliation of the voters, especially since the New Deal era. With the exception of a brief period around the Republican victory in the 1994-midterm elections,[18] the Democrats have held an advantage over the Republicans in terms of polling data from a number of different sources. Conversely, the tradition has also been for the Republicans to be at an advantage in terms of their ability to finance campaigns, with the 2008 presidential election being a notable exception.

While the Democrats enjoy this enrollment advantage, it comes with a built in down side. The coalition of demographic and interest groups that supports the Democrats is diverse enough to make agreement difficult and the task of getting out the vote even more so. Who are these people who identify as Democrats? Voters from lower- to middle-economic class, minorities, and women tend to be more supportive of the Democratic Party and its candidates. Voters who are white, middle- to upper-economic class, suburban, and male tend to be more supportive of the Republican Party and its candidates. Should these descriptors be taken as absolutes? No, there are many voters from lower-economic strata who vote Republican and there are many wealthy, white suburbanites who regularly support the Democratic Party. These statements are *tendencies*—meaning that suburban males *are more likely* to vote Republican. It is also true that the Republican base is usually easier to get out to the polls, they are more mobile and can afford (in terms of time and convenience) to take the time to vote. Democrats, however, often find it harder to get their voters to come to the polls. They may have transportation problems, child-care issues, and may find it less convenient or more costly to take the time to vote. Though there appears to be little support in the academic literature for it, there is an expression in politics, "good old fashioned Republican rain," which implies that rain on Election Day will tend to keep more transient Democratic voters at home, while Republicans seem to get to the polls no matter what the weather.

It is party identification (PID) that the parties count on for support from voters with an affinity for their positions and candidates. PID is an emotional or psychological attachment to one of the two major parties. It begins early in life, learned from family, friends, and coworkers. It does not change easily and tends to intensify over time. One does not go to bed at night as a Democrat and wake up in the morning as a Republican. But, if as you were falling asleep you may have been thinking about how frequently you have voted Republican over the last several years, and in the morning wake up and realize that you have slowly become a Republican over time. PID is measured in seven categories: Strong Republican, Weak Republican,

Independent Republican, Pure Independent, Independent Democrat, Weak Democrat, and Strong Democrat. It is those voters who identify as the strong partisans that we would think of as the bases of the two parties (for definitions and discussions of PID see work as early as Campbell, Gurin, and Miller 1954 or Fiorina 1981 for a review).

Each party must ensure that its base of supporters is sufficiently motivated to participate in the election and that the candidate at the head of the ticket is not too far out of the party's mainstream. At the same time, the party's candidate cannot be too far out of the general population mainstream either. Nominations are often won closer to the extremes, but general elections are won in the center. This sometimes poses difficulty for candidates who may appear to waffle or flip-flop on issues as they move to a more centrist position (or at least the appearance) on some issues. Barack Obama was criticized for apparent waffling, once Hillary Clinton had suspended her campaign in 2008, in the run up to the Democratic Convention. The same could be said of McCain's apparent moves back toward the center around the same time (Vennocchi 2008).

Like a Grim Reaper, time is ever present for the presidential candidate. There is far too little of it, especially for challengers who really have about 14 to 15 weeks where the voters are focused enough on the campaign for candidates' arguments to have any real meaning. Most campaigns will work backward from Election Day, planning the candidate's schedule and all of the other tasks that need to get done in such a way that little is left to chance. That's not to say that there is no flexibility in a campaign schedule—there must be some in order to address needed changes to strategy as the result of debate performances, scandals, events, and so on.

The Advantage of Incumbency

The 2008 campaign for president was an oddity, not just because the Democratic nomination battle included the first truly viable African American and female candidates, or that the first African American ended up being elected, but because it was the first time since 1952 that there was no incumbent president or vice president on the ballot. It was the first truly open seat campaign for president in 56 years. This is an important element to note because incumbency, while it has some disadvantages, often carries great advantages. In fact, in the 29 presidential elections between 1900 and 2012, 21 of them have involved an incumbent president and the incumbent has an impressive record of 16 wins and 5 losses—that would be a potential Cy Young performance for a major league pitcher these days.

Like any other incumbent, presidents have the ability to *make* news, more so than any other elected official does. That, however, is not the only advantage an incumbent president (or a sitting vice president running for president) has. Certainly, the ability to demand the attention of reporters and pundits at the drop of a hat is no small advantage, but there is the ability to actually deliver programs, policies, and benefits that challengers just don't have. With incumbents there is a sense of the familiar; we know this person, and it may be difficult for us to seek change unless there is a compelling reason such as scandal or obvious misconduct in office. Incumbents get to make use of their offices, to gain media attention, and to provide benefits to constituents. Presidents have all of the trappings of the office from the photo ops in and around the White House to the arrival of Air Force One in a city. Presidents can employ a strategy known as the Rose Garden Strategy, where they stay within the confines of the White House grounds (or at least in Washington, DC) to demonstrate that they are president. Challengers only get to "act presidential," to appear with foreign and domestic leaders, to make us comfortable with the notion of them actually *in* the office. Jimmy Carter attempted to use a Rose Garden strategy during the Iran Hostage Crisis in the 1980 election, but with declining poll numbers had to abandon it (PBS n.d.).

Challengers are not wholly without recourse against these incumbency advantages. Naturally, they have no record as president, and if their career has been primarily legislative, they can attack a president on his executive record with little managerial record of their own to be attacked. Also, challengers do not always have to provide a positive alternative program. A president with a terrible record and/ or low approval ratings can be attacked without the challenger offering much in substance.

The Role of TV

It would be difficult to imagine how campaigns functioned in the days before TV—as it soon may be difficult to imagine how campaigns functioned in the days before the Internet, social networking, blogs, and Twitter. In the grand scheme of history, it was not that long ago that TV made its first appearance in political campaigns—presidential campaigns in particular. We also need to distinguish between "earned media"—what used to be called free media—and paid media. Earned media is the coverage a candidate "earns" by being newsworthy and is much sought after, but has its drawbacks in that the campaign cannot control how it is presented in this format. Earned media has been around just bit longer, as network news coverage of politics was born at almost the same time as the technology. In fact, the first TV coverage of both national nominating conventions was in 1948[19] from Philadelphia, where both parties held their events at the same location to make things easier for the fledgling networks and their more modest technological capabilities at the time. It would be difficult to call this national coverage, however, as only 18 cities had TV stations and only half of those had access to the broadcast from the floor (Karabell 1998).

It was 1952 that saw the first national coverage of conventions and the first real application of TV advertising to presidential campaigns. Democratic candidate Adlai Stevenson stuck with a familiar format for his ads, a 30-minute speech a candidate might have given to a crowd in the days before TV. Some longer duration advertisements have worked on occasion to make a specific point or to highlight a candidate struggling to be heard, much like third party candidate Ross Perot did in 1992 and 1996.[20] Republican Dwight "Ike" Eisenhower took a very different approach, one that fit in with the evolving advertising industry. Eisenhower's

"I like Ike" ads in 1952 and 1956 were short and set political advertising on the course it has been on ever since. At the time, however, the ads—known as spot advertisements—were controversial. Governor Thomas Dewey had refused to use the format in his 1948 campaign referring to them as "undignified." In comparing his opponent's commercials (in 1956) to those for cereal, Stevenson agreed (Museum of the Moving Image 2008).

The 1960 presidential campaign brought with it great influence by TV, both in terms of paid media and earned media. The wealth of the Kennedy family was put to good use to ensure that plenty of advertising was purchased to get the John Kennedy message out to voters. If there was any doubt that Eisenhower's spot ads of 1952 and 1956 were not too undignified for use by potential presidents, certainly, 1960 made sure. Both the Nixon and Kennedy campaigns used TV ads rather heavily.

It was not the paid media that drew the spotlight for the 1960 campaign, it was the earned media. The election of 1960 brought us the first televised debates between presidential candidates and with a brief pause until 1976, they have been with us ever since.[21] It was his performance in, and the end result of, the 1960 debates that kept Richard Nixon away from the format in both his 1968 comeback and his 1972 reelection effort. The crucial debate took place at a time when Kennedy had been campaigning in the south and he came to the debate looking tanned and healthy. Nixon, however, was suffering from a cold or the flu and looked it; he had also injured his leg earlier in the day and was in some pain. His clothing blended into the stage backdrop—his advisers had not thought out how he might look on a black-and-white TV screen—and he had his trademark five o'clock shadow. Kennedy's suit was a nice contrast to the background and he used appropriate stage makeup to enhance his tanned appearance. On the substance many have argued that the debate was virtually a draw, and in fact people who only heard the debate on radio, thought Nixon had won. It was the viewable image that made Kennedy the apparent winner (White 1982).

The 1964 presidential campaign brought with it what is undoubtedly the most famous (or infamous depending on your point of view) political ad in history. Often referred to as "The Little Girl with the Daisy" ad, it might seem tame by the standards of political campaigns a few decades later, but it created such controversy that it ran on the air just once, but remained a news story for days after. On September 7th, 1964 (Labor Day), during the NBC "Movie of the Week" (*David and Bathsheba*), the ad opened with a cute little blonde-haired girl in field counting the petals on a daisy (Hamill 1964). As many small children sometimes do, she was having trouble counting and skipped around a bit. When she reached ten, the image froze and the camera zoomed in on her eye, focusing on the pupil and forcing the screen to go black. A deep, metallic, male voice took over at ten and began counting backward until it reached zero. At this point, a large nuclear explosion filled the screen and Lyndon Johnson's voice repeated lines from a speech about nuclear nonproliferation, implying that his opponent was incapable of negotiating limits on nuclear weapons and thus was dangerous to cute little girls in meadows.[22] It was the last time the ad would air as a paid commercial (Hamill 1964).[23]

In spite of all the public outcry over the harshness of the ad, it was quite effective. Certainly, we can point to the running of the ad as a news story after its initial airing as one measure of success (Ridout and Smith 2008). Additionally, it kicked off a conversation that continued for the remainder of the campaign that focused on Goldwater's lack of support for the nuclear nonproliferation treaty and his apparently more hawkish stance on Vietnam. One other ad, not long after the daisy ad, featured another little girl eating an ice cream cone and the female voiceover spoke about the dangers of strontium 90—a key ingredient of nuclear fallout that gets into the dairy chain (Hamill 1964). The implication of the two ads together was that if Goldwater couldn't incinerate children in a nuclear explosion, he would see to it that they died of cancer caused by consuming milk and ice cream laced with deadly strontium 90.

The daisy ad is in a category commonly known as negative advertising. These are attacks on one's opponent in one form or another. There are ads that simply go on the attack (either the opponent's character or record) and there are ads that attempt to contrast one candidate's position or record with the other candidate. The extent to which these ads are accepted often depends on the context and the severity of the message. Ads that focus on a candidate's record or positions on issues, as long as they are not too forceful (e.g., daisy ad) are often fine with voters. However, ads that focus on a candidate's behavior that has little or nothing to do with the office they seek are less accepted. For example, an ad emphasizing a candidate's flawed character because of a drunk-driving conviction when he or she was in college, with no accident involving property damage or injury would probably be rejected by voters as a desperate attempt at smearing someone's reputation unnecessarily. An ad involving an attempted cover-up of some action or an act that caused someone else harm would be seen as legitimate.

With the daisy ad becoming a news story, 1964 brought us the perfect combination of earned and paid media. In a way, it was a precursor of what has become known as "going viral," where a video clip spreads across the Internet with great rapidity. Viewers pass the link to their friends and it ends up being seen by many more than the originally intended audience. It also solidified the role of TV in modern presidential campaigns. The campaigns of 1968 and 1972[24] saw extensive use of TV advertising by Nixon. Beyond the early attempts at simplistic cartoon images (as in the "I like Ike" ads of 1952 and 1956) and talking heads, televised political advertisements were becoming an art form. By the 1990s the American Association of Political Consultants was awarding the political advertising industry's equivalent of the Oscars—the Pollie—to the creators of the best political advertising including TV commercials.

Innovative ads or ads that make outrageous claims certainly get covered by TV news, but what else does earned media cover? It has been said that media coverage—especially TV—of political campaigns, presidential campaigns in particular, is a great deal like coverage of sports. Coverage has most often been likened to that of a football game, but half-time coverage in particular. The stories and commentaries often seem to focus more on issues such as who has the momentum, who's ahead or behind, who's made the biggest blunder—in fact CNN used to highlight the "Political Play of the Week"; much like sports shows show the top-ten plays of the week.

Political scientists have studied news coverage of campaigns and what viewers take from that coverage. One study, done by McClure and Patterson (1976) involving the 1972 campaign, found that viewers who watched the ads appeared to be better informed about the issues than those who watched the evening broadcast news. More importantly, the ads did not do much to change the minds of voters. Also significant is the finding that, as we have already discussed, the TV news programs focused more on the horse races and hoopla material than on the issues or other substance, as measured by both viewer recollection and McClure and Patterson's content analysis. Of course, the race they studied was one of the nation's biggest landslide victories and there may not have been much room for persuasion, especially in the time period studied—the last seven weeks of the campaign. While it was important that TV could reach those voters who were less interested and less educated,[25] it was PID—a strong emotional or psychological attachment to one of the two parties—that dominated the vote choice of the subjects.

Today, it is not just the broadcast networks available to the voters at the time of the McClure and Patterson (1976) study, but also the proliferation of cable and satellite TV that has changed the influence or impact of media yet again. Since the 1970s we have seen the creation of three news networks (CNN, MSNBC, and FOX News),[26] that at least initially broadcast 24/7 news. Many criticize both FOX News and MSNBC for their partisan slant on the news and politics, but watchers would certainly know the positions of the parties and candidates. All three networks seem to exist for all things political. The cable networks carry and sponsor the debates in the primaries, they do countdowns to the next contest or contests, and each makes a special claim in the political realm—CNN is "the best political team on television"; FOX News is "fair and balanced"; and MSNBC is "the place for politics." Where in the 1970s we may not have had enough coverage of politics, in the early 2000s we may have too much. Even with all this coverage, society may wonder if the quality has improved much since the days of the McClure and Patterson study.

Certainly, since the advent of TV in politics, and its evolution, we have seen yet another technological innovation that has had a great impact on politics. The development of the Internet has been at least as revolutionary as the spread of TV, in terms of an impact on politics. The Internet has made newspaper and magazine coverage from far away locales available first on our desktops, then on our laptops, and then in the palms of our hands. With this technology have come web loggers or bloggers, individuals who seemingly spend, a great deal of their time following politics and posting their interpretation of it on the web for everyone else to read. Some bloggers come from the extremes of the political spectrum and serve to stir up passions of their readers. Other bloggers are more mainstream and adhere, at least somewhat, to journalistic standards and report and interpret the news. Bloggers have been responsible for keeping a wide range of political stories before the public, from the John Edwards affair to the rumors of Obama's Kenyan birth.[27] Some praise the Internet and these bloggers as real grassroots democracy (sometimes referred to as the netroots). Critics argue that because of who some of the bloggers are (some are professional bloggers) that it is undermining democracy by keeping us focused more on trivia and items that lack of substance. For example, the allegation that the health insurance reform proposal being considered by Congress during 2009 contained "death panels" began and was kept alive on the Internet by bloggers.

It has been the Internet, however, that has allowed candidates to break all sorts of records regarding fund raising and to make organizing far easier. The ability to send out e-mails and tweets (on the message service known as Twitter) instantaneously makes crowd building and communication of important information as easy as stroking a few keys.[28] Twists on this technology are helping campaigns to make efficient use of voter lists for canvassing and GOTV efforts.[29]

In Sum

In summary, the strategic environment of the general election is driven by a number of factors. Perhaps the most significant of these is time, followed by the strategies determined by the math of the Electoral College, the partisan makeup of the electorate, and the influence of media. Candidates seeking to reach the magical number of 270 have to make sure that their base stays motivated, while trying to reach out to those in the middle to put together a winning coalition. They must accomplish this in an era of a constant news cycle, and in an environment where rumor and innuendo make news before the accuracy and veracity of the information can be checked. At the same time, if they have declined public funding they must continue to raise money. Regardless of their decision regarding public financing, they must sprint from media market to media market to woo voters through TV appearances. By October of a presidential-election year, a candidate may long for those days of solitary campaigning outside a factory in New Hampshire or at a gathering of farmers in Iowa.

Part III

The Individual Presidency

Chapter 8

You've Been Elected, Why Is This Guy Asking How You Feel All the Time? The Vice President and Succession

American humorist Will Rogers once joked, "The man with the best job in the country is the vice president. All he ever has to do is get up every morning and say, 'How is the President?'" (Rogers n.d.). This political humor by Rogers certainly cuts right to the heart of the need for a vice president. As such, it also points to one of the, if not the, most significant decisions a president will make. It is so significant because it is an early decision, made even before the fall campaign begins—or soon after a vacancy. It is also a decision that is dissected by the media and academics, is debated by members of the party, and is the focus of nearly all the speculation just prior to a convention. Since the heart of this whole discussion has been about the individuality of the office, choosing one's potential successor is a singular indicator of the character, personality, and style any president brings to the office.

The individual who sits "a heart beat away" from the presidency occupies an office that has been ridiculed as long as the office has existed. It is only more recently in our history that the office of vice president has had real influence, and been held in relatively high regard. The president, if following the more recent model established by Jimmy Carter's pick of Walter Mondale in 1976, is thoughtful in his or her selection, and takes the time to fully vet the individual chosen. If not, there's an Eagleton, a Johnson, a Quayle, or a Palin sitting one heartbeat from the presidency. Some may wonder if who sits in the vice presidency is really all that important. Nine of our 47 vice presidents[1] have become president through the death or resignation of the president—close to 20 percent, or nearly one in every five. Four others have been elected on their own—John Adams, Thomas Jefferson, Richard Nixon, and George H. W. Bush. So, in actuality, 13 of our 47 vice presidents have eventually become president. Even though the Framers didn't spend much time discussing the office, it behooves us to pay attention to it.

Over the course of American history, many have described the office of vice president with derision. We have already seen how Will Rogers felt about the office, but there have been many others, including vice presidents, themselves who have felt the same. The nation's first occupant of the office, John Adams, referred to it as "everything and nothing"[2] and as "the most insignificant office" (Adams 1793). Franklin Roosevelt's vice president, John Nance Garner, is known for two references to the office he held. He referred to the vice presidency as "the spare tire on the automobile of government" and, perhaps more famously, he said the office "wasn't worth a warm bucket of spit."[3] Much more recently, Vice President George H. W. Bush, in commenting on his role as President Reagan's personal ambassador at funerals of world leaders—that seemed to be occurring with fair rapidity in the 1980s—noted that he seemed to be "traveling on the frequent *dier* plan." If that was all that Bush could comment on, the lot of the vice president had certainly improved.

As the Carter-Mondale relationship changed forever the process by which presidential candidates selected their running mates, so did their working relationship change the way presidents and vice presidents worked together. Carter had said that he picked Mondale to counter his own lack of Washington experience. Thus, unlike his predecessors, he actually had his vice president play a key role in making decisions and crafting policy. Reagan, while perhaps not as reliant on George H. W. Bush as Carter was on Mondale, certainly had Bush play a more significant role than most vice presidents. By all accounts, the Clinton-Gore relationship was more like that of Carter-Mondale and Gore was more a partner than most previous vice presidents were. The relationship that cemented the new role of the vice president was that between George W. Bush and Richard Cheney. In fact, some have argued that it was really Cheney who played the dominant role (Montgomery 2009), until it was no longer politically possible for Bush to allow even the appearance of Cheney's control within the administration.

Creation of the Office

While the creation of the presidency was debated early in the tenure of the Constitutional Convention,[4] one could say that the vice presidency was "an afterthought." Certainly, the seeming last minute treatment of the office in the waning days of the convention would confirm that assertion. Even then, the discussion revolved around two key points—the issue of succession and who should preside over the Senate. The historical character of the office of vice president is based on this inherent conflict of purpose. Essentially, the office was created as one-half in the executive branch and one-half in the legislative branch. Such ambiguous placement of the office leads to a natural animosity or suspicion regarding the loyalties of the individual. This is especially so when one considers that the first vice presidents were not selected by the president, at least theoretically, to work in concert to help achieve the goals of the administration, but as the second highest vote getter in the Electoral College contest.

According to Milkis and Nelson (2012), the vice presidency became the focus of some convention delegates when they returned home and engaged in the debates over ratification. Some feared a mixing of executive and legislative power in a single individual. Others feared that this person could become president without much effort or experience, especially given the lighter résumés of a number of post-Twelfth Amendment vice presidents. While garnering some modicum of attention among the writers of the *Anti-Federalist Papers*, the vice presidency is mentioned a mere single time in "Federalist #68." It would seem that the supporters of ratifying the Constitution were far less concerned with the office than were the opponents of ratification.

Though there seemed to be divided opinion about the office of vice president, ranging from whether there should be one at all, to what powers it should hold, and to the role of the vice president in succession to a vacancy in the presidency, the concept of a deputy executive was not unknown among the Framers. In the Postrevolutionary War period, a number of states had adopted the concept in the form of a lieutenant governor. For some states, it was a separate office, and for others it was the presiding officer of one chamber of the legislature or the other. As in a number of states, having the deputy executive—the vice president—preside over the upper chamber of the legislature removed the problem of having one of the members of that body lose his vote (except in cases of a tie), and thus fall short of living up to the republican ideal of the age in representing his constituents. Perhaps it was the varied usage of such an office from state to state that confused the delegates to the convention, or those delegates from states that saw no need for such a deputy may have simply felt no need for such an office, based on their lack of familiarity with it. Certainly, while the creation of the vice presidency solved this one problem, and it partly solved the problem of succession, the vague and confusing wording of the section left a shadow hanging over the issue of succession until decades later (Milkis and Nelson 2012).

Animosity to the Office

Where does this animosity that Carter and his successors had to work to overcome originate? Some place the beginnings of the history with John Adams, the first vice president, and the poor relationship he had with many of the members of the initial government established under the Constitution. Adams was often seen as a bit of a royalist, partly because of his suggestions for what to call the president. Combining this perception of Adams and his pomposity with his size, many of the members of Congress took to calling him "His Rotundity."[5]

By itself, Adams's personality would not be enough to create such long-lasting animosity. Other factors in the early history of the vice presidency would help in the process of growing ill will. First, the person elected to the office was designed to be the person receiving the second most votes. Theoretically, this would make the individual the second most qualified person for the job. An unintended consequence of such an arrangement would be a tension between the president and the vice president, who would be a natural rival to the president.[6] Second, the Constitution places the vice president into both the executive branch and the legislative branch by placing the individual next in line to the president and as presiding officer of the Senate,[7] setting up a lack of trust of the individual by both branches. Those who work more closely with the president over time have tended to see the vice president as a nuisance and head of the upper chamber of the legislature. Members of the legislature see the vice president as an interloper and more properly a member of the executive.

As political parties evolved, this animosity became more deeply rooted with the manner by which vice-presidential candidates were selected. As noted in chapter 6, until fairly recently in the process of presidential selection, the vice presidency was often not much more than an afterthought. In fact, it was often a peace offering to a vanquished rival (e.g., Kennedy's pick of Johnson) or a pick made to ensure no strong intraparty rival to the president four years later.

Goldstein (1982) argues, "The nineteenth century witnessed a sharp decline in the caliber of [v]ice [p]residents" (7). The last great vice president in the early history of the office, he claims, was Jefferson. I would agree and assert further that the next vice president of positive historical note would be Teddy Roosevelt. The constitutional construction of the office following the adoption of the Twelfth Amendment, the manner of selection accompanying the rise of political parties, and the lack of true responsibility combined to hinder any vice president with talent, and might discourage those with true skill, from accepting an offer in the first place.

Other Constitutional Duties

In addition to the role already described—presiding officer of the Senate—the vice president sits to take the place of the president in the event of the president's death, resignation, or removal. Until the Twenty-Fifth Amendment offered a clarification, the details of succession were uncertain. Early in our history of vice presidents, stepping up to fulfill the second of their constitutional duties created controversy. The original Constitution actually says that in the event of a vacancy in the office of president that the executive duties and powers "shall devolve upon" the vice president. It did not say that the vice president shall *become* president.

"His Accidency"[8] John Tyler was the first vice president to face the question of what duties and powers an ascending vice president could actually claim (McDonald 1994). President William Henry Harrison died a month after falling ill, supposedly from delivering his inaugural address in foul weather (Milkis and Nelson 2012), leaving the nation with its first vacancy in the office of president. Not only was the Constitution vague about what the place of the vice president truly was when having presidential power "devolve upon" him, but Tyler was caught in the middle of a political battle within his own Whig Party. There were many among the Whigs who sought to roll back the powers of the presidency that had been asserted by Andrew Jackson. This wing of the Whigs, in keeping with a view of a weaker executive, believed that a vice president who would ascend to the presidency would serve merely as an acting president, and should merely act upon the agenda set by the departed president (Morgan 1974).

Tyler, obviously, thought differently. Soon after his arrival in Washington, having received the news of Harrison's death, he took the oath of office from a judge with the members of Harrison's cabinet as witnesses. Within days, Tyler delivered the equivalent of an inaugural address of his own. By June, in spite of the internal battles in the Whig Party, Congress was able to reject efforts to diminish the "legitimacy" of Tyler's claims by defeating amendments to resolutions that would have referred to Tyler as the vice president *acting as president* (Morgan 1974). It was Tyler's affirmative steps *to be president*, however, that set the precedent we followed until the ratification of the Twenty-Fifth Amendment in 1967, which then rooted his actions in firm constitutional ground.

It took a more modern age with the threat of rapid worldwide destruction from nuclear weapons to force the issue. The assassination of John Kennedy, and the consequent assumption of power by Lyndon Johnson, naturally created a vacancy in the office of vice president. Coupling this vacancy with the reality that in the 1960s we were faced, for the first time, with a world in which foreign attack could occur in mere minutes, many felt that there was a need for a way to ensure a smoother and quicker succession. As a result, Congress proposed an amendment to the Constitution that would accomplish that smoother and quicker succession.[9] The Twenty-Fifth Amendment stated clearly that the vice president would become president, and that the new president would then have the duty to nominate someone to fill the vacancy in the vice presidency with the advice and consent of *both* houses of Congress.

Additionally, the Twenty-Fifth Amendment provided for a mechanism to allow for presidential disability, such as the stroke suffered by Woodrow Wilson or the heart attacks suffered by Dwight Eisenhower. It also created a mechanism for the temporary transfer of power if the president were unable to do so himself. For example, under President Reagan, presidential power was transferred to Vice President George H. W. Bush while Reagan was undergoing surgery.[10] In an instance such as this, the president knows about a disability and can voluntarily invoke the disability clause.[11] As we've noted before in this discussion, there have been a number of fictional treatments—"what if scenarios"—of such disability (and of those disabilities where a president is unable to voluntarily declare it). Among the most well known of these is an episode of the TV drama *The West Wing*, where fictional President Bartlet voluntarily stepped aside when his daughter was kidnapped. If a president didn't do so voluntarily, or was unable to do so as a result of a medical incapacity, the cabinet and the vice president may invoke the disability clause by majority vote.[12]

Extraconstitutional Duties

If checking the president's health each morning were all the vice president had to do, certainly Will Rogers's comments would be more than humorous. Over the course of American history, presidents have assigned many other duties or roles to their vice presidents. Certainly, some of these duties or roles have been with the intention of getting the vice president out of the way, while others have had legitimate purpose. Many vice presidents have served as "ambassador without portfolio," traveling all over the globe to represent the nation and the president. Vice presidents also serve as members of the National Security Council (see chapter 10 for a discussion of the NSC) and as members of the board of the Smithsonian Institution.

Sometimes a vice president will be given a rather specific area of policy to coordinate. Lyndon Johnson, for example, had two main areas of concern (among others) as John Kennedy's vice president. First, he was placed in charge of the US Space Program, and as such, formalized the role for future vice presidents. Second, he was given a fact-finding role regarding US policy toward Vietnam.

Order of Succession to the Presidency

Naturally, the discussion above demonstrates that it is clearly the vice president who rises to assume the office and duties of the president and *becomes* president upon a vacancy, whether due to death, resignation, or removal of the president. But, what happens if the offices are vacant simultaneously, or if there is a vacancy in the office of vice president?

The second part of that question is the simpler one to answer and we've already touched on the broader answer, so I'll dispense with that one first. If the office of vice president is vacant, for whatever reason (death, resignation, removal, elevation), the president gets to nominate a replacement. As with most other executive appointments, this requires the advice and consent of the Senate. What is different, however, is that the approval of a vice-presidential nominee under the Twenty-Fifth Amendment requires the advice and consent of both the Senate *and the House*. Two vice presidents have been nominated, approved, and served under this procedure—Gerald Ford (who later became president) and Nelson Rockefeller (whom Ford nominated to replace himself when he became president).

The first and more complex question has a two-part response. The law governing this succession is the 1947 Act of Succession. It provides that in the event of a simultaneous vacancy in the presidency and vice presidency, the Speaker of the House of Representatives becomes president. And, if there is no Speaker or the Speaker is unable to assume the office, the president pro tempore[13] of the Senate becomes president. In each case, the Speaker or senator must meet the constitutional qualifications for president (see chapter 1). Since the Constitution prohibits the simultaneous holding of an office in the executive and legislative branches of the government, these individuals must resign their seats in Congress with their assumption of the executive office.[14]

In the unlikely event of a simultaneous vacancy in all four of these elected offices (president, vice president, Speaker of the House, and president pro tempore of the Senate) the duties of the office would devolve upon the officers of the president's cabinet in the chronological order of the creation of the department. As of 2010, that order stands as follows: the secretary of state, secretary of the Treasury, secretary of Defense (as the successor agency to the Department of War), secretary of the Interior, attorney general (Department of Justice), secretary of Agriculture, secretary of Commerce, secretary of Labor, secretary of Health and Human Services (successor agency to the Department of Health, Education, and Welfare), secretary of Housing and Urban Development, secretary of Transportation, secretary of Energy, secretary of Education, secretary of Veterans Affairs, and the secretary of Homeland Security. Writers of fiction—books, movies, and TV—often find the possibilities offered by this sequence of succession and the disability clause of the Twenty-Fifth Amendment to be fertile ground for their imaginations and plot lines. It should also be noted here that any cabinet secretary not meeting the minimum constitutional qualifications to be president, just as with the Speaker or president pro tempore, would be passed over and the next ranking cabinet officer would assume the duties of president. Secretaries of state Henry Kissinger and Madeline Albright are two such examples. Neither Kissinger nor Albright was born a citizen of the United States.

Cabinet officers who assume the duties of the presidency do so only as acting president. The logic here is that the person who actually becomes president should be serving in an elective office, even if it is to be the representative of a single congressional district as it would be in the case of the Speaker assuming the office. They would continue to serve as acting president until such time as one or the other chamber of Congress could meet to elect a new and qualifying Speaker or president pro tempore, respectively. The individual selected by the chamber being the first to elect such an officer would serve out the remainder of the departed president's term.

Positives of Such a Seemingly Negative Office

It would seem from the comments made by vice presidents themselves, or by others in making reference to vice presidents, that the office lacks certain desirability. This would be from the perspective of both the president and the vice president, and their staffs. There is a natural or inherent rivalry in the offices, a certain amount of distrust—the vice president is sometimes seen by the Oval Office as a legislative interloper and the legislature sees the vice president as an executive interloper. Perhaps gone are the days when vice presidents see their only real task as checking on the president's health each morning, but awaiting the president's death or removal from office, remains the vice president's penultimate constitutional task.

So, the very first positive to having a vice president, given all the baggage, is to provide for an orderly transition. Can we imagine the chaos that might have ensued following the assassination of John Kennedy if there had been no vice president? In an age where nuclear missiles can arrive on our doorstep only minutes after detection, or when a terrorist attack can happen virtually anywhere, at anytime, would we want the question of who becomes president left to political argument or debate in the Senate or the House?

The vice president is a ready representative for the nation and the president when the president is unavailable, or his or her attendance would be impractical. Certainly while not the president, an appearance of the vice president of the United States at a diplomatic event sends a strong signal to the world. The word of a vice president, or the image of a vice president standing with another world leader, is almost as powerful as the word or image of the president, and certainly stronger than a "simple" ambassador.

Even in domestic politics, the ability of the president to make use of the vice president for policy or political reasons is a great benefit. Vice presidents, in their very traditional roles, were to reach out to other factions in the party, to mend fences, or to cut deals. They are meant, in a political sense, to fill gaps in the president's background or skill set. Jimmy Carter chose Walter Mondale because Carter lacked knowledge of the Washington political scene. The same might be said of Reagan's choice of George H. W. Bush. Mondale brought not only knowledge of how Washington worked to someone who had no Washington experience, but also connections to interest groups traditionally supportive of Democrats in Washington, which Carter lacked.

All in all, vice presidents provide an array of benefits to the American political system. They certainly provide grist for the late-night comedy mill. From Dick Cheney's poor aim with a shotgun,[15] to Joe Biden's unequaled ability to put his foot in his mouth, vice president's will, at the very least, deflect direct attention away from the president.

Chapter 9

Presidential Character: Everybody Has One

Richard Nixon's strange behavior following the break-in at Democratic National Committee Headquarters in the Watergate Complex is among the many bits of information that made many wonder about the president's psychological makeup. Exemplary of this curiosity about a president's psychological shortcomings was comedian/mimic David Frye's depiction of Nixon devolving into Humphrey Bogart's Captain Queeg from *The Caine Mutiny*.[1] One political scientist became well known as a result of our curiosity about Nixon's psychology. James David Barber had predicted, back in 1969, what Nixon's response to a scandal might be. Barber's good fortune begs the question, "Can we predict the behavior of elected officials, especially the president?"

Up to this point, we have examined the basic parameters of the office of president of the United States. We have looked at its historical underpinnings, and different ways to view the institution and those who occupy it. We have discussed the manner by which the individuals have been and are selected. We've taken a look at the first indication of a president's individual character, style, and judgment—the selection of a vice president. The discussion now turns to the individuals resulting from that long process, and how they impact the office for themselves and those who follow.

Our Fascination with the Presidency

In April of 2011, much of America was spellbound by the British royal wedding of Prince William to Kate Middleton. Some might argue that this is a form of transference, making up for our lack of royalty in the United States. This is similar to what we do with our obsession with celebrities and certain political figures (e.g., Britney Spears or the Kennedy family, respectively). Lacking royalty and, perhaps, seeking more substance than celebrities usually provide, we tend to focus our attention on the president and his or her family. Political scientist James David Barber put it this way, "We have no king. The sentiments English children—and adults—direct to the Queen have no place to go in our system but to the President...the President is the only available object for such national-religious-monarchical sentiments as Americans possess" (Barber 1992, 3).

We have but one president at a time and the individual in the office is, politically speaking, without peer in our society (with the possible exception of former presidents). There is no elected official who may claim the same kind of presence or the same level of respect. Even governors, though without peer in their home states, must rise when the president enters the room. The deference and respect with which a president is treated is on the same level as that of a royal figure. As mentioned in chapter 1, the president does, in fact, hold the same diplomatic rank as a royal head of state, the equivalent of a king or queen, and no one else in the US political arena holds that rank.

It could be argued then, that perhaps our focus on the president is somewhat justified, and serves as an outlet for our own psychological needs. Could it be that we, as a nation, need a parental figure in a position of leadership? It is possible that having such a figure allows us to sleep soundly at night, knowing that mom or dad is watching out for us,[2] but at the same time, we wonder what makes them tick. How often do teens try to figure out their parents, determine their motives?

In the same way, the American people often try—more likely, it is the media and the punditry—to figure out what makes the president tick. A number of political scientists have attempted to provide us, both the large number of political scientists who teach courses on the presidency, and the American people who simply desire information about their leaders, with the tools to do so. Perhaps the best known among them is James David Barber, whose series of works is titled *The Presidential Character* and concludes with his fourth edition (1992). Barber first rose to national notoriety in January of 1969, on the eve of the inauguration of Richard Nixon to his first term, when he predicted that when confronted with a scandal that would threaten his presidency, Nixon's reaction would be "hush it up, to conceal it, bring down the blinds. If it breaks open and Nixon cannot avoid commenting on it, there is a real setup here for another crisis" (Barber 1969). Later that same year, according to *The New York Times*, Barber addressed the American Political Science Association and said much the same thing, "The danger is that Nixon will commit himself irrevocably to some disastrous course of action" (Fox 2004).

Barber is just one of many social scientists who have engaged in this line of work. The list includes, but is certainly not limited to Erwin Hargrove (Hargrove 1966, 1974; Hargrove and Nelson 1984), Alexander and Juliette George (1988), Michael Nelson (Hargrove and Nelson 1984), Michael Lyons (1997), George Goethals (2005), Dean Keith Simonton (1987), James Pfiffner (1998), and, the "granddaddy" of political psychology, Harold Lasswell (1948). We will briefly examine the work of each of these scholars a bit later in this chapter. Barber was a contemporary of Hargrove's, and they attended graduate school together, where they studied closely the work of Lasswell. Though Barber became most well known for his work on the psychological makeup of presidents, he also did similar work on legislators (Barber 1965) and members of committees (Barber 1966).

Why Is Character or Personality Important?

Certainly, in the context of this discussion, we are primarily concerned with the influence of a single individual on the institution as he or she occupies it, and on the condition in which he or she leaves it for successors. To better understand that, we need to understand, as I put it before, "What makes this person tick?" One of the reasons this discussion spent so much time on the process by which we select our presidents is that it may have an effect on the kinds of personality types that are drawn, not just to the office, but to the run itself.

Questions of the relationship between personality and performance in political settings have long been a question of interest to political scientists. Among the earliest work in this area was work done at the University of Chicago in the 1920s and 1930s, just around the time a young man by the name of Harold D. Lasswell was doing his undergraduate work. Lasswell's mentor, Charles Merriam, was among the early political scientists to examine behavior at the individual level in a systematic way and, with others, launched serious survey-based quantitative work on nonvoters in local elections in Chicago. As a graduate student at the University of Chicago, Lasswell continued this work and is often considered to have kicked off a long line of research into the interaction of psychology and politics (Almond 1987). His early work, *Psychopathology and Politics* (1930), made use of Freudian concepts to explain why people in politics behaved in particular ways (Marvick 1980; Simon 1985).[3] It was his later work, *Power and Personality* (1948), which spawned attempts by others to categorize the behavior of politicians by character or personality traits. Lasswell relied, primarily on two character types: the compulsive character and the dramatizing character. The compulsive character "is distinguished by the degree to which it relies on rigid, obsessive ways of handling human relations" (62). The dramatizing character, he claims, is defined by its "unifying demand for immediate affective response in others" (62). It also tends to "resort to traces of exhibitionism, flirtatiousness, provocativeness, indignation," and a desire to "'get a rise out of' the other person" (62), not unlike what we today might refer to as a "drama queen." Lasswell's focus is more broad, and deals with the behaviors that result from a compulsive character or a dramatizing character pursuing office. He discusses the development of a "democratic personality" that sounds a good deal like the concept of "civic republicanism" used by the Founders in discussing the role of individuals in a representative democracy.

In an essay for an anthology on researching the presidency, Erwin Hargrove (1993) discussed the difficulties for social scientists, in general, and political scientists in particular, to evaluate the importance of individuals on the course of history and on the institutions and actions therein. He wrote, "Surely the issue is not, Do individuals make a difference? but Under what conditions do they make a difference?" (70). Of course, many presidents have had very little impact on changes in the institution and seem, with the 20/20 vision of hindsight, to have had little to no impact on history. Why? Was it the individual personality of the president? Was it politics, his or her particular outlook, or the conditions under which he or she served? Or, was it just an unexciting time in history to be president? Perhaps it was some combination of all those factors. Louis Pasteur once said, "Chance favors the prepared mind"[4] (BrainyQuote.com "Louis Pasteur Quotes" n.d.). For our circumstances, we might alter the statement to say, "Fortune favors the appropriate personality."

We are not concerned here, though voters may be, with questions of sanity or mental illness as we discuss the psychology of the presidency. We are concerned with aspects of the president's background, and mental or emotional makeup, which might lead to his or her being able to make a difference. In other words, will he or she have the "strength" to adapt to the situation, be forceful when needed, or be more docile when appropriate? We would also be concerned with how a president might react under stressful conditions (recall the disquiet about McGovern's first vice-presidential pick of Eagleton and his having undergone electroshock therapy).[5]

Most of the efforts along these lines involve some sort of scheme to categorize the presidents by trait, tendency, past behavior, or whatever set of measures the researcher deemed appropriate. Barber and Hargrove both favor a two-dimensional approach, where one attribute is placed on the horizontal axis and another attribute placed on the vertical axis. The handy outcome of this approach is the creation of four fairly simple categories or typologies. The most well known of these typologies deserves some of our attention, while fully acknowledging that there are a multitude of approaches. Because Barber has, perhaps, been criticized the most, we'll begin with Barber's concept of presidential character.

James D. Barber's Presidential Character

Key to Barber's approach to the study of what he calls "presidential character" is the president's, or potential president's, self-esteem. Some who enter politics may do so to compensate for low self-esteem. In a way, they become addicted to the attention and the admiration, both of which substitute for their own lack of esteem. Others, once in politics, will seek to avoid any challenges to self-esteem, surrounding themselves with "yes men," and not engaging in thorough examination of the issues before them.

The traits necessary to observe this, according to Barber, emerge early in life. It is in the varied attempts children make to establish self-esteem that, Barber believed, helped to create character. This was accomplished, he argued, through "the child's experiments in relating to parents, brothers and sisters, and peers at play and in school" (1992, 7). By extension, one could argue it is the establishment of their place in the political environments of home, playground, and school that set the pattern for their lives. Success in one of those environments could impact success in others. For example, being able to garner parental attention from among the demands for similar attention by siblings might instruct the child in how to garner similar attention from teachers in school. Or, interactions with siblings may prove to be good training for interacting on the playground. Naturally, if the child finds success, or learns how to deal with failure (in a healthy manner) in these environments, that child will use those lessons in the political arena later in life.[6]

Barber goes on to discuss the development and importance of aspects of personality such as style and worldview. These two concepts are closely related to character, and the three aspects of personality interact with each other. We will discuss these two concepts a bit later. For now, understand that, according to Barber, these three aspects of personality seem to develop at different times in life: character in childhood, worldview in the teen years, and style as the child enters adulthood.

For Barber, a president's character is determined by the individual's placement on two dimensions or axes. The first is activity, running from active to passive. The second is affect, measured as positive or negative and is how the individual feels about the level of activity in which he or she engages. If we intersect these two dimensions (what Barber calls "baselines") at their mid points we get a 2 × 2 matrix containing four cells, each corresponding to one of Barber's character types (see figure 9.1).

The four categories, or types, of character are thus combinations of the position of each individual on each of the two dimensions. The first is the *active-positive*. This individual is very active and enjoys all aspects of the activity. He or she is flexible, has high self-esteem, and, as Barber puts it, "growing toward his [or her] image of himself [or herself] as he [or she] might yet be" (1992, 9). Presidents with this character type will admit to and correct mistakes. John F. Kennedy stands out as Barber's archetype for the category. According to Barber, this is the most desirable type for voters to choose.[7] They are the most flexible characters and have the greatest proclivity to learn from experience.

The second type is the *active-negative*, exemplified by Lyndon Johnson and Richard Nixon. This individual works hard, but gets little psychological or emotional reward for his or her efforts. He or she may be a bit of a perfectionist, but suffers from low self-esteem. Barber says it's as though he or she "were trying to make up for something or to escape from anxiety into hard work" (1992, 9). Just as the active-positive type was the most desirable, the active-negative is the most dangerous, the character most likely to run into policy problems or to "stonewall" as protection against a scandal.

The *passive-positive* character is an affection seeker, not personally assertive, such as William H. Taft. This type, as well, argues Barber, suffers from low self-esteem. This individual compensates with what he calls "a superficial optimism."

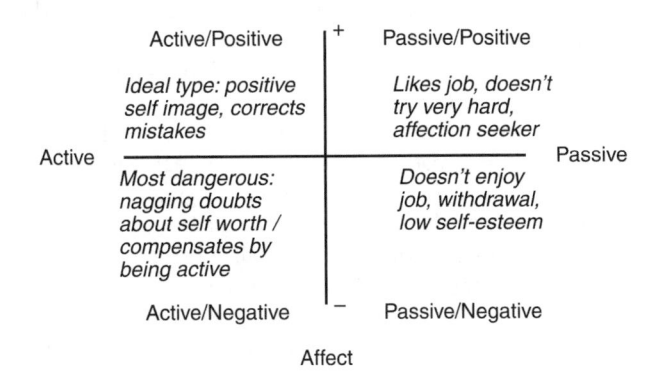

Figure 9.1 Barber's personality matrix.
Source: Figure created by author based on information in James Barber (1992).

Apparently, the attraction these individuals have for voters is that optimism and the ability to be agreeable and cooperative. So, it is his or her compliance that makes him or her successful in politics, while at the same time sets up disappointment for the individual and the voters.

The last type, the *passive-negative*, sees politics as "dutiful service," which is also compensation for low self-esteem. These individuals, like Dwight Eisenhower, will appear to be withdrawn, to avoid conflict. Barber argues that it is likely that their policies and statements will tend toward prohibitions and will emphasize "vague principles...and procedural arrangements" (1992, 10).

Barber summarizes these four types with the following:

> Active-positive Presidents want to achieve results. Active-negatives aim to get and keep power. Passive-positives are after love. Passive-negatives emphasize their civic virtue. (Barber 1992, 10)[8]

It can easily be extrapolated from these descriptions that there are some types that are more likely to be elected president, given the system we discussed in the earlier chapters. Naturally, with the rigorous schedule of contests to achieve a party nomination, and the need to be constantly selling oneself to raise money, the two activist character types are more likely to choose to run and be successful at it. A passive-positive, through his or her affability and optimism, might hoodwink voters sufficiently to be successful. The passive-negative, on the other hand, is not likely to even choose to run under this current regime of presidential selection. Such an individual could, in theory, be chosen to serve as vice president and succeed to the office upon the death, resignation, or removal of the president.

At this point you may be wondering which presidents (other than the examples already given) fall into which categories. Barber starts out with the first four of our presidents and argues that they "ran through this gamut of character types" (1992, 10). Washington was not to seek out the job, but his role as commanding general of the army during the Revolutionary War earned him sufficient respect that others sought him out. Thus, our very first president, argues Barber, was a passive-negative. John Adams, Barber asserts, was the typical compulsive whose actions seemed directed at maintaining his power and position, and thus fits the active-negative type. Adams's reaction to being defeated by Jefferson would indicate a less than strong level of self-esteem. Jefferson, according to Barber, "was clearly active-positive" (1992, 11). Jefferson was also among the very first presidents to seek expansion of the government, somewhat in contrast to his partisan position, a key element among the later presidents Barber would add to the category. Lastly, Barber asserts, our fourth president—James Madison—was most likely a passive-positive. Barber demonstrates this by pointing to many compromises made by Madison, allowing the country to "drift" into war. Madison was, says Barber, "the constitutional philosopher thrown into the White House"[9] (1992, 11). For more recent presidents, readers are encouraged to consult Barber's volume. A small sample of more recent presidents is available in figure 9.2.

Barber intended that his work would serve as a guide to voters in making selections among presidential candidates. He hoped that with his categorization of

```
                Active/Positive    +    Passive/Positive

                J. F. Kennedy,
                F. D. Roosevelt,          W. H. Taft
                H. S. Truman,
                T. Roosevelt

Active  ─────────────────────────┼───────────────────────── Passive

                L. B. Johnson,         J. C. Coolidge,
                R. Nixon               D. D. Eisenhower


                Active/Negative   −    Passive/Negative
                             Affect
```

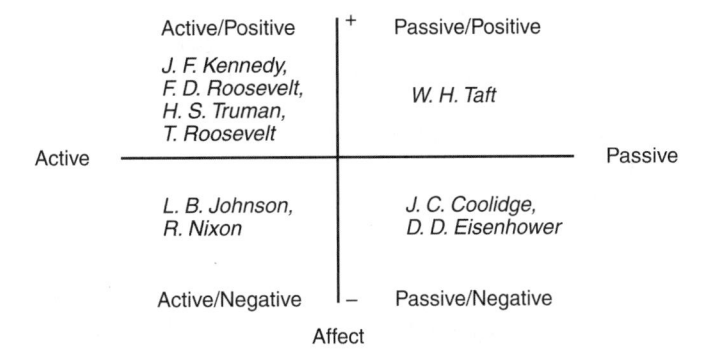

Figure 9.2 Sample of more recent presidents in Barber's personality matrix.

Source: Figure created by author based on information in James Barber (1992).

behavior we could avoid electing the more dangerous personality types. There were two things wrong with this approach. First, presidential candidates began reading his work and controlling information and behaving in such a way as to appear to be in Barber's best personality type. Second, much of the information was hard for the ordinary voter to obtain. It is also the case that Barber was criticized for fitting the data he used to the placement of presidents on his personality matrix.

Critiques of Barber

As previously noted, Barber's work has its critics, some justified, some not. Soon after the publication of the first edition of *The Presidential Character* in 1972, there were some in the social science community who accused him of making a partisan attack on Richard Nixon, who was running for reelection, by placing him in the active-negative category (Patterson 1973; Rogow 1976).[10] With Barber having made his comments and predictions about Nixon three years earlier (see earlier in this chapter), it could be argued that the partisan allegation is of lesser merit.

What is of more concern, however, for us as political scientists and students of politics, are other issues raised by critics. In his review of Barber's work, Patterson (1973) says that "this engagingly written book is not only faulty but perhaps dangerous" based on what he calls "sketchy research" (63).[11] Harry Bailey, Jr. (1975) praises Barber's effort and presentation, but says, "I find the difficulties with his approach to the presidency infinite" (550). Ruth Morgan (1975) makes the point that Barber tries to argue for predicting the behavior of *future* presidents based on his "retrodiction" of past presidents. Morgan's point gets right to the heart of the problem for a number of critics—availability and accessibility of appropriate data for doing the analysis. All of Barber's analyses (at least up to 1972), many point out, use biographical data available after the individual being considered had *already become president*.[12]

If Barber's goal was to provide a tool by which voters could make better choices among presidential contenders, then basing it on data that is not readily available to voters, would seem to make the tool inherently flawed with respect to meeting its intended goal. By no means should we simply dismiss Barber's work. Barber's typology is still of use to students of the presidency in making comparisons between presidents and in pointing us, and voters, to aspects of candidate character that might be of concern and that might point to a potential problem once the individual is in office.

Erwin Hargrove's Critique *and Praise* of Barber, and a Typology of His Own

Hargrove (1973) simultaneously criticizes Barber for what appears to be a liberal bias—making his active-positives all liberals—and praises him, as others have, for this bold extension of the work of Harold Lasswell (1948). "Barber gives us the best typology to date, but its very virtues raise questions about the usefulness of typology," states Hargrove (831). He praises Barber's typology as "clear and plausible, and it can be used by scholars who are not psychologists" (831). But, being easy could lead to misuse. Hargrove goes on to say, "The great risk in a typology is that we will be lazy, relying on the type to explain the individual, thereby distorting individuality" (832). While this is true, Barber reminds us that his typology is about tendencies, and much is determined by the situation in which a president may or may not exhibit the tendencies.

Up to the point of Barber's work, much of what political scientists did to understand presidents and the presidency was to write biographies and discuss the interactions of institutions and systems. Hargrove notes that Barber has taken the next step in the study of the presidency. In a later work, as part of an anthology about doing research on the presidency (1993), Hargrove again notes that while he has criticisms of Barber's "contribution," "they illustrate the difficulty of creating a comprehensive typology of political personalities" (1993, 97). Hargrove offers his own "simpler schema," where the two dimensions are democratic character and level of political skill. While this approach is a bit less psychological, there is still a difficulty that Hargrove acknowledges, in determining a president's democratic character as this, too, involves "judgments about the degree of ego strength and self-esteem" (97). In what sounds a good deal like Barber's active-negative type, Hargrove describes a president with low democratic character and high skill levels as someone who will perceive "challenges as threats to the self and to act accordingly" (97).[13]

Working with Michael Nelson, Hargrove (Hargrove and Nelson 1984) developed the 2×2–matrix approach in a different way. The dimensions involved in this approach are two questions: (1) is the presidency strong or weak, and (2) is this strength or weakness good or bad? Using biblical metaphors, Hargrove and Nelson arrive at four categories. The *Savior* is when the institution is strong and that strength is good for the nation. This was the prevailing model for the period from the 1940s through the 1960s and thus reflects the presidencies of Franklin

Roosevelt, Harry Truman, John Kennedy, and Lyndon Johnson (through 1966). The *Satan* is when the institution is strong and that strength is bad and can lead to bad policy or scandals (usually involving the maintenance of power). According to Hargrove and Nelson (1984), this reflects the period of the early to mid-1970s, but would include the latter Johnson's presidency as well as Nixon's. The *Samson* president occurs when the president is weak and that weakness is bad for the country. This often occurs when other institutions are also weak and none takes a lead role in politics. This would be the mid- to late 1970s and would include Ford and Carter. The last category, the *Seraph*, occurs when the president is weak and that weakness is good for the nation and would include Eisenhower.

Adding Complexity

One of the themes among these critiques seems to be that Barber's categories do not allow for much nuance. You are in the category, or not, with no matter of degree or relative position. Another theme is the inaccessibility of the necessary data *prior* to the individual under study becoming president. The latter seems rather significant if the intention is to try to *predict* behavior. One other theme of critique is the difficult, highly psychological nature of the analysis, despite the fact that Hargrove praised Barber for making the psychology more accessible for nonpsychologists.

In a much more complex analysis, a number of social scientists have begun adapting the Myers-Briggs Type Indicator (MBTI)[14] to analyze presidents and their behavior (Choiniere and Keirsey 1992; Lyons 1997). Lyons (1997) adds to the critiques of Barber by arguing that the four types may not "correspond consistently and meaningfully with observable differences in personality and behavior" (795). Lyons is using a more sophisticated way, perhaps, to say that Barber's categories are "squishy." While there is a great appeal in attempting to apply an established measure of personality to the American presidency, the MBTI is rather confusing for those not trained in psychology. The resulting 16 different types, and the subtle differences between them, seem to take us further from what Barber was trying to do, and certainly further from Lasswell's original intentions. Lastly, the addition of 12 more character types is still reliant on data that is not all that accessible and is subject to the interpretive biases of the researcher.

Choiniere and Keirsey (1992) look at the same question from the perspective of what they refer to as temperament.[15] This is different from character, they argue, in that it "is a lifelong predisposition toward certain identifiable patterns of behavior" (7), as opposed to character, which is closer to habit. "Character is a pattern of behavior, and therefore observable, while temperament is the biological substrate out of which character emerges" (8). They, too, use a two-dimensional construct that results in four categories of temperament. On one axis is expectations about the behavior of others, from a sanctioning outlook where the politician wants others to obey the rules and engage in legitimate behavior, to a utilizing outlook, where the expectation is that people will do things that work, that achieve some end. The second axis relates to communication and emphasizes concrete versus abstract speech.

The result is a matrix with "sanctioners" and "utilitarians" on the horizontal axis and "abstract" and "concrete" speech on the vertical axis. A sanctioner, who expects people to follow the rules, who is also an abstract communicator, is an "Idealist." Choiniere and Keirsey argue that we had not had an Idealist president through the timeframe covered by their analysis, but in other venues, someone like Gandhi would fit the category. Idealists tend to be nurturing and "promote individual growth" (494). They tend to be focused on the "Self" within others and seek ethics over regulation. Idealists have a powerful conscience and are benevolent. They strive to be authentic. A sanctioner who also utilizes concrete communication is a "Guardian," members of this category "quickly take note of the transgressions of others" (160). Such individuals will not only be rooted in tradition and preservation of resources, but will also be concerned with reward and punishment and have a sense of duty. In this category, claim Choiniere and Keirsey, are presidents Washington, Monroe, Taft, Wilson, Truman, Nixon,[16] Ford, Carter, and George H. W. Bush (to name a few).

A utilitarian, who wants to get things done, who uses concrete communication, is an "Artisan." These individuals are "skilled in *any* of the arts" (17), they "are drawn to change" (17), and "we see the Artisan's love of impulse and excitement showing up in their behavior toward women" (19). This category includes Andrew Jackson, Martin Van Buren, Teddy Roosevelt, Warren Harding, Franklin Roosevelt, John Kennedy, Lyndon Johnson, and Ronald Reagan. The "Rationals" are "get it done" utilitarians, who use more abstract communication. The category includes John Adams, Jefferson, Madison, John Quincy Adams, Lincoln, Grant, Hoover, and Eisenhower. Such individuals, argue Choiniere and Keirsey, "want to be able to understand and control anything in their lives that seems important to them" (373). They seek competence, often in more than one field or skill, and "rely upon an iron will to see them through the most difficult situations" (375–376). By the very name of the category, one would not expect Rationals to be very emotional, but will rely heavily on words and "on precision in their use" (376).

Choiniere and Keirsey's analysis is interesting, especially in its attempt to get at something "deeper" than Barber's character. Their categorizations suffer, however, from the same subjectivity as Barber's in that it still relies on their collective subject use of data and interpretation. They also add levels of unnecessary complexity by adding subcategories and linking their work more closely to the complex MBTI.

Summarizing the Critiques and Competition

It is evident that Barber's work has some difficulties and some drawbacks. Most would likely agree that Barber's work cannot live up to his original intentions. Compounding the previously stated reasons is the simple fact that many presidential candidates, starting with Jimmy Carter, have been exposed to Barber's work and would, most likely, try to manage information and spin interpretations to appear to be an active-positive character type.

This does not necessarily invalidate all of what Barber did, or sought to do. Admittedly, the data is hard to come by, the *predictive value* of the typology may be lost, the methodology may be tainted by Barber's preferences, but nonetheless, there is some *explanatory value* in Barber's work. Looking at the various attributes or traits associated with each type, and knowing that certain presidents are one type or another, may help us to understand why those presidents behaved the way they did.[17] Perhaps all it serves to do for the general public is to answer that fascination, mentioned earlier, that Americans have with their presidents as pseudoroyalty. On the other hand, social scientists, especially historians and political scientists, could use such oversimplification to help draw parallels and contrasts between presidents, and thus better understand how the institution functions and how decisions are made.

Hargrove and Nelson (1984) add a different set of explanations and a richness of color to our understanding of presidential behavior. Their interesting biblical references certainly bring some clarity to their typology. Perhaps if Barber had been as imaginative in naming the categories there would have been more clarity to his end product. To be sure, Hargrove and Nelson's Savior is easy to understand, as is their Satan. There may be slightly more confusion with respect to their Samson and Seraph categories, but Samson is still rather straightforward for those who can easily recall the story of Samson and Delilah.

No typology for categorizing human behavior, especially behavior of elected officials, will be perfect. Each attempt at doing so, however, leads us farther down the road of explanation. The emphasis on the institution within a political situation gives us one perspective, the emphasis on self-esteem or ego gives us another. Bringing in typologies from other areas or research[18] sheds new light on different aspects of the presidency and different skills of the presidents.

The More Observable Style

Recall that Barber had three aspects to his assessment of presidents and the patterns of their behavior—character, style, and worldview. We have already dealt with his classification of character. Style is much easier to observe than character. It can be argued that style itself has three components—rhetoric, interpersonal relations, and work. Rhetoric, naturally, deals with the way the president communicates; interpersonal relations deals with how the president relates to others, especially in close relationships; and work being the way a president approaches the more mundane aspects of the job—reading briefing papers, doing paperwork, attention to detail, and so forth. The combination of these aspects and the amount of emphasis a president puts on each determines his or her style.

Jerry Ford, never really considered a great speaker, was alleged to have been very good at interpersonal relations (Mieczkowski 2004). Certainly, his career in the House of Representatives demonstrates ability in this area. Generally, one does not rise to positions of leadership in Congress without being able to engage successfully in small-group dynamics, to glad hand and back slap.[19] The same perhaps could be said of the elder George Bush, especially when one looks at his ability to bring a group of disparate and diverse nations together in coalition against Saddam Hussein's 1990 invasion of Kuwait.

Jimmy Carter, also not known for his ability as a great speaker, was known as a bit of a workaholic who would take stacks of briefing materials to the residence each night for homework. One of Carter's most significant speeches, the infamous "malaise speech," seemed to be lost in his inability to communicate the key theme. Stories of his discomfort in dealing with Washington politics would indicate a less than successful approach to interpersonal relations (Barber 1992).

Ronald Reagan was best known for his rhetorical style. In fact, he was so good at addressing large audiences, whether live or on TV, that he earned the nickname "the Great Communicator." Stories did surface that, in contrast to Carter, Reagan preferred short summaries of briefing materials, indicating less of a conviction to the work aspect of the job (Greenstein 2000).

Bill Clinton seemed to have abilities spanning all three aspects of the job. His ability to deliver a speech to a large audience was on par with Reagan's. His ability to charm small groups, even House Speaker Newt Gingrich, helped in policy negotiations. Clinton was also known for his ability to soak up much information and to engage his advisers on a very high level, such that some have commented that policy meetings often resembled graduate seminars or "college bull sessions" (Stephanopoulos 1999).

Other Factors beyond Character—Worldview, Situation, and Ideology

Of course, all of what we have been discussing must be considered in two other contexts, the contemporary political-historical situation and the president's ideology. The first is beyond the president's control, but often character is about how one handles the cards one has been dealt. Will the president rise to meet the challenge or seek to avoid conflict? The answer often lies in his or her underlying character and the particular political outlook or ideology that helped to elect him or her.

The worldview a president holds "consists of his [or her] primary, politically relevant beliefs, particularly his conceptions of social causality, human nature, and the central moral conflicts of the time" (Barber 1992, 5). For Barber, the worldview is how presidents, or anyone for that matter, see the world and interpret it. Worldview is rather hard to discern and is perhaps best analyzed as the sum total of an individual's life and work.

Not all presidents are presented with opportunities to demonstrate whatever skills they may possess. Other presidents may feel as though they are presented with far too many opportunities. Certainly, Abraham Lincoln would have preferred not to have had to demonstrate how capable he was at managing a Civil War. It is doubtful that Franklin Roosevelt needed to demonstrate his wartime leadership after having managed the economic crisis of the 1930s. At the same time, presidents who served during calmer moments of history, and are thus less notable, would have appreciated some way to demonstrate their skills.

Ideology will affect what choices a president makes. Ideology, in this day and age of being a liberal or conservative,[20] might push a president to choose diplomacy over military action or shift the emphasis of legislation he or she would propose to Congress, for instance. Given, for example, that Barber classifies both Lyndon Johnson and Richard Nixon as active-negatives and they served as temporally proximate presidents, a comparison between them is apt. Would Nixon, more socially conservative than Johnson, have pushed for, and achieved passage of the Civil Rights Act and the Voting Rights Act? I would argue no, but some might disagree. Or, take two recent active-positive presidents, George H. W. Bush (the elder Bush) and Bill Clinton. If Bush had won reelection in 1992 instead of being defeated by Clinton, would there have even been a debate about health care and the subsequent defeat of Clinton's Democratic Party in Congress, which also led to the budget battles of 1995 and 1996? Not likely, since Bush's ideological perspective probably would not have moved him to weigh in on such a controversial policy debate.

Similarly, if not for the American failure during the Bay of Pigs invasion of Cuba in 1961, would President Kennedy have recognized his decision-making shortcomings and been successful during the subsequent Cuban Missile Crisis?[21] If not for the Tet Offensive in 1968, would Lyndon Johnson have remained in the race for the Democratic Party nomination for president? Would George W. Bush (the younger Bush) have been a two-term president without the events of 9/11?

A Less Observable Style

Naturally, we can try to discern a president's style from his or her choices about rhetoric, the types of performers he or she invites to the White House, the kinds of vacations he or she goes on, or from any number of other activities. The problem with this approach is that much of it can be staged to try to place a certain image in the minds of voters. George W. Bush's "aw shucks" approach and down home, ranch vacations complete with brush clearing and hunting, made him appear less aristocratic than his family's more patrician New England background might. Recall the contrast in the 2004 campaign with his opponent John Kerry being shown in more aristocratic light, from his wife with a foreign accent, to wind surfing, to a poor attempt at hunting that ended with a discussion of his designer hunting clothes. This is more image than style.

Less directly observable, but still obtainable by intrepid journalists, is how the president relates to his or her advisers. We can classify these interactive styles with three categories. The first is a formalistic style, the second a competitive style, and the third is a collegial style. Each approach says something about the president who adopts it.[22]

In a more formalistic organization, the classical hierarchical structure, as in a pyramid, can be readily observed. Usually this would mean an all-powerful chief of staff having the complete trust of the president and guarding access to him or her. The authority would be concentrated at the top of this pyramid with the chief of staff and/or the president wielding all the power. While this style promotes efficiency and limits access to the president, it also has the great drawback of the flow of information being blocked or distorted, with the president perhaps not getting sufficient diversity of opinion. The classical breakdown of such a system could result in a Watergate-like failure.

In a competitive approach to dealing with advisers, the president must be a skilled manager, as this approach often involves pitting one or more advisers against others. In this way, the advisers compete for the attention of the president and are, supposedly, motivated to provide him or her with the best possible information. If one were to plot this on an organizational chart it would look like a hub-and-spoke system with overlapping areas of responsibility. Some have argued that the only real successful use of this style was by Franklin Roosevelt (Hess 2002).

The collegial approach would look quite a bit like the hub-and-spoke system used in the competitive model, but the emphasis would be quite different. In this approach, allegedly used by John Kennedy, there is a greater sense of collective decision making and collective responsibility. There is little to no competition among the advisers, but they are encouraged to offer competing viewpoints. The danger with this style is the possibility that through concerted efforts to avoid competition and losing the collective sense of responsibility, a phenomenon known as groupthink could occur. This is where the members of a group value their membership in the group more than they value a positive outcome (Janis 1972). The end result is a rather large and embarrassing policy failure. More detailed discussion of this phenomenon is available in chapter 12.

Coming Back to the Individual

In this chapter, we have dealt with the issues at the heart of our overall discussion, the individual as president. What we have learned is that what is at the heart of the president's makeup is his or her character, the way he or she sees the world, and how he or she responds to and interacts with it. The individual may be active regardless of political persuasion, but that persuasion will guide the actions the president takes. The individual may have a negative view of the job before him or her, again regardless of partisanship or ideology. It is, however, the political outlook filtered through an individual's character and style that will determine the kind of presidency he or she leaves to the next person to occupy the office.

Being able to recognize these factors helps us to better understand the central institution in American politics. Certainly, the presidency is a "coequal branch" along with Congress and the courts, but as we have seen and will continue to see throughout our discussion, it is the presidency that gets all the attention, whether from the media, other political actors, or even schools. Much of the history and civics we are taught in elementary school, and sometimes beyond that level, focuses on the historical contributions of the president and what the president wants as policy goals. Knowing what drives them to do what they do helps us understand that better.

Chapter 10

The Presidential Advisory System: For Good or Ill, There Really Is One

The contemporary system for advising presidents is a reflection of the modern presidency. It could also be seen as a remnant of the modern presidency in a postmodern era. The dawn of the modern presidency wasn't, however, the beginning of the presidential advisory system, but the reforms associated with the New Deal administration of Franklin Roosevelt certainly provide the foundation of the system we can observe today.

Early History of Presidential Advising

Naturally, the first formalization of a presidential advisory system comes from the mention in Article II of the Constitution of the president's authority to appoint, with the advice and consent of the Senate:

> ...public Ministers and Consuls, Judges of the supreme court, and all other Officers of the United States, whose appointments are not herein otherwise provided for, and which shall be established by Law: but Congress may by Law vest the Appointment of such inferior Officers as they think proper, in the President alone, in the Courts of Law, or in the Heads of Departments. (Constitution of the United States, Article II, Section 2)

This reference indicates that there will be "departments" within the executive branch, presumably to assist the president in the carrying out of his or her duties. The first among these were created "before the end of summer, 1789: State Department, War Department, and Treasury Department"[1] (McDonald 1994, 224). Two "lesser" agencies were also created by Congress—the Post Office that existed under the Articles of Confederation was continued and the Office of Attorney General was created. The Office of Attorney General was much smaller than what we are familiar with, and what we know of today as US attorneys reported to the secretary of state (McDonald 1994). The first presidential cabinet had three advisers to the president. Other than household staff, the assistance to Washington beyond these officers was next to nil.

As the nation and the scope and authority of the central government grew, so did the power of the presidency. With this growth in the power of the presidency came a need to expand the cabinet and provide the president with more advisers. Similarly, as the range of authority of the executive branch grew, so did the need for staff help for the president above and beyond the cabinet.

FDR and the Evolution of the Contemporary System

We can easily trace the current system of presidential advisement back to the reforms implemented during Franklin Roosevelt's time in the White House. As part of the federal government's response to the economic crisis of the Great Depression, the scope and size of the federal government grew considerably. This growth, naturally, was in the executive branch where Congress delegated much of its regulatory authority at Roosevelt's request.[2] The executive branch was becoming unwieldy and hard to manage. Prior to this time, the cabinet had grown much larger as well, and the heads of the departments, while still technically under the control of the president, sometimes seemed to answer more to external constituencies than to the president.

To deal with this managerial problem, Roosevelt appointed a commission to make recommendations to him about how he might better control the branch of government he was purported to lead. The commission came to be known by the name of one of its members, Louis Brownlow, a well-known political scientist specializing in public administration. Serving with Brownlow were Charles Edward Merriam, another well-known political scientist, and Luther Gulick, an expert in the field of public administration. The Brownlow Commission, more formally known as the Committee on Administrative Management, made a number of recommendations to Roosevelt about how the executive branch should be reorganized. The report of the commission led to the creation of the Reorganization Act of 1939, which when passed created the Executive Office of the President (EOP) (Fesler 1987). It should be noted here, however, that the EOP envisioned by the commission and its report was of a much smaller scale than the EOP we know today. In addition, Warshaw notes, "The intent of the reorganization plan was not to alter the Cabinet's advisory role, but rather to improve presidential management of the executive branch" (1996, 25).

Though the Act included only two of the major recommendations in the report, it led to the creation of the White House staff, as we know it today. It created the EOP and several senior-level staff assistants to the president to provide advice and management assistance to the president. It led to the development of the president's *personal bureaucracy*, which reported only to him with no allegiance to any external constituency, and which served at the pleasure of the president.

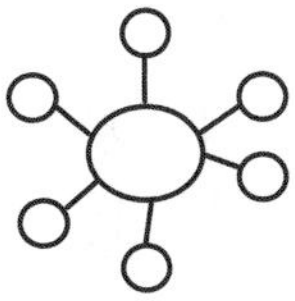

Figure 10.1 Hub-and-spoke organizational style.

In general, the report asserted that the president should be the center of managerial direction and control of executive branch departments and agencies. However, it also pointed out that there was no adequate mechanism, either legal or administrative, at that time to provide that direction. Obviously, the recommendation to create a "White House secretariat" was adopted, but so was the recommendation to grant continuing reorganization authority.

In the end, the president did become the center of things. If we diagrammed the organization of the EOP, we would see a series of concentric circles with the president at the center, the White House Staff in the next circle, the large EOP in the next, then the cabinet, and the rest of the executive branch in the outer circle—a bit like a bull's eye. In the case of Franklin Roosevelt, the arrangement would have been closer to the hub-and-spoke concept of the competitive model of organization (see figure 10.1).[3] It has been said that Roosevelt preferred to keep his staff competing while he stayed above the fray until the end.

Growth in the Advisory System

There have been a number of policy areas in which the presidential advisory system has exhibited growth over the years. Two of the largest growth areas have been economic policy and national security policy. The 1960s and 1970s saw expansion in what might be called service areas, particularly regarding the creation of new cabinet departments.

With World War II behind us and a system of government regulation of the economy in place in response to the Depression, presidents saw a need for a better system of getting advice about the economy. The Council of Economic Advisors was created in 1946 to address this shortcoming (WhiteHouse.gov "About CEA"). Its focus was academic in nature and was made up of leading economists, who often saw policy from a similar perspective as the president.

As time has progressed, presidents tinkered with their economic advising system to suit the circumstances and their ideological perspective. To help implement the president's economic agenda, President Clinton established the National Economic Council, made up of department and agency heads with policy responsibility for aspects of the economy.[4] It is a sort of task force to facilitate coordination. There is a director and a staff to work with the council. As we'll see shortly, the function of the National Economic Council parallels in the economic realm what the National Security Council (NSC, see further on for definition) does in the area of national security.

So too, following World War II, the United States had a much larger role in world affairs and we now had a greater responsibility, like it or not, for the security of a large portion of the world. Due to the onset of the Cold War and the attainment of nuclear weapons by other countries, we also had a more elevated threat level for our own security. As a result, the NSC was created to coordinate the military, diplomatic, and intelligence capabilities of the executive branch (WhiteHouse.gov "National Security Council"). While the president chairs the council, its staff is headed by the National Security Advisor, a key adviser to the president who often becomes an important administration spokesperson. Some have become well known to the American public. Two National Security Advisors were later appointed secretary of state (Henry Kissinger under Nixon and Ford and Condoleezza Rice under George W. Bush), another was fairly well known during and after his tenure (Zbigniew Brzezinski, during the Carter administration), but may today be best known as the father of MSNBC journalist and morning talk show host Mika Brzezinski.

As with a great deal of the centralization of policymaking in the White House, the creation of the NSC could be said to come from a growing sense of distance between the president, the White House Staff, and the career bureaucrats in the Departments of Defense and State. Particularly, the State Department came to be seen as mired in diplomacy and protocol and unable to quickly respond to the changing international environment and carry out the president's directives.

As the federal government began providing more and more services and the public and local governments demanded more from the federal government, the executive branch grew to meet the demand. Key among this growth was the creation of service bureaus. The Departments of Health, Education, and Welfare (HEW, now Health and Human Services); of Transportation (DOT); and of Housing and Urban Development (HUD)[5] were just three examples of this growth within the cabinet. Passage of Civil Rights legislation in the 1960s also delegated a large set of new responsibilities to the executive branch across a number of agencies and perceived needs helped to create other agencies like the Department of Energy[6] (Pika and Maltese 2010).

In a similar but smaller way, the management concerns were raised by the expansion of the government's economic regulatory power in the 1930s; this further expansion of the executive branch created some new difficulties for executive management. Presidents during the time of this new expansion struggled with ways to manage a much larger executive branch and, to some extent, a larger EOP. A number of different mechanisms were used by presidents to gain control over the policy process. Some would employ a group of cabinet members and heads of other agencies, usually referred to as a domestic council, with overlapping jurisdiction in domestic policy areas. Other presidents created a specific office within the EOP for the direction of policy. The former process usually involved development of policy out in the departments and agencies with coordination at the White House. The latter approach often involved centralization of policymaking, where the executive branch beyond the White House was simply given directives about policy implementation while the policy had been developed in the domestic policy office at the White House (Lamb and Twombly 2001).

One other area of growth within the EOP in the more recent past has been in the area of interest group communications and relations. Here, the term *interest group* is used more broadly and refers not just to the organized interests we think of as lobbying the government on a daily basis, but also the legislative branch and the voters. The most visible among these efforts is the Office of the Press Secretary and the Press Office. This is the president's main means of communicating beyond the physical boundaries of the White House. The White House press secretary is usually in front of the White House Press Corps at least once a day, making announcements and fielding questions. The press secretary and his or her staff do much more than simply stand behind a podium in the Briefing Room before a bank of cameras and microphones. The press secretary must develop a working relationship with what he or she may view as more of an unruly mob than colleagues, but they must treat them like colleagues, look after their professional needs, and make the task of the Press Corps easier. All of this is done with the goal of achieving a more positive interpretation of the news for the president and the administration. Sometimes, however, this work takes on the tone of a war between the president and the media (Jacobs 2003). Jacobs uses the examples of the Clinton administration's pushback on health care and social security reform to demonstrate this concept and in particular points to the use of "the war room" mentality in making his point.

Since May 11th, 2009, the operation formerly known as the White House Office of Public Liaison has been named the White House Office of Public Engagement (Office of the Press Secretary 2009). The new name more appropriately calls attention to President Obama's background as a community organizer in Chicago before he entered politics. The function is still much the same as its predecessor office. While Public Liaison was, perhaps, more of a one-way street, with the White House attempting to organize support among the public for its policies and programs, the Office of Public Engagement seems more two way. That is, while the goal of making the president look good to the American people may still loom large, the new mission provides a mechanism for citizens to attempt to engage the administration on issues of concern to them, as well.

Decline in the Role of the Cabinet

Difficulty in management of a disparate and diverse branch of government is not the sole reason for the centralization of decision making in the White House. In some ways, it has to do with the nature of the cabinet and what it has evolved into, or what some specific departments have become. As we will see in the discussion in the next chapter, sometimes cabinet departments, and their heads, stop speaking for the president and begin acting like representatives of the very groups in society they are supposed to regulate.[7]

At one time in our history, starting actually under George Washington and continuing for quite some time, at least through Lincoln's administration,[8] the president's cabinet worked more like a cabinet in a parliamentary system with collective decision making and responsibility. While this was Alexander Hamilton's[9] preferred approach, though he probably would have preferred a cabinet more closely styled after a parliamentary system, it came about more as a result of the political situation existing at the time (McDonald 1974). According to Forrest McDonald's (1974) history of the Washington presidency, there were some members of the Senate who saw themselves as an aristocratic council to the president. Difficulty in getting cooperation from that "council" led Washington to rely more heavily upon his appointed cabinet. The tradition based on that precedent lasted for many decades.

Even today, we see that presidents start out with the best of intentions with respect to maintaining lines of communication among their cabinet members. They begin their administrations with regular cabinet meetings, but time and the pressures of office often combine to reduce the frequency of those meetings. By the end of a president's term in office, it is most likely that the cabinet is meeting infrequently at best.

As the scope and size of government grew, naturally so did the size of the cabinet. Thus, it became a bit more difficult for the cabinet to act as a unified, cohesive decision-making body. As the strength of special interests also began to grow (the railroads in the nineteenth century, for example) there was more opportunity for direct interaction between such interests and leaders of executive branch agencies. So too, cabinet appointments became more political, in that such appointments were often used to seal political deals either within the president's party or with strong interests. Figure 10.2 depicts the relationship between the legislature, the executive branch agency, and the special interest group—often referred to as the "Iron Triangle." Where this political subsystem has become so dominated by the interest group, such that it serves more as an agent for the interest than as an agent for the president, we have an example of "capture theory" or capture. When this occurs it is said that the agency head has "gone native," where the individual is in a state of capture and is doing more the bidding of the regulated group than that of the president, and usually loses the trust of other cabinet members and the White House staff. This was certainly the case in the late 1960s and early 1970s under Richard Nixon when he and his closest advisers in the White House felt that HUD Secretary George Romney (father of former Massachusetts governor and candidate for the Republican presidential nomination in 2008 and 2012, Mitt Romney) had gone native. They believed Romney was so supportive of a constituency in need of low-income housing that it would threaten their suburban, white, Republican base. As a result, they offered him a number of other administration positions, including ambassador to Mexico, to try to get him out of housing policy. In the end, once reelected, Nixon called for the resignations of all staff; he rejected some, but Romney's was among those he accepted[10] (Lamb and Twombly 2001).

Capture theory, and the condition of an agency being captured, does not happen every day, and the impression left by the system depicted in figure 10.2 is a bit overly simplistic. In discussing how the relationship actually works, I have often used the image of what I have called the "Double-Sided Triangle." It maintains the image of strong relationship,[11] but tempers it with the depiction of competition among

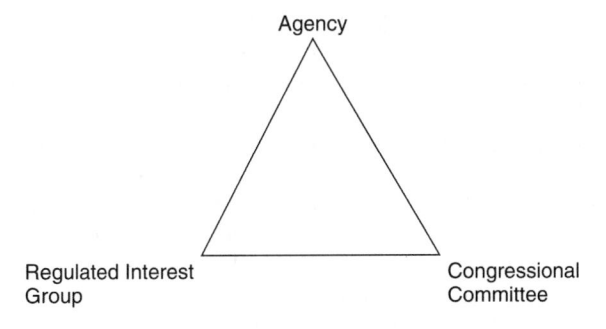

Figure 10.2 Iron Triangle.

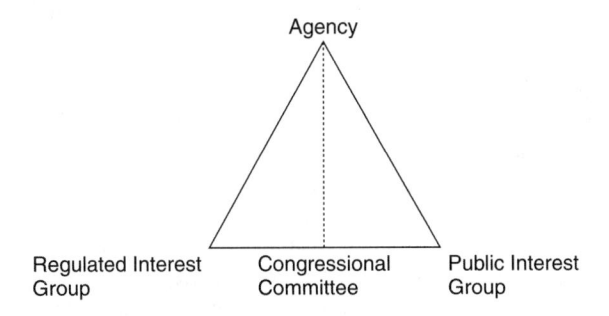

Figure 10.3 Double-Sided or Folded Triangle.

interests. Figure 10.3 more clearly illustrates this competitive aspect of the policy subsystem.

Even in the case of a more competitive subsystem, however, the agency head can still go native and adopt the political outlook of either one of the interest groups or the professional bureaucrats working under him or her. This sets up a condition where the president's closest advisers may begin to view the agency head as an outsider, or worse a competitor. In some cases, especially where the individual is a more high-profile cabinet member, the staff may see him or her as developing an independent political base for a possible challenge to the incumbent. Certainly, this was the case with George Romney as discussed earlier.

Part of what develops as a result of this mistrust is alienation. Occasionally, other members of the cabinet may begin to ostracize their rogue colleague. There has also developed an informal dichotomy between members of the "inner cabinet" and the rest of the cabinet, or the "outer cabinet." The inner cabinet is generally the four most senior officers—State, Defense, Treasury, and Justice—in part, because they are often individuals appointed for their close relationship with the president or such a relationship develops over time because of the necessity of working closely with the president. Political scientist Thomas Cronin has called these the "nonclientele departments," referring to the fact that they are less likely to have easily identifiable special interests in domestic politics associated with them. The inner cabinet might also contain a secretary from a department that is a primary focus of the incumbent president's political agenda. An argument could also be made that given the importance of the issue area in contemporary politics; the secretary of Homeland Security could be a member of the inner cabinet.

In Richard Nixon's attempt to further reorganize the executive branch, he attempted to formalize the concept of the inner cabinet by creating a small number of "super departments," the heads of which the other cabinet officers would report. While Congress rejected this proposal, they did agree to a beefing up of the Bureau of the Budget and gave it a new title to reflect its broader responsibilities. The Office of Management and Budget (OMB) was perhaps the most well known of the surviving proposals from Nixon's reorganization plan.

Who Gets Appointed to the Cabinet and Why

One of the most effective cabinets in US history, it could be argued, was Abraham Lincoln's. The individuals Lincoln chose were, primarily, his rivals for the Republican nomination for president in 1860, thus supposedly among the most qualified individuals in the country to serve. It took Lincoln's special talents to reign in this rather "healthy-egoed" group of individuals.[12]

In a similar fashion, John Kennedy's cabinet was at least once dubbed "the best and the brightest" (Halberstam 1972). Supposedly, Kennedy selected a wide range of individuals from politics and business, not for the political points he would score by their appointment, but for their ability and, in one particular case—Bobby Kennedy as attorney general—for loyalty (Schlesinger 1965). Even this group, as we will see in chapter 12, had difficulty overcoming some powerful group dynamics to arrive at the right plan of action.

Though we would hope that presidents would pick well-qualified individuals to serve as the heads of these executive branch agencies, politics cannot be ignored. Certainly, both could be satisfied—quality appointees and political concerns. Early in our history, in particular, a consideration like geographic diversity was important in trying to balance the membership of the cabinet. During the period of the Brokered Convention, especially, building bridges within one's political party played a significant role in cabinet selection. More recently, presidents like Clinton and Obama have touted their efforts to make the cabinet look more like America by increasing gender and ethnic representation. Some presidents have also sought to ensure some measure of bipartisanship by appointing cabinet members from the opposing party. One might think that these bipartisan appointees would serve in lesser positions, outside the inner cabinet, but some, like Obama's appointment of Robert Gates to continue on as Defense secretary, demonstrate that keeping such appointees at arm's length is not necessarily the case.

Whether a part of the inner cabinet or the outer cabinet, whether trusted or distrusted, whether of the president's party or not, and regardless of the reason for their appointment, these high-ranking government officials are considered representatives of the administration and surrogates for the president. They are also there to provide advice to the president about their particular area of expertise, both in terms of policy and management. These individuals are also responsible, ultimately, for the management of their agencies. Collectively, the cabinet still performs an important function, and even though they are no longer a collective decision-making body, the body provides a mechanism by which conflict between agencies may be resolved (Warshaw 2000). Such conflict resolution is not always successful, as is easily evidenced by many "tell all" books by former presidential staff or books by journalists in which former staff are interviewed (e.g., many of the books by journalist Bob Woodward).

One might ask if the management of agencies should be left in political hands or if we should move to a system with career civil servants running these government agencies. Even in the British system of parliamentary government, the highest-ranking careerist serves under a political appointee. The fact that the cabinet no longer functions as a collective decision-making body does not eliminate its value. The symbolism of group representation and qualification has political value for the appointing president, which in turn can help him or her, over the long term, to achieve political goals.

Part IV

The Presidency in Isolation

Chapter 11

The President and the Bureaucracy

Of all the parts of government the president must interact with, it is the bureaucracy that is most pervasive. The president must work with the bureaucracy on a daily basis and must appear to be in command of it. Few expect the president's relationship with Congress to be smooth or commanding in the same way. The president's impact on the judiciary, especially the Supreme Court, is more long term and in many ways more complex.

Since dealing with the bureaucracy—the core of the branch he or she is supposed to head—is both a daily and vital function of the presidency, we should take time to examine it further. The manner in which the president deals with the massive federal bureaucracy is yet another way to get at what makes him or her tick, and leaves a lasting impact on the executive branch for subsequent presidents.

What Is a Bureaucracy?

At the most basic level, a bureaucracy is defined as rule or government by bureau or department.[1] This definition refers to a very specific form of organization that has become a pervasive feature of modern life where we see most organizations we interact with on a daily basis making use of the form. Many in society also attach a strong negative feeling to the term; perhaps this comes from waiting on seemingly endless lines[2] at the department of motor vehicles, or being treated like a number at some social services agency.

Our current conception of bureaucracy comes to us from the man considered to be the "father of bureaucracy"—sociologist, Max Weber. Among other things, Weber studied the organization of the Prussian Army and the Catholic Church. From that study, he devised what he saw as an ideal organizational form with what could be argued is six characteristics.[3] The first of these characteristics is that the organization has a *hierarchy*, a series of superior-subordinate relationships. Part of this hierarchy, and the second characteristic, is a *division of labor*, where the emphasis is on specialization based on training and background. The third characteristic and one that is often the source of misunderstanding, leading to our contemporary disdain for bureaucracy, is the *use of impersonal rules and procedures*. We often mistake this to mean impersonal treatment as opposed to impersonal rules. The distinction is that the rules are designed to treat people equally, and the treatment we often associate with the calling of us by number as opposed to by name, makes us feel alienated from the service we expect to receive. The fourth characteristic listed by Weber is that the rules of the organization are not arbitrary but are based on *precedent and experience*. Fifth, the organization must display *routinization* and have predictable behavior based on these routines. Last, but not least, is that the work of the organization is seen by the employees as their *vocation*, preferably a job to which they feel some sense of being "called" and to which they bring an attitude of professionalism. In other words, this is not a part time occupation or merely a job.[4]

In Weber's mind, bureaucracy was not an evil monstrosity or not even a bad organization, bureaucracy was an organizational form correlated and compatible with the Industrial Revolution. For Weber, it would help lead us out of feudal arrangements and create efficient organizations better suited to the business, economic, social, and political demands of a new era. Weber's ideal organizational form was designed to eliminate favoritism, arbitrary decision making, and inefficiency. As a society, we generally disapprove of special treatment for individuals based on their position, status, or wealth and the Weberian notion of bureaucracy certainly eliminates that. The concept that work should be done by those with specific training and appropriate background seems natural, as does the concept that in a large organization the worker should view his or her role as a vocation and not just a temporary job. Those who approach what they do as a vocation—a career—often take a more professional line to the tasks they perform (Freund 1968; Weber 1997).

Somewhere along the way, our perception of bureaucracy, and its performance, has deviated from Weber's expectations. We now see bureaucracy as a hindrance (Hill 1989; Kaufman 1981; Meier 1993), where Weber saw it as organizational salvation. We use the word bureaucracy to describe a whole host of organizational ills, from long lines to being treated as a number to overspecialization. Perhaps our sense of the negative has been enhanced by the idea that the workers perpetuating these wrongs work for us. We also fear the abuse of government bureaucracy to serve, not the public will, but to benefit a small group or an individual at our expense. In a way similar to Weber, some political scientists developed an approach that seems to be intended to prevent such abuse.

Politics/Administration Dichotomy and Presidential Management

Tracing its roots, at least as far back as the work of Woodrow Wilson (1887), while he was still a practicing political scientist, is what has come to be known as the politics/administration dichotomy.[5] This dichotomy refers to what was thought to be a real separation between the political side of government and the nonpolitical, administrative side. Practice has demonstrated, however, that the dichotomy works best as an intellectual tool, allowing us to look at the two sides of public policy as individual snapshots. In our current context, it allows us a better understanding of the struggle presidents face in managing the executive branch.

What the dichotomy really allows us to do, with respect to the administration of policy, is to have a science of administration, where policymaking is political, and the study of administration or bureaucracy is more mechanical. As such, we can examine the process of staff allocation, rule enforcement, and other aspects of administration separate from the more political process of policy making. That does not mean, however, that there is no political aspect to administration and today we tend to recognize that the two are not really separable.

Following the mid-1970s, for a time, most states accepted the federally recommended speed limit of 55 mph. In those states it was often recognized that while this was the politically accepted speed limit, it was the law, the reality was a different story. In a number of states, word on the street was that the state police would not pull you over and give you a ticket for speeding as long as you didn't exceed 65 mph. This practice by the state police was a political act that effectively changed the speed limit back to 65 mph.[6] What this example tells us is that, while we may intellectually separate politics and administration, we cannot actually do so.

More directly connected to our concerns is the example we will discuss in more detail in chapter 12 involving presidential control over the military, intelligence, and Foreign Service apparatus. During the Cuban Missile Crisis, President Kennedy was greatly concerned about subordinates carrying out his wishes without interpretation or discretion. As we will see later, Kennedy was walking a diplomatic and military tightrope and worried that someone down the line in the chain of command would revert to the rulebook or use his or her own discretion, thus acting in a way that would send the crisis spiraling much further out of control than it was. Such was the case on the opposing side when one of our U-2 spy planes was shot down in spite of an agreement by Kennedy and Soviet premier Nikita Khrushchev to allow the flights of the planes for monitoring purposes.

Political Support and Autonomy of Government Agencies

One of the difficulties for the president in dealing with the bureaucracy on a daily basis is the level of public support, and the resulting political autonomy, enjoyed by many agencies. Naturally, government agencies gain much of their support and autonomy from the expertise they wield. By and large, we trust government agencies to perform their jobs and to perform them well because they have been doing those jobs for some time and the individuals working at those agencies were, supposedly, hired because of their background and training. In chapter 10, we also discussed the power of the "Iron Triangle" in American politics. One additional negative not mentioned in that earlier discussion is the revolving door of job placements between agencies, congressional committees, and the relevant interests. While such practices have a certain professional incestuous aspect to them, there is the benefit that individuals who know the policy area are circulating among these organizations and gaining new perspective as they negotiate the revolving door.

Some government agencies gain their support and decision-making autonomy because of the esoteric nature of the field in which they work. In spite of our everyday disappointment with our local weather forecaster, we generally support the National Weather Service (NWS) for its handling of the varied nature of the weather and providing warnings for dangerous situations. Meteorology is a relatively complex field and as such, it is rare that politicians seek to cut funding dramatically or interfere in the work of the NWS. Similarly, except when processes seem to have led to problems—sometimes-catastrophic problems—politicians pretty much leave NASA (the National Aeronautical and Space Administration) alone.[7] NASA generally enjoys fairly high levels of support among the American public (Jones 2007), in part because of the complexity of what NASA does. We recognize that complexity everyday with the common expression to demonstrate that some task is not as hard as one might have thought—"it's not rocket science." If it were easy, private sector operations or private citizens would have also placed humans on the moon by now.

One agency to note here that regularly enjoys high levels of public support is the National Forest Service. The Forest Service enjoys this support not only because of what it provides the public, but also for an advertising campaign. Smokey the Bear has been one of the most recognizable icons in all of advertising, but especially among advertising for government agencies, for decades.[8] Other agencies may seek to develop public support by helping to create public interest groups as the US Department of Agriculture (USDA) did with the Farm Bureau Federation.

Often the end result of this public support and autonomy, coupled with a political cycle that leaves agencies in place even during the terms of presidents *opposed* to the agencies' goals, is an agency operating seemingly independent of any presidential direction. Agencies seek to survive, at the very least, and to expand their scope, size, and power if possible. In this endeavor, agencies are often at odds with a president who does not support their agenda or sees the agency's budget as cannon fodder in a budget battle. Agencies may also fall into the conundrum where if they achieve the goals laid out for them, they eliminate the need for them to exist, which would fly in the face of the goal of survival. It could be argued then that an agency will never actually complete the assignment given by its political superiors, for to do so would mean the agency's termination.

Presidential Control

Given this conflict of goals and the level of autonomy often attained by government agencies, presidents seek to control the behavior of the bureaucracy they are purported to head. Presidents cannot, obviously, take for granted that their wishes will be carried out. This is even the case in agencies where one might think that the president could more easily exert control—the military, for example, where the "commander in chief" role of the president might allow us to believe that there would be control.[9]

Presidents are not without options or ability to control the behavior of reluctant bureaucrats (Kagan 2001). Many of the president's powers in this area are shared with Congress and the president must work that relationship with care (see chapter 15 for a discussion of the relationship between the president and Congress), especially in order for his ability to control the bureaucracy to work effectively. Among these shared abilities are appointments, the budget, reorganization, and the creation of new agencies (and presumably the elimination of old ones as well).

Through the appointments process, the president controls the individuals directing the activities of the bureaucracy. Certainly, the upper-level appointees must have the advice and consent of the Senate before they can serve, but many lower-level functionaries may be appointed by the president, or his or her designee (the department or agency head, for instance), without involving Congress directly (Ingraham 1991; Meier 1993). These individuals set the tone for the agency, direct resources, and with some public input, control the rule making process. Naturally, as we have already discussed, presidents need to be mindful of the potential for an appointee to go native and take on the "persona" of the agency or interest group (see chapter 10).

The production of a budget for presentation and passage by Congress (in the best of all possible worlds) sets an administration's, and thus a president's, priorities. Cutting a bit from one agency or adding some to another makes quite clear what a president hopes to accomplish. Money means resources, from personnel to paper clips. Without adequate resources, an agency might not be able to perform its assigned tasks well, if at all. By restricting (or expanding) the agency's access to such resources, a president can further influence the direction of bureaucratic behavior (Carpenter 1996; Meier 1993).[10] Nixon's impoundment of funding for several programs including those under the jurisdiction of the Department of Housing and Urban Development (HUD) and the Equal Employment Opportunity Commission was an extreme example of budgetary limitations impeding agency performance—in this case had Nixon succeeded, the programs would have been shut down.

Reorganization is yet another tool presidents may use to help direct the behavior of the bureaucracy (Seidman and Gilmour 1986; Meier 1993). Here too, for any substantial reorganization Congress would have to provide authorization to the president, by writing a law granting the president his or her request. Perhaps the law would make an independent agency report to a cabinet department, or create a new agency altogether. We have already seen (chapter 10) how Presidents Franklin Roosevelt and Richard Nixon made use of reorganization to gain control of, what in their view, was a rogue bureaucracy. In an attempt to gain better control over the nation's intelligence and security apparatus, the George W. Bush administration asked Congress to reorganize the intelligence community and to create the Department of Homeland Security (DHS), mostly by taking offices and bureaus from existing agencies and bringing them together under one roof. In the aftermath of 9/11, Congress granted the request.[11]

Less orthodox, in the sense of having laws passed, budgets created, and organizational structure manipulated, a president may resort to persuasion. Just as a president may persuade the public or the Congress to see things his or her way, so too, a president may persuade bureaucrats to follow his lead. This is done less directly than a presidential address to the nation, but may be a part of such an address. Certainly, members of the government bureaucracy are citizens too and watch TV, read the newspaper, and live the same lives as other citizens. In other words, they get the same news, and the same speeches by the president as the rest of us. By attempting to change the tone of public debate, by getting the public to focus on a particular policy, presidents are aligning forces in the political environment. Bureaucrats, seeing or hearing the speech or reacting to the public's response to it, can have their minds changed or be made more susceptible to the president's intended policy outcome (Lewis 2004; Whitford and Yates 2003).

In some ways, a last resort for presidents is to centralize decision making in the White House. The term *centralization* has also been used to refer to the practice of bringing policy making back to the federal government, but here it is simply taking responsibility for the development of policy away from the agency with the usual responsibility in the policy area. Earlier, we discussed the situation in the Nixon administration where HUD Secretary George Romney seemed to be about to develop a housing policy that would undermine Nixon's political efforts to create a base for himself and the Republican Party among white suburban voters. To prevent Romney from developing a policy that might injure Nixon's political position, the administration took HUD out of the loop and created a task force in the White House to develop the policy (Lamb and Twombly 2001).

In Sum

The bureaucracy is responsible for much of what government does, but no one elected the members of this branch of government and most of the street-level workers are careerists with little or no loyalty to a particular president and his or her agenda. To overcome this potential lack of cooperation or commitment, presidents have a number of tools at their disposal. Some tools are more effective than others are, but almost all require the cooperation of other actors in the political system.

Certainly, the perceived need for tighter executive control and interagency cooperation following the 9/11 attacks demonstrated the failure of some tools and led to the use of others to enhance control. Perrow (2006) does point out that the organizational approach employed as a solution is fraught with its own perils. Still, what may have been of greater significance in a time of fear was the *appearance* of presidential control. In political science, we are well aware of the need of cabinet-level agencies to serve at least two masters—the president *and* Congress—but the public's understanding is often quite different. From the perspective of a frightened public, the creation of the DHS as a full-fledged cabinet department signals importance to the public. Additionally, with presidential nomination of the secretary and Senate advice and consent seems to be a presidentially controlled agency. Naturally, for the sake of more direct presidential control, the creation of an Executive Office of the President bureau with all the same powers and responsibilities would have made presidential control far easier. As a cabinet department, DHS comes with all of the same managerial baggage of HUD that may force a president to employ mechanisms like centralization, budget control, and so forth. In the end, such baggage may be necessary and tolerable given the overall political environment where the demands of Congress, interest groups, and the public all need consideration and, *perhaps*, concession.

Chapter 12

Presidential Decision Making

When discussing vice-presidential selection a few chapters ago, I stated that one of the reasons why this was so important was that it was an early indicator of the president's character and his ability to make decisions. Certainly, picking a vice president is not the only decision a president will make over the course of his or her tenure. Many decisions are made, some rather small and with relatively little impact on politics or history, while others can be monumental and change the political landscape or the course of history. In this chapter, we will discuss two rather significant decisions in the area of national security and foreign relations, decisions that could have led to war in each scenario. Both decisions come from the same presidency and demonstrate what Barber (1992) and others would argue are positive characteristics for a president to have, namely the ability to admit to a mistake and learn from it.

To get an idea about the process presidents engage in when making major decisions we can turn to John Kennedy's handling of the Bay of Pigs invasion and the Cuban Missile Crisis, examples of a process "gone bad" and a process that worked, respectively. Conveniently, both of these situations occurred during the same administration and both dealt with US–Cuban relations, with implications for the relationship between the United States and the Soviet Union (USSR). The similarity of circumstance and implications makes the decision-making process in these two situations more readily comparable.

The Bay of Pigs invasion has been rather roundly criticized as an abject failure of decision making in foreign policy. Others believe that the process of decision making during the Cuban Missile Crisis, while not perfect, was about as good a process as one could hope for, especially given the stakes.

Flawed Decision Making and Groupthink

Noted organizational psychologist, Irving Janis (1972) stumbled across a name for a failed decision-making process while reading Arthur Schlesinger's history of the Kennedy administration, *A Thousand Days*. What struck Janis so profoundly was the ability of such supposedly smart men to make what appeared to be such a "dumb" decision with regard to the attempted invasion of Cuba. He wondered why Kennedy's advisers had not seen the pitfalls that were so obvious in retrospect. His reading and rereading of the sections of Schlesinger's book that dealt with the Bay of Pigs were of particular concern to Janis.[1]

His contemplation of Schlesinger's account led Janis to question the process of group decision making. He wondered what dynamic might be at work to lead a group of intelligent, powerful individuals to ignore evidence, to miss opportunities, to question logic, and to go along with what they *imagine* is the group leader's preferences. Janis saw this as a psychological contagion. His first attempt to understand what he observed was to discuss these processes with his graduate seminar. What emerged from that discussion was the suggestion that, perhaps Kennedy's advisers were more concerned with the approval of their colleagues than they were with adhering to critical thinking and analysis. After this discussion with his graduate students, Janis went back to *A Thousand Days* and reread the material on the Bay of Pigs through the lens of that discussion. What he found is what he referred to as a high level of cohesiveness, that members of the group were more concerned with maintaining the group than with the process itself, and the ultimate outcome—the decision. In short then, this flawed process is driven by a need to belong illustrating a high level of situational insecurity.

Intrigued, Janis dug deeper and used the Bay of Pigs decision process as the exemplar for what he called "groupthink." He didn't stop there, however, Janis applied the concept to other flawed decisions, those he deemed *fiascos*.[2] That is not to say that a groupthink-afflicted process must always end in failure, but there is a strong chance that it will. Janis wrote, "Groupthink is conducive to errors in decision making, and such errors increase the likelihood of a poor outcome. Often the result is a fiasco, but not always" (1972, 11–12). A decision-making process that suffers from groupthink can be successful, but has an inherent tendency toward failure. So, while it might be possible for a decision-making process infected by groupthink to arrive at a successful outcome, it *is not likely*.

What then, is this process of groupthink and what causes the process to be flawed? First, groupthink is not about the negatives of a simple "rubberstamp process." The group leader is sincere in his or her attempt to seek honest opinions and analysis from the members of the group. The members of the group are not necessarily afraid to speak their minds, but there are subtle constraints placed upon them by their membership and inadvertently reinforced by the leader.[3] Together, these conditions prevent members from fully exercising critical judgment and applying their analytical powers. These constraints come about from, as mentioned before, the high level of group cohesiveness, where the members highly value their membership in the group (so much that they may be blind to flaws in their decisions and the process used to arrive at it) and their prime motivation is to remain in the group. In part, this is because there is a tendency to ostracize members who "don't go along" (recall our earlier discussion of cabinet members who appear to have "gone native"). Outsiders and competing groups are dehumanized, stripped of identity, and generally referred to as "they" or "them," quite naturally setting up the typical "us versus them" mentality.

Janis identified six major defects in decision making that contribute to the high likelihood of failure. The *first* defect is that discussion is limited to few alternative solutions. *Second*, there is a failure to reexamine early consensus solutions. *Third*, little time is devoted to an attempt to reduce the costs of previously dismissed alternatives to make them more viable solutions. *Fourth*, the group also makes little or no effort to gain further expert advice or to seek possible alternatives. *Fifth*, there tends to be a selective bias that limits the factual information and expert judgments used by the group. *Lastly*, there is little time devoted to playing devil's advocate to try to find the negatives in the agreed upon plan.

The Bay of Pigs Invasion

This ill-fated plan that was the result of groupthink was, in retrospect, quite typical of what one might expect in the early 1960s. Simply put, it was a plan to invade Cuba using Cuban expatriates (to minimize the appearance of US involvement), who were trained by the Central Intelligence Agency (CIA) to spark a civil uprising in Cuba that would ultimately overthrow the Castro regime. While John Kennedy acted upon the plan, it had its origins during the Eisenhower administration and was apparently the policy baby of then vice president Richard Nixon. Kennedy was briefed about the planned operation soon after his election and subsequently, soon after his inauguration, he had regular meetings with a group of key advisers to approve and implement the plan.

In the early 1960s, the political environment was such that Democrats could not appear to be soft on communism and regimes that followed far-left ideologies. Add to that environment the fact that one such government in particular, was just 90 miles off our coast. The junta became a communist dominated regime after being refused aid by the US government during their rebellion against a corrupt and the oppressive regime of Fulgencio Batista, which was capitalist in its orientation. In short, Kennedy appeared to welcome the opportunity to be the president that would remove this annoying outpost of the Soviet system.

John Kennedy assembled a number of top advisers to help him with the weighty decision to send this band of Cuban exiles into harm's way. Among these advisers were his brother, Bobby; Allen Dulles, director of the CIA; Richard Bissel, deputy director of the CIA; Lyman Lemnitzer, chairman of the Joint Chiefs of Staff; Dean Rusk, secretary of state; Robert McNamara, secretary of Defense; and Arthur Schlesinger, special adviser to the president. It was their job to make a recommendation to President Kennedy whether to go ahead with the planned invasion or not. After much discussion—all in secret—the decision was to invade a sovereign state. Naturally, this group of advisers did have questions and concerns (as we will see in the discussion of the process) about the CIA plan.

The basic plan was for the CIA to train the exiles in various locations, including Nicaragua, Puerto Rico, and Louisiana. After landing on shore at the Bay of Pigs, the exile brigade would establish a "beachhead" and set up a provisional government of exiles. The United States, in turn, would recognize the provisional government as the legitimate government of Cuba and could then provide assistance to its new ally. It all sounded so simple, but there were a number of problems.

Janis cited what he called six miscalculations, or false assumptions, that were associated with the plan and led to its inevitable failure. The first miscalculation was that US involvement would remain secret and that the CIA cover story of mercenaries helping the exiles would work. Unfortunately, the mission and the involvement of the United States would not remain so secret. In fact, *The New York Times* had a front-page story about the training. Kennedy insisted on and expected there to be no US involvement in the actual operation, even if our involvement in training might come to light. In the end, the first combatants on shore during the invasion were Navy Seals whose mission it was to mark the landing site for the Cubans who would follow them. Ultimately, US Navy planes had to be called in to help the exiles who were pinned down on the beaches, but even that was too little and too late.

Second, based on apparently faulty intelligence, it was assumed that the Cuban Air Force would be no match for the well-trained exile pilots and that the skies over the battlefield would be controlled by the exiles. Instead, many of the older aircraft we had provided the exiles did not function properly and the Cubans were far more capable than had been anticipated. In fact, they were able to sink a number of the ships containing supplies the invading force would need.

Third, it was also assumed that the soldiers in the exile brigade all had high morale and were ready to carry out the mission with or without US aid. The truth was much, much different. A number of the soldiers ended up serving time in the brig, even on the day of the invasion. There had been a number of instances of fighting among the men, not an unlikely occurrence given that the officers tended to come from the Cuban military under the prior regime, and though the men desired to take back their country from Castro, they had no love for the regime Castro had defeated either.

Fourth, the CIA had led Kennedy's team to believe that Castro's army was weak and inept. Instead, they responded quickly to the threat and took many prisoners. Fifth, the CIA expected that news of the invasion would get out and inspire the populous to sabotage and rebellion. The reaction of the Cuban people was just the opposite; they held pro-Castro and anti-US demonstrations. Sixth, the backup plan was also flawed. Kennedy's advisers were told that if the invasion failed, the exiles could escape to a hilly, forested area known as the Escambray Mountains, where they could connect with the Cuban underground and begin guerrilla warfare. There were two problems with this scenario, one of which was that the Cuban underground was nowhere near as strong as intelligence indicated. Second, the CIA had stopped training the exiles in guerrilla tactics because the invasion site was moved to a point more than 80 miles from the mountains—a virtually impassable, swampy 80 miles.

Explaining What Went Wrong

Janis first attempted to explain how these otherwise highly intelligent men could get it so wrong by looking at what he called a "four factor analysis." *First*, he sought explanation from Kennedy's domestic political situation and his need to appear to be tough on communism. This was not enough to explain why he and his advisers would be led down this disastrous path. *Second*, was it, Janis asked, that this was a new administration and they were not yet used to working with each other? Such tentativeness could be a contributing factor, but Janis thought it was not sufficient by itself. *Third*, could the high level of secrecy have been a factor? While one would expect that the government would want to keep the planning of and involvement in, such an operation a secret, perhaps this went a bit far. For example, members of the team were not allowed to take their notes with them when they left meetings and were discouraged from discussing the operation with potential experts at their home agencies. This high level of secrecy prevented the group from seeking expert opinion outside of their circle. The *fourth and last* of these factors, threats to personal reputation and status leading to a reluctance to disagree, seemed, to Janis, to be the strongest possible explanation, but not by itself.

It is this desire to be a part of a group, to be valued by the other members, perhaps partly as a result of newness, which would lead the members of Kennedy's team to fall victim to groupthink. Characteristic of groupthink are shared illusions and related norms that help to ensure the failure of the process. The group would see itself as invulnerable. There would be nearly unlimited confidence in the ability of the group to accomplish its goals. Similarly, the members of the group would see no need to raise strong opposition to solutions to which they had apparently agreed. Seeing this invulnerability and unanimity, members, placing membership in the group above other concerns, would be likely to self-censor and suppress any personal doubts they might have about the arrived at solution.

Janis also argued that certain individuals would come forward and serve as "mindguards"[4] to protect the consensus. Supposedly, on at least two occasions this occurred. Arthur Schlesinger voiced his concern about the CIA's plans to Attorney General Bobby Kennedy, who told him to keep quiet, because this is what the president wanted. Similarly, when Undersecretary of State Chester Bowles, having sat in for Secretary Rusk, expressed his concerns to Rusk, he too was told that this was what the president wanted and he should get on board.[5] While, as mentioned earlier, the group leader is sincere in seeking critical judgment and analysis, he or she very subtly lets the group know that he or she has a preferred outcome, thus creating a sense of docility among the members of the group. Lastly, groups suffering from groupthink tend to exhibit a taboo against antagonizing new members. Janis argues that with Dulles and Bissell being holdover appointees from the Eisenhower administration they were new to the Kennedy team and thus the others perhaps were too willing to accept their presentation at face value and not ask the critical questions that might have prevented what Janis called a fiasco.[6]

Preventing Groupthink

Janis divides the mechanisms for preventing groupthink into two categories. The first category contains those strategies that are "not so desirable." The second category contains those strategies that are a bit better and he refers to them as "not so *un*desirable." The major distinction between the two is that the first set of strategies seems to have a smaller likelihood of success.

Among the not so desirable preventatives is that the leader could *assign the role of critical evaluator* to one individual. Here, the problem is that through lengthy evaluation and questioning, this could prolong debate when time may well be of the essence. The role is not simply of playing devil's advocate, which could help, but to ask the key skeptical questions at the right time to break up a quick consensus. The problem in this approach lies in the impact it could have on the evaluator, as constantly asking such questions could lead to the member being ostracized or at least losing a level of respect. Kennedy had the advantage in the Cuban Missile Crisis of having his brother, Attorney General Robert Kennedy—someone who clearly could not lose the respect of the group—play the role. Second, *the leader could make a greater effort to be impartial* and present no biased facts by way of introducing the problem to solve and avoid any hint of what his or her preferences might be. The problem with this solution is that group members may still try to determine for themselves what the leader's preferences are and then not only engage in a flawed process, but one that starts with a potential misinterpretation of the goal. Or, it may be a perfect process with no groupthink-like errors, but aimed at the wrong target. Last among these solutions would be to *have independent consideration of the problem by several bodies*. Again, there are problems with this solution. One such problem is that there may be a sense of "let the other guy do it" and at least one of the considering bodies does not provide a solution. It is also possible that with consideration by so many others there could be leaks—rather problematic if secrecy is important.

In Janis's, other category of the "*not so un*desirable" is to divide the decision-making group into *subgroups* and work on smaller parts of the problem. This avoids adding to the number of people who could potentially leak information and it avoids the problem of letting "the other guy" solve the problem because they are working on different aspects of the problem. In this category of preventatives would also be allowing the members to *hold outside discussions* with their own trusted advisers. The group could also *bring in outside experts* on a rotating basis; these individuals could deal with a small portion of the problem and thus not be in a position to leak vital information about the whole problem/proposed solution. One member of the group could play *Devil's Advocate*, but, like the role of critical evaluator, this could consume valuable time and place the individual in a position to be ostracized by the group. The group could also take steps to *pay closer attention to warning signals* from rival out groups. For example, the State Department had information that the Cuban underground was unorganized and would not be effective in mounting a resistance to Castro, which went unused. The group could have sought intelligence from allies to check the CIA's information. Lastly, they could have held a second chance session where all were given the opportunity to pick apart the proposed solution.

We should also note that members of decision-making groups with a little bit of knowledge about what groupthink is and how it creates a flawed process could use it to manipulate the outcome to their advantage. However, it is probably better to have some knowledge to be aware of the pitfalls of groupthink. In the end, the best way to prevent it from happening may be for one member to simply ask, "Are we becoming victims of groupthink?"

A Demonstration of Character—
the Cuban Missile Crisis

Clearly, John Kennedy's approach to decision making during the lead up to, and the implementation of, the Bay of Pigs Invasion was flawed. His handling of the aftermath, however, it could be argued, was stellar. His instinct to go on national TV to accept responsibility and take the blame for the mistakes, worked well for him in terms of public approval and his overall political situation. The national apology could also be seen as an indicator of his willingness to make changes. Kennedy's handling of the Cuban Missile Crisis just a year and a half later it could be seen as an example of a president willing to make positive changes.

These two situations are ones where we might believe that a president would have a much greater expectation that the bureaucracy he or she is purported to command would follow those commands. Both the Bay of Pigs and the Cuban Missile Crisis involved foreign and military policy, where the president, as chief diplomat and commander in chief, respectively, should have had little difficulty in having his or her orders carried out. As we have seen however, in dealing with the bureaucracy, the policy implemented is not always that which was intended. The advice presidents receive from the bureaucracy can be self-serving of the agency's needs as opposed to the president's. The communication of advice up the chain of command, or directives down, may become distorted and result in an outcome far different from that which was intended.

In the case of the Cuban Missile Crisis, following so soon after the Bay of Pigs Invasion, the United States was still in the early part of the Cold War with the Soviet Union. The Castro regime in Cuba was still relatively new in the fall of 1962. The climax of the incident took place just a few short weeks before what the Kennedy team assumed would be their first midterm elections, creating an extra level of domestic political importance.[7] During that campaign, given the fallout from the failed invasion a year and a half before and the apparent poor performance by Kennedy in a summit meeting with Soviet leader Khrushchev, US relations with the Soviet Union were a major issue. As a result, Kennedy did not want to appear to be "soft" on communist expansion, especially so close to home. Over the summer of 1962, in diplomatic and intelligence communities, there were rumors that the Soviet Union was engaged in some sort of military buildup on the island of Cuba. In order to check the veracity of these rumors, US intelligence agencies began aerial surveillance of Cuba using the well-known U-2 spy plane.

There were reports during the summer and ultimately, confirmation by U-2s that some sort of military activity was going on. The first problem the Kennedy administration faced in this crisis was how to get better evidence. At the time, the U-2 spy planes operated by the CIA had more sophisticated cameras and could take more detailed photos from much higher altitudes than could cameras onboard Air Force U-2s. The problem was that if one of the CIA planes was shot down and the pilot survived, he wouldn't have the protections that the Geneva Convention extended to military personnel. While it might seem that the simplest solution would be to place Air Force pilots in the CIA planes, it took time. First, agency rivalry between the Air Force and the CIA would get in the way. Second, it would take time to train the Air Force pilots in the use of the more sophisticated equipment. Last, once all this had been accomplished, Mother Nature intervened and covered much of the island with clouds through which even the more sophisticated CIA cameras could not penetrate. As a result, the first photographic evidence of the existence of Soviet Intercontinental Ballistic Missile (ICBM) sites in Cuba was not taken until October 14th, 1962. It was two days later (October 16th), allowing time for the photo to be analyzed to be sure of its contents, that National Security Advisor McGeorge Bundy was able to tell President Kennedy that we had "hard photographic evidence that the Russians have offensive missiles in Cuba" (*LA Times* 1996).

Kennedy convened a special meeting of a subgroup of the National Security Council, known as the ExComm[8] to review the situation. Initially, there were four options on the table for discussion. The first was to ignore it and make no reaction. We, after all, had missiles in Turkey, much closer to the Soviet Union than the missiles in Cuba were to us. Ironically, the only supporter of this option was the Secretary of Defense Robert McNamara. The second option was a naval blockade of Cuba. The problem with this approach was that it would, under international law, be considered an act of war. The third option was a "surgical air strike" in an attempt to take out the missiles. Among other difficulties with this approach was that this was 1962 and our technological capability to be "surgical," compared with the accuracy of weapons today, was like the difference between Civil War Era battlefield surgery and our ability today to save and/or reattach limbs. The last option was an all-out invasion of Cuba. In the end, this would be considered the last resort, first because of how "well" the last invasion of Cuba went, and second because Bobby Kennedy said he didn't want his brother to go down in history as an "American Tojo"[9] (Kennedy 1969; Schlesinger 1965).

Ultimately, the ExComm chose to respond with what in common language we would call a blockade. However, they called it a "quarantine," a simple manipulation of language to avoid appearing to commit an act of war. And, rather than ban all goods from coming in to Cuban ports, the ships enforcing the quarantine were given a list of embargoed materials—contraband—that could be used in the construction or operation of ICBMs. They could not simply ignore the provocation by the Soviets and the Cubans. These intermediate range ICBMs could reach nearly all of the continental United States and Washington, DC, itself was in the most effective range of the missiles, which was sufficient to reach most of the United States except the extreme Northwest. To ignore the threat could be seen as weakness, both in terms of domestic politics by Kennedy's opponents and by the Soviet Union.

Graham Allison's Analysis: Three Questions, Three Models

To understand this decision-making process, political scientist Graham Allison (1971) initially proposed three questions. The first question was, "Why did the

Soviet Union put the missiles in Cuba?" The second question was, "Why did the U.S. respond with a 'blockade'?" And the last question was, "Why did the Soviet Union concede?" What Allison (and then later with Phillip Zelikow 1999) did was to seek answers to these questions through the lenses of three different models of decision making. Observers sometimes attribute the models to Allison, when it was others who developed the models. It was, Allison, however, who applied them in such a way as to demonstrate how the models can lead us to different conclusions about how decisions are made.

Before looking at Allison's application of these models, we need to understand what a model is. When demonstrating this concept to a group (or a class) I have often drawn a two-dimensional representation of a house on the board. When asked what it is, the audience usually responds with "a house!" When I note that this is an incorrect answer someone will usually respond with "a picture of a house!" I acknowledge the individual's answer and move on to say that yes, it is a picture, but couldn't it also be a two-dimensional model of a house? The definition in use here is that a model is a representation of real world phenomena, which utilizes key distinguishing characteristics of that phenomenon. So, with a house, one might expect that a drawing would present a peaked roof, windows with frames, a solid door, perhaps curtains in the windows, and so forth. Such a drawing could be compared to one of a more industrial or commercial building and the audience could easily note the differences. While in these cases, certainly, models can be used to help create the object—the house or the building—in our case the models are for the purpose of analyzing a process—before or after the fact—and are not models of *how to* make a decision.

The first of these models could be considered the foundation or cornerstone for the other two. It lays out the basic theoretical premise that underlies the others. The *rational actor model* (Arrow 1951; Buchanan and Tullock 1962; Rothschild 1946)[10] is the broadest approach and usually requires the most assumptions about other actors. It has the following four key distinguishing characteristics: (1) all alternative solutions are known, (2) all the consequences of those alternatives are known, (3) the actor has a set of ordered preferences among the outcomes, and (4) the decision rule is usually some form of utility maximization or more appropriately utility optimization.[11] Using this model to answer Allison's three questions, we see that the reason the Soviets placed the missiles in Cuba has to do with their assumption that they lagged behind in the number of missiles and in the technology to fire them accurately, placing them at a strategic disadvantage. To overcome this disadvantage, without investing resources in increasing their missiles and upgrading their technology, moving what they had closer to the intended target made sense. If we use this lens to look at why the United States chose the blockade option, it was the one option that would demonstrate a strong response without overescalation and bought time for diplomacy to work. Regarding the Soviet concession and eventual removal of the missiles, the rational actor model allows us to see that the Soviet Union recognized that we responded far more strongly than anticipated. They were still at a strategic disadvantage and attempting to push their position further would only result in an escalation they could not win without resorting to nuclear weapons.

The *organizational process model* provides for a greater depth of explanation. While still rational in its approach, the organizational process model recognizes the limits of human cognitive capacity and that it is not possible to know all alternatives and all of the consequences of those alternatives. Many scholars have dubbed the model the bounded or "intendedly" rational model (Simon 1957). In using this model as an analytical lens, we see that it is no less rational than the simpler rational actor model, but may instead be emphasizing a different utility. The key characteristics here include the recognition that organizations, especially governments, are often made up of complex, diverse actors. In recognition of the need to organize the flow of information, this approach recognizes routines, repertoires, heuristics, and standard operating procedures (SOPs). The decision rule observed is often referred to as *satisficing*, a term combining satisfactory and sufficient. It is that solution that is both, and thus does not necessarily make the criteria of maximizing utility in the way we might normally think of doing so. Naturally, it could be said that the utility being optimized is time or effort rather than move the decision maker(s) closer to the stated objective. That is, in order to save time or effort a decision maker may unwittingly choose a solution that does not provide the maximum utility with respect to the stated goal. From the perspective of the organizational process model, the first question about Soviet placement of the missiles is likely based on their routines and traditions. Being more concerned, historically speaking, with western European threats (Germany and France, for example) the missile technology they developed would be aimed at reaching targets on the European continent and thus not have the range needed to reach the United States. In addition, we can explain the manner in which the United States discovered the missiles through the SOPs of the Soviet Union's agencies involved. The shipment of the missiles and the equipment to build them was the responsibility of military intelligence and thus done in great secrecy. The construction and operation of the sites once in Cuba was left to the Strategic Rocket Forces (SRF), who were accustomed to operating in the Soviet Union or its close neighbors with no care or need for secrecy. In fact, one of the telltale signs to US analysts was that the SRF personnel decorated the sites with white rocks depicting their unit logo, completely visible to a view from aerial reconnaissance. For our part, the blockade, or quarantine, was chosen in part due to the SOPs of our agencies. An air strike would have been the equivalent of a preinvasion bombing and could not guarantee the removal of the missiles, especially with minimal human casualties. An invasion would have led to a complete occupation of the island and would likely have resulted in taking Soviet military personnel prisoner, thus having a high potential for escalation. Even the ultimate choice of the blockade had its SOP problems. The Navy wanted the blockade line far enough out to sea to be out of range of land based aircraft from Cuba and Kennedy wanted it closer to give the Soviet ships time to turn around. The Soviet concession could be explained by the underlying assumptions (routines) of Politburo members who had not interacted with Kennedy at the summit with Khrushchev in June of 1961, thus leading them to misread the level of resolve Kennedy would have on this matter.

For the *governmental politics* or *bargaining model* (March 1962; Neustadt 1990; Snyder and Diesing 1977), the focus is on the outcome and that such policy outcomes are the result of debates between relevant actors, each of whom has different relative positions of power. It is still a rational approach to the analysis of decision making, but there are many more actors, each pursuing their own utility optimization. What becomes important then is the set of power relationships among the actors and the process by which the bargaining takes place. In attempting to answer Allison's questions, it is competition between hardliners and moderates in the Soviet government that may have forced Khrushchev to agree to the placing of the missiles in Cuba in the first place. Additionally, territoriality among agencies almost certainly could have led to two different organizations being responsible for the delivery and set up, respectively, of the missiles. Some have argued that contradictory letters to Kennedy from Khrushchev at the height of the crisis may be indicative of the political pressure Khrushchev was under to force Kennedy's hand. With respect to the US response of a naval blockade, some have argued that it should have been expected given that both Jack and Bobby Kennedy had served in the Navy, putting the Navy in the more powerful position in the bargaining for a piece of the action. The Soviet Union's concession may have been forced by John Kennedy's artful ignoring of the second more combative letter mentioned earlier. Responding to Khrushchev's more conciliatory letter that Kennedy thought had been written by Khrushchev himself, where the more combative one sounded like it had been written by other hands and Khrushchev had been forced to sign it, put Khrushchev back into a position of power opposing the hardliners in the Politburo.[12]

Comparison and Conclusion

So, what do we learn by looking at these two crisis situations and use these various lenses to make closer examination? The closest similarities can be seen in terms of group dynamics in looking at groupthink and the bargaining models. The relationship a leader has with his or her advisers is crucial to successful decision making. To be sure, no president, or any executive for that matter, starts out wanting to be non-rational. The problem is in the choice of what utility to maximize and sometimes that is determined by which adviser is closest to the leader and why they have that relationship. Leaders, particularly those who can make life or death decisions, must be aware of the dynamics of the group, the process by which information gets to him or her, and the time and resources available.

Kennedy certainly seems to have made changes from the Bay of Pigs to the Missile Crisis. He behaved as Barber suggested the typical active-positive president would behave, he owned up to and corrected his mistakes. In the fall of 1962, Kennedy made use of subgroups, occasionally having smaller groups of the ExComm working on parts of the problem; the advisers sought advice from others outside the group; and multiple sources were used to verify information. Details of activity on the ground in Cuba were checked with foreign intelligence services, a journalist was employed as a go between with the KGB (Komitet gosudarstvennoy bezopasnosti or Committee for State Security) Washington station chief, and Kennedy used the CIA to ensure that the Air Force had obeyed his orders. None of this cross-checking and trust was employed during the spring of 1961, hence Janis and Barber would both likely argue that the Bay of Pigs was doomed to fail and the Missile Crisis decision making had at least a chance of success.

Naturally, presidents make decisions all the time that have little to do with national security, from the mundane to major domestic policy initiatives. Bill Clinton is said to have run meetings where advice was discussed as though he were conducting graduate seminars in public policy (Hermann 1995). Other presidents have preferred a more formal approach, as we saw in the discussion of styles of management, where information is filtered through a handful of top advisers (or perhaps just one). Certainly, in many more dangerous situations, as with the Bay of Pigs and the Cuban Missile Crisis, information may be hard to come by, time may place extra pressure on the players, and the stakes could elevate quickly. Would Jimmy Carter have made a better decision about the hostage rescue mission attempted in the spring of 1980 if they had better weather data? Could a different process have led to a different outcome regarding our invasion of Iraq in 2003? These questions are beyond the scope of this discussion, but they serve to remind us that the stakes of presidential decisions, whether to go to war or to seek approval of a controversial reform of health insurance can be high, and many factors may influence the outcome. The best decision processes are ones that allow for flexibility in response to changing conditions, and perhaps some presidential personalities are better suited to more flexible processes.

Part V

The Presidency Interacting

Chapter 13

The President and the Media

The relationship between the president and the media is crucial to any president's success, particularly in this age when there is 24-hour access to news and information. The so-called news cycle doesn't end with the later edition of the newspaper or the evening news on three major TV networks anymore. Certainly, the media is important in any democracy (or republic) where citizens need to have information in order to make educated choices among candidates for office or on ballot propositions. With 535 elected members of Congress, too many bureaucrats to count, and justices who operate more out of the public eye, the presidency, with its singular nature, is much easier to cover. As viewers of broadcast and cable news, we gain some measure of familiarity with the individuals assigned to cover the president and would no doubt have an easier time identifying a White House correspondent over one assigned to cover Congress.

News coverage is the primary mechanism by which any president can get his or her message to the nation, to the voters. As such, as technology has advanced and has helped to hasten the news cycle, the relationship between the president and the media has become much more important and in need of great attention by the president and his or her staff. The individual serving as White House press secretary doesn't just brief the press and answer their questions, but is responsible for the "care and feeding"—both literally and figuratively—of the press and, as a result, is one of the president's key advisers. The press secretary is more than just a reader of official statements. He or she may be the key in an administration's attempts to manipulate the press to its advantage, to create the most appropriate pro-administration spin. The media, however, seeks information to fill its stories and also often seeks the more sensational story in order to draw attention to the headlines in the newspaper, or the top story on radio and TV, all to drive up advertising revenue. Essentially, this creates an adversarial relationship, at times, between much of the media and the administration.

Some History

Governments, social movements, and political candidates all seek to influence public opinion in support of their cause. One of the simplest ways to do so is to make use of the media, to attempt to get newspapers, radio reporters, and TV correspondents to tell the story in the way that sheds the best possible light on the government, the movement, or the candidate. One of the earliest attempts at using the available media to gain support for a cause here in the United States (at the time of the revolution) was Thomas Paine's *Common Sense* (2003). This early political pamphlet was written by Paine to stir up support for the revolutionary cause, and to legitimize the actions of the rebels. George Washington saw Paine's arguments as a way to rally the troops and had it read to the troops at Valley Forge.

With the first daily newspaper in 1783 (National Park Service n.d.; Stephens n.d.), the battle for control of the spin the media would put on stories about the government had begun. Of course, back then most newspapers were a part of the partisan press and the fight was more about getting the paper from *your side* to issue a counter argument as quickly as possible. Today, it is much more nuanced than that (perhaps except for FOX News and MSNBC) and dueling "spin-doctors"[1] argue over interpretations of speeches and reactions to events. This could leave the viewer wondering if the opposing individuals had heard the same speech or witnessed the same event.

Adversarial Relationship

The press is in need of information, something on which the White House or the administration more generally, has a near monopoly. In addition to there being an adversarial relationship between news organizations and the administration, there is often much competition between the reporters, and the organizations they represent, for the scoop or the first headline. It is nearly impossible to win such competitions by waiting passively for the press secretary to hold a briefing or to be granted an audience with a high-ranking administration official (the president being the ultimate coup). Reporters need to cultivate relationships with White House staffers and with contacts in executive branch agencies beyond the White House in order to remain competitive.

This environment and relationship is greatly changed from the earliest days, even as recently as the mid-twentieth century, of White House reporting. It is said that Franklin Roosevelt would hold a press conference in the Oval Office where he would suggest to the reporters what their stories might be—right down to what the lead paragraph would say. It was a much more informal in setting than the press conference of today, a bit like "sitting around shooting the breeze," but there was still the imposing presence of the president of the United States (Kernell 1997).

The modern press conference does little to reduce the adversarial relationship between the press and the White House. Regular briefings, and sometimes, announcements by the president are done in the briefing room, just a short walk from the Oval Office. This room and the working area for the press corps, close to the offices in the West Wing of the White House, give reporters a real feeling of being able to access the highest advisers to the president, if not the president him- or herself. It is set up much like a small college lecture hall with someone at the front of the room calling on people after having delivered information to them—like the question and answer that, at least in theory, would occur after a class lecture. The biggest difference, perhaps, is that this audience is usually at the opposite end of the spectrum in terms of the quantity of questions they ask.

The press conference is even more formal when the president shows up. For more important addresses and interactions with the press, a different venue might be arranged; the Rose Garden is sometimes used. The East Room has been a popular location for press conferences. It is the location from which President George W. Bush discussed the lead up to the Iraq War and the place from which President Barack Obama let the world know that US Navy Seals had located and killed Osama bin Laden.

Both forms of the press conference have given the White House some measure of control over the press and the spin on stories. In part, this is accomplished through which reporters get called on and when. Reporters who have been friendlier to the administration get to ask their questions either at the beginning or near the very end of the event. Favorable questions and positive coverage might also bring the reward of a sit down with the president or a "backgrounder"[2] with a senior staffer.

Where there is the least control is when an unplanned "leak" occurs. This would be when someone in the administration is feeling that some wrong has been done and that someone wishes to play the part of the whistleblower to let the world know that all is not as it seems. The now infamous "Plumbers Squad" from the Nixon administration was set up initially to "plug leaks" to the press. It eventually morphed into the group that broke into a psychiatrist's office in an attempt to discredit Daniel Ellsberg—the leaker of the Pentagon Papers (a series of government documents)—which revealed rather negative information about government decision making regarding the Vietnam War.

Administrations, however, have made use of planned leaks. Sometimes, in order to "test" a story, an unnamed official will let friendly reporters know about certain items. Similarly, some reporters may be given the opportunity to break a negative story about an administration official who is in trouble with the White House or a story about the opposition to make them look bad.

Presidents, and their press operations, seek to control the image of themselves that is transmitted to the American public. This is at the core of the adversarial relationship. A positive portrayal of those in power is not always the best way for the competitive press to gain readers or viewers. That is why each administration is concerned with the appropriate venue for addressing the American public and how it will play before citizens—the Briefing Room, the East Room, a direct address by the president from the Oval Office, or a major speech before a joint session of Congress.

Attempts to create that positive image include the concept mentioned earlier—the use of spin-doctors. As noted, these are individuals offered as guests to TV and radio operations to help interpret or put the right spin on, statements made by the president or about events. Following presidential debates, for example, the practice is so prevalent that special areas, sometimes referred to as "Spin Alley," are set up for the media to seek out the experts in various subject areas in support of one candidate or the other. The individuals may be members of the administration (staff or agency heads) or other advisers and consultants.

Certainly, the use of spin-doctors is an inexact method, often subject to the questions asked by the reporters, anchors, and talking heads of the media. From the White House perspective, one would hope that there is a more direct way to influence the kind of coverage a president gets. However, there is one small problem for an administration dead set on direct manipulation of the media—the First Amendment's protection of the press. While some (e.g., Nixon) have tried using the tax code and the Federal Communication Commission (FCC) licensing procedure to intimidate less compliant operations, such presidents would come under great criticism for attempted infringement on the media's constitutional freedom.[3]

The reward side of things was alluded to earlier in the discussion of exclusives and backgrounders. Such opportunities can be awarded to news operations that are cooperative, though not necessarily positive all the time, but perhaps holding back on a hot story until it is more convenient for the administration. Reporters who do this will get more favorable treatment from the Press Office than those who do not play ball with the administration. To some this may seem like simple infringement of First Amendment rights, but it is more subtle than that. Certainly, the administration is seeking favorable coverage through a system of rewards, but is not using its "legal" authority to gain the reporting outcome it desires. The press is still free to write what it pleases. We've looked at leaks as something the White House might seek to control or eliminate. It is also the case, however, that the administration might try to strategically place a leak to deflate the impact of a story's timing or to "float a trial balloon" to see what the reaction might be to a policy proposal they themselves are unsure of.

Still, presidents and their advisers need more. They can't always rely on the media to make their case to the American people for them. They do have ways of speaking directly to the public about their policies and programs, but even then, their words are subject to the interpretation of others.

Going Public

Political scientist Samuel Kernell (1997) describes a strategy (or set of strategies) that may be helpful to presidents in getting their unfettered message out to the public. He describes "going public" in a book by the same title, a process where the president goes over the heads of Congress and the media directly to the people. It is an effective mechanism if people listen to what the president is saying and interpret the meaning for themselves instead of relying solely on the interpretations of the media. Certainly, presidents can reach large audiences because the broadcast and cable news networks rarely refuse to give the president airtime. A notable exception is when Ronald Reagan sought time to address the American people about an upcoming vote in Congress on aid to the Contra rebels in Nicaragua. Some media outlets[4] thought that Reagan's intended use was solely political and not in the broader public interest—after all, Reagan had already addressed the public during prime time about US policy in Latin America. There are a number of different forms of the practice of going public, including the direct address, the formal press conference, the "impromptu" press conference, and public appearances.

The *direct address* is a speech delivered with the intention that most of America's viewing audience will see it at the same time. It may be delivered from a venue in the White House or during a joint session of Congress.[5] The most familiar form of the address to a joint session of Congress is the State of the Union Address, traditionally given early in the year. The direct address from the White House can be from the Oval Office, somewhere in the residence, the East Room, or perhaps from the Rose Garden, all depending on the kind of tone the president and his or her advisers seek to impart. It could also take the form of a short statement made in the press briefing room. For example, Jimmy Carter delivered a sort of updated Fireside Chat[6] in the less formal setting of a rocking chair in front of a fireplace,[7] while Bill Clinton sought the more personal venue of the residence to talk to us about his testimony before a grand jury about his affair with Monica Lewinski. In each case, the point was to be less formal. For Carter it was about being in our homes with us and showing shared sacrifice during the energy crisis of the mid-1970s. Thus, Carter had the symbol of the fire and a sweater to demonstrate he, too, was turning down the heat. Clinton sought to distance his explanation of bad personal behavior from his official role as president and by making the address from the residence provided the symbol that this was about his *personal* behavior. When the nation needed solace after the Challenger explosion in 1986, Ronald Reagan addressed us from the Oval Office. The same is true of George W. Bush's more formal address later on 9/11 from the Oval Office.

The *formal press conference* is another form of address with which most of us are familiar. Earlier in this chapter we discussed this arrangement, with the scene much like a college lecture hall or classroom with the president as the instructor and the reporters as students. The first formal press conference was held by Woodrow Wilson, who "saw it as a vehicle for uniting public opinion behind his programs…[but] he spoke off the record" (White House Historical Association n.d.) and the physical layout was different from what we are familiar with today. The contemporary version is scheduled by requesting time from the TV networks and we might know about it a day or so (or perhaps just hours) in advance. The "impromptu" press conference occurs when reporters get a chance at an event to stop the president and fire a few questions at him or her while he or she is on the way somewhere. One of the best examples of this is when the president might pause to answer a few questions on the way to Marine One, before being whisked off to Camp David or to catch Air Force One.[8] A hybrid of the two might be the more formal setting within the White House as described earlier, but it happens quickly with little to no advance notice as when Barack Obama called a late-night session to announce that Seal Team Six had killed Osama bin Laden.

Presidents have also been known to try to make their case directly to the American people by *traveling around the country and speaking with smaller groups*—public appearances—than their typical direct address audience. A president trying to emphasize an employment proposal might make appearances at a few locations around the country where unemployment is particularly high. Similarly, promoting a package of environmental protection policies might involve stops at national parks or environmentally sensitive locations. A more recent example in the realm of economic policy would be Barack Obama's speech on ensuring everyone a "fair share" at the same location—Osawatomie, Kansas—where Teddy Roosevelt gave his famous speech on "New Nationalism," which laid out his "square deal" agenda.

Which form of going public a president uses may depend on his or her individual skills, the subject matter involved, and the tone sought. A president known as a great public speaker might stick to formal speeches. A president more skilled at interpersonal relations might do better with public appearances. A president best known as someone who does his or her homework and can handle the details might be better off with press conferences. If a president uses the wrong form for addressing an issue, it could lead to negative ramifications, such as when the media criticized Carter's imitation of Franklin Roosevelt's fireside chats, in the most well-known Carter discussed energy policy.

In the end, however, the direct address offers the most control for the president. There are usually no questions and it is a prepared script. Again, the particular location may be chosen for its effect on the delivery of the speech, but certain props may prove even more useful. If the speech is delivered from the White House, photos and paintings of family or historical figures in the background may aid the president in the delivery of his or her message. The view through the windows behind the president may remind viewers of who this is and where he or she is sitting. Our familiarity with the presidential seal helps to lend further credibility to the words being spoken.

Presidential Rhetoric

When we use the term rhetoric outside of our everyday conversational or colloquial use it has an entirely different meaning than what we might recognize. In everyday usage, we view the term rhetoric as something bad, usually associated with less than true statements or self-serving language. Here, however, the usage is more traditional and refers to the time-honored practice of debate and argument, the use of words to convince others. As such, it describes a very important presidential activity, closely related to our discussion above about shaping the image and the message a president seeks to present to the public.

When the president is making a direct address or using the setting of a press conference or other appearance, it is for the explicit purpose of convincing some audience of the correctness of his or her approach. In other words, such events are designed to persuade. Political scientist Richard Neustadt (1990) has argued that the true power of the president is the power to persuade, even more important than any constitutional or statutory grant of authority.[9] If Neustadt is correct, it is important to understand what it is that presidents say to us and why.

What is it then that presidents say when they speak to us? Presidents often make use of what is commonly known as "the royal 'we,'" using a plural pronoun to refer to himself or herself. It is also likely that the royal we is not the intent at all, but "we" refers to the president and his or her advisers and staff—the administration. Or, its use is to refer to the American people. In this case, the president is more often clear and will state the distinction between him or herself and his or her association with those he or she represents. Except in very specific circumstances, as in seeking the public's help in convincing Congress or drawing a distinction between him or herself and the legislature, the president rarely refers to Congress. There is little mention of the cabinet, especially as a collective decision-making body, except if the address is about a program or policy directly under the purview of a particular cabinet department.

The president might also make references to subnational groups, but not those we might usually associate in a negative way with special interests (lobbyists, PACs [political action committees], and so on) or those the public would deem to have "an agenda." The references might be to states, demographic groups, veterans, men and women in the armed forces, and so on, not those with a specific economic or other policy agenda. For example, in dealing with labor-related issues, a president would refer, not to labor unions, but to "the hard working men and women of this great country." Similarly, positions that might be held by organized interests may be referred to, but only as positions held by individuals, perhaps expressed to the president in a letter or during an encounter on a rope line at a public appearance. Interestingly, presidents will tend to ignore earlier presidents as a group, but will mention a former president with whom he or she feels a specific connection or to divert blame from themselves onto their predecessors. This latter tactic only works for so long until the public begins to believe that problems legitimately belong to the incumbent.

We now have an idea what presidents are saying, but what is it that they are doing when they speak to us? First and foremost, they are educating the public, about either facts and circumstances or the correctness of their position on an issue. Accompanying explanations of their positions and the reason for those positions, naturally, is a request for support. Often such a request is quite straightforward, using words like, "In this endeavor, I ask for your support." Though it is more the case in recent years, presidents (when addressing us in the manner under discussion) don't engage in direct partisan activity. The evolution of politics in the last 30 or so years has limited this to the president's avoidance of asking for our votes for his or her favored candidate in an election. Naturally, presidents will do this, but just not from a venue in the White House or before Congress. They reserve such pleas for what is clearly a partisan venue—a campaign stop or fund raising event. When they are being partisan in their comments, more often than not, they are attempting to draw distinctions between themselves and opponents in Congress in order to gain our help.

What presidents are doing is invoking a sense of moral higher ground in attempts to sometimes create an aura of divine appointment—yes, as in they are doing God's work. In doing so, there are three general themes employed. *First*, our nation seeks only noble and worthy goals. We didn't form a vast international coalition to kick Saddam Hussein out of Kuwait to ensure our access to Kuwaiti oil, but to preserve the right of Kuwaiti citizens the right of self-determination of their government. *Second*, we are a moral society and thus our actions are moral because of our association with God. A stark example is George W. Bush's invocation of God and "good and evil" in his first State of the Union Address to Congress following the attacks of September 11th, 2001. "In his speech, Bush called the war in Afghanistan a 'just cause' and announced that times of tragedy have made Americans realize that 'God is near'" (Shogan 2006, 3). *Third*, our intentions are completely altruistic and not necessarily motivated by our self-interest. We assist in the creation and enforcement of a no-fly zone over Libya in support of our allies and because we must support all popular movements for democracy in the Middle East. Yet, there are some movements we don't support because the governments they seek to overthrow are our allies in the War on Terror.

Evidence does indicate that there is some support for the notion that making speeches, going public over the heads of Congress and the media helps presidents. Obviously, Kernell would not have published the book referenced earlier if he had not found evidence of the success of going public. Brace and Hinckley (1993) point to a generally positive impact on a president's approval rating from what they refer to as "major addresses." In unpublished work with a graduate student, I have found similar impacts, but we noted that just as with other events that boost approval ratings there is a decaying effect of the impact. Further, we found that there was a negative aspect from "going to the well" too often, in that too many speeches affected approval negatively, and speeches or addresses about scandals only served to remind the public of the scandal (Howes and Twombly 1995).

Wrapping Up

The relationship between the president and the media is a contentious one, to say the least. Each party to the relationship has something the other wants, and is afraid of giving that something away, for fear of being abused. Reporters don't want to be used to achieve the political ends of a president, and the White House does not want to give out information it controls without some positive result.

To cope, presidents have developed a wide range of strategies to deal with an adversarial press. The most effective strategy may well be to go public by speaking directly to the American people without the editing that normally attaches to a press conference. Certainly, even when going public, subsequent showings of the president delivering his or her own words will be subject to selective editing by the media, but at least there is that initial chance to make his or her case, without edits and without comment. The use of spin doctoring after the fact can help to mitigate any negative interpretation from the media or opposing spin-doctors.

Chapter 14

Presidential Popularity: How Do I Approve of Thee? Let Gallup Count the Ways

Every recent president has been well aware of his[1] standing in the polls and has often commissioned his own polls. One should not take from this that presidents are passive observers of public opinion. Rather, they actively engage in activities to shape opinion. As noted in chapter 13, presidents employ strategies to ensure that interpretation of their statements and actions favor them, and these same strategies are used to influence how their policies are viewed by the American public. Other than to massage their own egos, why would presidents feel the need to shape opinion, whether about themselves or their policies? The answer lies in their ability to work with others, both domestically and in foreign affairs. A president's standing and reputation, both partly a function of popularity, impact whether he or she is in a position of dominance when dealing with leaders of Congress or foreign leaders.

Presidential Approval Defined

For most political scientists, journalists, and the American public, presidential approval and popularity are one and the same and come from a familiar question asked by pollsters, based on the Gallup Poll question, "Do you approve or disapprove of the way (insert incumbent's name here) is doing his job as president?" Notice that the question does not ask about specifics and also avoids the concept of "likeability." If a president has low approval, we might ask why. We might also be faced with the conundrum present during the Reagan years, where the president was much more popular than were his positions on issues. Reagan was *likable* while his positions on issues were not (Lipset 1986).

We usually think of the response to this standard question as having three dimensions. First, of course, is job performance—after all, it is right in the question,

"Do you approve or disapprove of the job the incumbent is doing?" Certainly, some respondents will separate out how well the president is doing his or her job from other factors, but for most it is likely that both of those factors—likeability and job performance—and other considerations will be lumped together in total or at least in some measure.

The second dimension here is that of likeability. Do we *like* this person? Is this someone you'd like to have a beer[2] with, or play cards[3] with, for example. Reagan's grandfatherly demeanor, Clinton's empathy, and George W. Bush's "aw shucks" mannerisms made them all very likable. Of course, scandal and war cut into that likeability at points during each of their presidencies. Think back over the presidents we have already discussed and imagine whether or not you could find yourself *liking* them. Might you want to get into a touch football game with John Kennedy? Could you imagine trying to hang out with Lyndon Johnson? Or, Richard Nixon? Most people today think highly of Jimmy Carter, in part, because of his charitable work and his ethical approach to life, but during his presidency these were seen as "holier than thou," or naive, behaviors. Thus, while he was in one respect a breath of fresh air, he seemed too much above it all.[4]

The third dimension has less to do with the particular individual than with the office itself and how the public sees the institution of the presidency. Now, certainly since the focus of this work is to demonstrate the influence each *individual president* has on the office and the institution, we know the two aspects are not necessarily separable. Respondents to surveys, however, may not see that intertwining of the individual with the institution. What they may see is an impression of a long-term lack of trust in the office or that it is too strong, or too weak. They may not see any of these as a reflection on or caused by the particular individual in the office. Thus, part of their response may be based on their evaluation of the institution and not just the individual in the office at the time.

Decline over Time

One important aspect of presidential approval is that since we have begun measuring it, it has been on the decline. Measures of approval or popularity for individual presidents *tend* to decline over the course of their presidency. Since presidential approval has been measured on a regular basis, only two presidents have finished their presidency with an approval rating higher than when they entered office. Eisenhower, president during a less turbulent time and having ended the war in Korea fairly early in his tenure, makes sense as one of these presidents. The second president whose approval was higher when he left office than when he entered usually surprises people. Most might think it was Reagan, but, in fact, it was Bill Clinton, who actually ended with the highest approval rating of any exiting president.[5]

Why would it be that approval has generally declined over the course of time we have measured it? A number of events and circumstances since Eisenhower's time have left us with less than the greatest level of confidence in the office of the presidency. For most, it would begin with Johnson's escalation of US involvement in Vietnam in the mid-1960s. Nightly footage of the dead and wounded being helicoptered from the battlefield, coupled with a nightly scroll at the end of the local news of the recent local casualties, left a negative impression in the minds of the public. This was, of course, reinforced by protestors chanting outside of the White House on a regular basis: "Hey, Hey, LBJ, how many kids did you kill today?"[6] We moved from that experience to the scandal surrounding the break-in at Watergate and its cover-up, along with what seemed to be a deeper, unsuccessful involvement in Vietnam under Nixon. This was followed immediately by Ford, who was never really forgiven for pardoning Nixon (CBS News 2009). Jimmy Carter seemed to be a well-intentioned, good-natured man who was in way over his head. Even Ronald Reagan, who seemed to offer a more optimistic view of America, became caught up in the Iran-Contra Scandal of the mid-1980s. The first George Bush neglected domestic affairs and at the last minute was named an unindicted coconspirator in the Iran-Contra Scandal,[7] and was limited to one term. Clinton, while certainly having his own problems with scandal, had the good fortune to preside over a healthy economy. The second George Bush, of course, though reelected, finished with one of the lowest approval ratings of any president, primarily because of public perception of his handling of the War on Terror. Naturally, such a backdrop would seem to provide an environment in which presidents would have to work hard, or have exceedingly good fortune, to overcome the overall negativity people seem to hold toward the office.

For individual presidents, the explanation is fairly simple. Over the course of their term, presidents make decisions or take actions that will, inevitably, disappoint some voters. The accumulation of these disappointed voters results in declining approval for the incumbent president. Naturally, the rate and extent of the decline over the course of a single presidency vary from president to president, with the events and conditions outside of a president's control in areas such as foreign affairs or certain economic markets.

There is a great deal of literature demonstrating the relationship between events and presidential approval. Among the best documented of these relationships is that between the performance of the economy and approval. As measures of the economy indicate a poorly performing economy, a president's approval rating will suffer (Gronke and Newman 2003 provide a very good review of this literature).[8] For example, as unemployment rises, a president's approval rating falls.[9] Similarly, as inflation increases, approval decreases. Given those two relationships, it might be natural to expect that an improving economy would lead to a better approval rating for a president. While that is mostly true, there is also what researchers have referred to as an asymmetric relationship, where the public more quickly blames the president for economic failure than they reward the president for an economic turnaround. This has sometimes been referred to as the congratulation/rationalization effect (Abramowitz et al. 1988). This occurs because we congratulate ourselves for our own success and blame others for our failures. In other words, if we get a new job we take credit for it, but if we lose a job we blame the president's handling of the economy. That is not to say, however, that presidents cannot benefit from a healthy economy. Bill Clinton was able to maintain a higher level of approval, mostly due to the economic boom that coincided with his tenure in office.

War also has an impact on the public's approval of the president. Short-term military involvements often will have a positive impact on a president's popularity[10] (Brace and Hinckley 1993; Mueller 1973). Reagan's use of troops in Grenada to help oust a government that had come to power by virtue of a military coup in 1983, helped to stabilize an approval rating that appeared to be suffering after the terrorist bombing of our Marine Headquarters in Beirut. George H. W. Bush received a positive impact from our quick success in the 1991 Persian Gulf War, which ousted Saddam Hussein from neighboring Kuwait. Usually, longer-term military engagements can have a devastating negative effect on presidential approval. Lyndon Johnson suffered greatly from the length of time we spent in Vietnam. Recall the discussion in chapter 4 of the impact the Tet Offensive had on the public's perception of how the war effort was going, and thus negatively affected Johnson's approval rating. The same could be said of the impact of the length of the wars in Iraq and Afghanistan on the public's approval of George W. Bush. The wars maintained his approval rating high enough after three years of engagement such that he was reelected in 2004, but soon thereafter the public grew weary of the wars and Bush's popularity suffered, as is the case for most presidents, when such conflicts linger and American casualties mount.

This short-term impact is more generically referred to as the "rally 'round the flag" effect (Baum 2002). We see the president as the embodiment of the nation—a symbol—not just a human being. As a result, if the nation is attacked or threatened, we rally around the president in a very patriotic response. Military engagements of short duration qualify in most cases.[11] Intense diplomatic confrontations involving attempts to settle crises or negotiate agreements also have the same effect. The issue becomes one of national pride, and this trumps partisanship or other differences of opinion voters may have with the president. In more recent history, rally 'round the flag effects have resulted from the news that US Navy Seal Team Six had found and killed Osama bin Laden and, naturally, from the al Qaeda attack on September 11th, 2001. This is not strictly an American phenomenon. Back in the 1980s, when the United Kingdom had its dispute with Argentina over who owned the Falkland Islands, Prime Minister Margaret Thatcher benefited greatly from the diplomatic crisis and the ensuing military action (Norpoth 1987).

Obviously, the human frailties that lead to political scandal can also impact a president's approval rating. Scandals can be of several different varieties: abuse of power, financial wrongdoing, hypocrisy, and sexual behavior (or any combination of them). The scandals that include all of the varieties are those that seem to be sustained stories.[12] We should pause to note, however, that it is often not the scandalous behavior itself that has the most devastating impact on the career and public approval of the elected official. Whether the individual is a member of Congress, a governor, or the president, it is either the attempt to cover-up, or the hypocrisy of behavior in direct opposition to the stated values or issue positions that determines the extent of impact.[13] It could be argued that one of the reasons Bill Clinton was able to survive the Monica Lewinsky scandal (and the allegations of other liaisons) was that he had never presented himself as saintly in his behaviors, thus there was no perceived hypocrisy.[14] Richard Nixon's involvement in the Watergate Scandal, which surrounded the break-in at Democratic National Headquarters in June of 1972, was his effort to cover-up the roles played by key campaign aides and White House staff in interacting with the actual burglars. Nixon's abuse of power was the real concern for most Americans, and was the focus of the impeachment hearings held by the House Judiciary Committee. Nixon fought the charges until a ruling by the US

Supreme Court forced the release of what came to be known as the "smoking gun" tape, a recording of Nixon instructing his top aides to obstruct the investigation—a clear violation of the law (which was exactly what he continued to tell the American people he had not done). It became clear that Nixon no longer enjoyed the support of a sufficient number of senators to avoid a conviction on charges of impeachment, so he resigned to avoid the embarrassment of the trial.[15] Sometimes the scandal doesn't rise to that level and involves the pursuit of a particular policy objective, as in the Iran-Contra scandal. Here, the issue was not covering up an attempt at partisan espionage or an affair, but had to do with efforts to circumvent (as opposed to break) the law in order to pursue the objective of stopping the spread of communist regimes in the Western Hemisphere. In every case, there was a negative impact on the public's approval of the president—how much and how long depended on other factors, such as the economy and events outside the president's control.

Many of these effects are lumped together under the heading of "rally points," points in time where there is a rally effect. Some have argued that these points can be positive or negative, not just a "rally 'round the flag" effect, in which the public supports the leader in times of international crisis, but a rallying of support of, or opposition to, the president. As we have already seen, short-term international events—diplomatic or military—have a positive effect, while longer-term conflicts tend to have a depressive effect. Even the widely recognized failure of the Bay of Pigs Invasion had a positive effect on John Kennedy's popularity, as did, of course, the Cuban Missile Crisis, which was deemed successful.[16] Nixon's trip to China and the opening of relations with that nation, naturally, had a positive effect on his popularity. The early days of the Iran Hostage Crisis in 1979 and 1980 had a very positive impact on Carter's approval rating, but the longer the crisis lasted, the more it had a negative impact on his approval. While there was no down side, there was a short-term positive impact from the signing of the Camp David Accords in 1978, which established an initial framework for peace in the Middle East.

One should not come away from this discussion with the idea that *only* international events or scandals can serve as rally points. Winning the Nobel Prize, passage of popular legislation, winning an election, and other types of events in domestic politics can also serve as rally points. The same is true of occasions when presidents address the American public, as we learned in chapter 13. They need to avoid talking too much about scandals or at all. Reminding us too much of the initial scandal is more likely to have a negative impact as opposed to a positive one. Going to the well of public support, or speaking to us too frequently, is likely to have diminishing marginal returns and may turn entirely negative if done too often.

How to Maintain Public Approval

It might seem as though there is little a president can do to keep his or her approval rating from falling, yet there is the fairly recent example of Bill Clinton bucking the trend and ending his tenure with approval ratings higher than when he entered the office. As we have seen, Clinton had the help of a booming economy, especially in the later years of his presidency. Certainly, some of that was fortunate timing and some of it was the impact of his administration's policies. It is often difficult to predict with any real accuracy what the impact of any given policy will be on the economy's performance, let alone the president's approval rating.

It would seem cynical to advise presidents to engage in short-term international conflict for the sole purpose of boosting their popularity via the rally 'round the flag effect. This was, of course, the very point of the movie *Wag the Dog*. A president accused of inappropriate contact with a young "Firefly Girl" visiting the White House as part of an event involving a girl scout-like group, hires a consultant who fabricates an international conflict—first diplomatic then military—with Albania to distract the media and the public from the allegations made against him.[17] One would like to believe that presidents don't decide to bomb a foreign country to divert attention from some domestic problem. Here again, some accused Clinton of doing this just before Christmas of 1998. With the House of Representatives ready to vote on impeachment resolutions, he ordered the bombing of select targets in Iraq for Sadam Hussein's failure to comply with UN resolutions on inspectors for weapons of mass destruction. What is more likely, one hopes, is that, at worst, it was the timing of the attack, and not the decision to make the attack, that is in any way influenced by polls.

So, short of declaring war on Albania, what can presidents do to nurture their approval ratings? Naturally, they should attempt to encourage a healthy economy; the types of approaches to this would be influenced by partisanship and ideology. But, since the difficulty of getting the economy to respond in a particular way is not an easy task, what else is there? Presidents should certainly avoid scandalous behavior of any kind. If underlings have engaged in improper behavior, the behavior should be acknowledged and the offender removed (if the behavior is sufficiently scandalous). Attempts should be made to keep any crisis situation to a shorter duration, especially if US military personnel are involved. Last, presidents need to act presidential, stay above domestic political infighting and look like a world leader by meeting with foreign leaders, here or abroad. Such measures should help maintain higher approval ratings, or at least slow the natural decline.

Thus, presidents need to shape events to the best of their ability or respond appropriately to those they cannot directly control. We have seen that there are many actions that presidents can choose not to take, that are totally within their control, to help keep their approval rating up, even if other things outside of their control may threaten to bring it down. As we saw in chapter 13, they need to engage in spin control to try to influence the interpretation of their words and deeds by the media. And, once again, as we learned in chapter 13, presidents sometimes need to make direct appeals to the American people, to go public, over the heads of the media and do an end run around the Congress. Without this direct connection to the American people, the natural decline of approval ratings cannot be slowed.

Chapter 15

The President and Congress

So far, we have talked about the importance of the president's relationship with the bureaucracy, the people, and the media as significant to his or her ability to succeed. Looking at the overall success of a president, those relationships are but mere tools he or she has to call upon in building or maintaining the relationship between the president and Congress. With all of the constitutional powers these two branches share, there must be some form of cooperation between them. It would be hard to imagine the government functioning for any extended period of time with all legislation being passed through the mechanism of a veto override. LeLoup and Shull (2003) have written, "No relationship in American politics is more important" (1).

Certainly, the ability of a president to get his or her way with the national legislature is dependent upon a certain level of prestige. This prestige is built upon his or her ability to be cordial with the press, to maintain a respectable image with the public, and to demonstrate some reasonable level of managerial skill over the branch of government theoretically reporting to the president—the bureaucracy. The relative strength of the two institutions plays a key role in how the two branches get along. There are also structural aspects to the relationship that shape their interactions, such as the schedule of elections, the way members of each branch see their representational role, the greater focus on decentralized control in Congress (whether with respect to committee structure or political parties), and the different timeframes through which the two branches see the political landscape.

In this chapter we will examine the above concerns and look at what tools might be available to presidents trying to shape the relationship he or she has with Congress. Political environments seem to have become more highly charged partisan environments than ever and so, the following questions must be addressed: (1) Is it possible for any president to successfully navigate what might appear to be a legislative obstacle course? (2) Which of these tools we will look at work best, or do the least damage, and which tools should a president avoid?

Important Structural Characteristics of the Relationship—Midterms and Term Limits

Among the structural characteristics of the relationship is the election schedule each branch follows. This schedule is important in two key ways. First, with the House of Representatives and one-third of the Senate being elected every two years, while the president is elected every four, an interesting dynamic is established. We have a situation that consists of, essentially, two types of national elections—one, a presidential election and the other, a midterm election. Second, combining this schedule with the limitation of two terms placed on the president by the Twenty-Second Amendment to the Constitution,[1] we have created an automatic "lame duck"[2] period following a president's reelection.

The simpler issue of the automatic lame duck is, basically, that in a president's second term—if he or she is lucky enough to have one—there is a diminished ability for a president to hold electoral consequences over the heads of members of Congress. He or she will never be on the ballot again and thus cannot use his or her popularity among voters as a threat to members of Congress from districts where the president performed well in the previous election. This factor is heightened even more for the last two years of a presidential administration. The Congress elected in the sixth year of a presidency—the president's second midterm—feels little or no electoral connection to the president and that their collective fate lies along a different path from that of the incumbent president. Naturally, this creates a much rockier road for the president and alters his or her approach to Congress.

The impact of midterm elections is far more complex. Most importantly, however, we need to note that the strength of the president's political party in Congress is almost always determined by a phenomenon known as "surge and decline." There are two aspects to this phenomenon and the second is highly dependent on the first. The first aspect relates to general voter turnout. Political scientists (e.g., A. Campbell, Converse, Miller, and Stokes 1966; J. Campbell 1987) have noted that in presidential election years turnout "surges" and that in midterm elections turnout "declines." A graph of voter turnout would display a fairly clear "saw tooth pattern" with the percentage of turnout represented as peaks in presidential years and as troughs in midterm years. Such a pattern of voting behavior has consequences for the political party that might have gained seats in a surge or presidential year—that party's voters are more likely to stay home two years later in the midterm. One needs to look no further than the 2008 election of Barack Obama as president and his party's (the Democratic Party) massive losses in the subsequent 2010-midterm elections. Naturally, such a loss has negative consequences for a president still attempting to pass major pieces of a legislative agenda.

This pattern of surge and decline in presidential party success is one of those observations in a "softer science,"[3] like political science, that is closest to a scientific law (Davidson, Oleszek, and Lee 2012). In the current era of political parties, dating back to 1860, the president's party has lost seats in Congress in all but three midterm elections, and each seat gain was under some rather special circumstances. The 1934 midterm election during Franklin Roosevelt's first term came during the still early stages of the Great Depression and voters were willing to give Roosevelt more members of his party in Congress with whom to work. The 1998 midterm election came during a period of relative economic prosperity, but also during a time when Congress was actively considering the impeachment of Bill Clinton. It could be argued that voters were sending the Republican majority in Congress a message that they were happy with their current circumstances and that the allegations against the president were a private matter. In 2002, the first midterm election during George W. Bush's tenure came on the heels of our invasion of Iraq and while Bush was riding high in the opinion polls due to the Iraq War and the residual effects of 9/11.

What is it then that explains this pattern? First and foremost is that presidential elections tend to draw to the polls more "peripheral voters," those voters who are less tied to the fortunes of one party or the other. Part of the reason these voters come out in such elections is that one aspect of the cost of voting—information—diminishes greatly in presidential years.[4] Every day, for months, voters are inundated with the flow of information through newspapers, magazines, radio, TV, and the Internet. In other years this information flow is much less plentiful and voters might have to search for the information they feel they need to make an informed voting decision. The extreme case would be an election for a very local office such as a school board or village council, where without major controversy over tax rates or zoning issues, information would be hard to come by except for very personal connections. As a result of limited information, and limited media attention, turnout is low. Certainly, an election for Congress has a much greater flow of information than most school board races, but the difference between the amount of information in such an election and a presidential one is still sufficient to keep those peripheral voters at home. Voters, who may have been drawn to a presidential candidate by his or her charisma or for a particular cause, don't necessarily feel the same enthusiasm for members of the House and Senate.

Second, the political conditions at the time of the midterm play an important role in determining the extent of the seat loss experienced by the president's party. The two largest considerations are the performance of the economy and the president's popularity. If both the president's approval rating and the economy are healthy, high public approval with low unemployment and inflation, the president can expect that his or her party will lose a minimum number of seats. If both are weak, low approval coupled with high unemployment and inflation, the president's party is in for a disastrous election outcome. If the two sets of measures are mixed, seat loss should be about average, around 32 seats (starting with the 1862 elections and running through 2006). Thus, the midterm election becomes a referendum on the performance of the president and his or her party over the most recent two years.

Presidents are concerned about their reelection, but only once since they are term limited. Members of the House of Representatives are concerned with reelection on a constant basis. House elections are held once every two years, so given that short timeframe members are constantly campaigning. Also, with the high cost of media, members must raise a great deal of money and to do so must start as soon as their oath of office is complete. Even without this more public or formal aspect of campaigning brought on by modern necessity, it has long been the case that members engage in other behavior more directly related to their job description, but that is also aimed at boosting their reelectoral chances. This is, without a doubt, the single biggest motivating factor in congressional behavior. Even if members seek to create good public policy and engage in good government, they need to establish a measure of seniority in order to achieve those goals.

Three scholars—David Mayhew (1974), Morris Fiorina (1977), and Richard Fenno (1978)—were at the forefront of research into the motivations behind the behavior of members of Congress. The primary focus of their work, though from slightly different perspectives, has been the drive to be reelected. Mayhew approached the subject through a set of strategies—advertising, credit claiming, and position taking. Fiorina postulated that members created a federal bureaucracy that would often require citizens to seek out the assistance of their elected representative to cut through the red tape, and that helping constituents with these requests did not require them to take a political position on the value of the agency. Fenno examined the actions members took to respond to their perceptions of what their constituents wanted with respect to the allocation of their office, staff, and personal resources—how much of their office budget and staff were spent on the district, and how much time the members spent at home as opposed to Washington.

These political scientists would argue that members were sufficiently insecure about their reelectoral chances that they would engage in behaviors they felt insulated them from the vagaries of national politics. For the most part, members of Congress have been successful, with 80 to 90 percent of them seeking reelection, and the rate at which those members are successfully returned to office often approaching 100 percent.[5] It is more likely that members of Congress will leave office of their own volition to run for another office or to retire. To be sure, their retirement might well be hastened by a scandal of one sort or another.[6] It is when the party that does not hold the White House (and often in the minority in the legislature) can sufficiently "nationalize" the issues in the midterm election that the president's party suffers the most. In 1994, Clinton's inability to deliver on his biggest promise of national health insurance reform led the Republicans, then in the minority, to develop the "Contract with America." It highlighted the perceived failings of Clinton and his party, and as a result, the Republicans were successful in gaining a huge victory of 54 seats in the House. In 2006, the Democratic Party, also expected to gain seats as the out party in a midterm election, not only gained seats, but made the increasingly unpopular wars in Iraq and Afghanistan the centerpiece of their attack on the Republicans and Bush and won back the majority in the House for the first time since the 1994 midterms.

It is hard to think of an institution of government that could be designed better to meet the reelectoral needs of its members than the United States Congress. The committee structure alone provides excellent opportunities for members to carve out areas of policy expertise and to bring real benefits home to their constituents. The combination of the committee structure and the party structures allows members the opportunity to advance and thus enhance their power and prestige, both aimed at bringing more benefits home to their district, and making a strong case for reelection.

Mayhew (1974), as mentioned earlier, using similar concepts as Fenno (1978) and Fiorina (1977) regarding the need for member insulation from national politics, explicated the strategies of advertising, credit claiming, and position taking. Advertising is defined as "any effort to disseminate one's name among constituents in such a fashion as to create a favorable image but in messages having little or no issue content" (Mayhew 1974, 49). This would include images of the member with the most recent Eagle Scout or the local high school valedictorians or throwing out a first pitch at a charity softball game or other activities of that nature. Credit claiming is defined "as acting to generate a belief in a relevant political actor (or actors) that one is personally responsible for causing the government, or some unit thereof, to do something that the actor (or actors) considers desirable" (52–53). This is, perhaps, best exemplified by the member taking credit for the "particularized benefits" received by the district. In other words, this would be taking credit for just about any federal expenditure in the member's district, from new public infrastructure to senior or low-income housing. It would also include the awarding of various federal grants to nongovernmental organizations to carry out certain privatized government policies or programs (e.g., job training programs, daycare, etc.). The last strategy, position taking, Mayhew defines "as the public enunciation of a judgmental statement on anything likely to be of interest to political actors" (61). The most common occurrence of this practice is when an elected official states a position on something outside the normal jurisdiction of the office to which he or she was elected. A member of Congress might comment on a local zoning issue or member of a local city council might state a position on US troop deployments in Afghanistan.

In addition to Mayhew's strategies, there are many other ways members can help to sustain themselves in office, from the use of the perquisites (franked mail, staff, travel allowances) of office to addressing the casework concerns of their constituents (solving problems voters face in dealing with the federal bureaucracy). Discussion of the details on the entire range of activities in which members engage have filled volumes of work on congressional behavior and is beyond the scope of what we seek to accomplish here. It is most important to take away from this discussion that members seek insulation from the whims of national politics, including the popularity of the president and his or her policies, in order to assure their own political success. Fenno (1978) referred to these activities as "constituency cultivation." This, naturally, sets up a dynamic where there is a potential conflict between the president and Congress, even with members of his or her own party.

Most of the work that Congress does is really done in committees and most of what we see regularly on C-SPAN and the news as occurring on the floor of either chamber is mostly for show and dissemination back home. Even when we might see a filibuster[7] or threat of one in the Senate, the negotiations to try to prevent or shorten it take place behind closed doors, out of the public view. By the time legislation actually does come to the floor for debate and vote, most often all of the details have been hammered out in committee or by agreement of the leadership. Certainly, we can see last minute maneuvering and proposed amendments, but these are the exception and not the norm. Even more importantly, the committee structure of Congress is well suited to the reelectoral needs of the members, by providing opportunities for the members to develop expertise and relationships with, in Mayhew's (1974) words, relevant political actors.[8] Similarly, committees and the ability of members to use the structure to advance through the ranks of their chamber, provide opportunities for members to access resources[9] that may be brought home to the district, further enhancing the member's stature with his or her constituents. Here again, the structure creates an environment where, in many cases, the president becomes far less relevant to the member's reelectoral needs.

More important for the president is the fact that the committee structure fragments and decentralizes power in both chambers, but especially in the House. You may now be wondering why, since you may also be familiar with the phrase "divide and conquer." What is different in this case is that the fragmentation creates many "veto points" or places where a single committee chair or subcommittee chair could refuse to consider an administration proposal or a committee might vote in opposition to the proposal. The structure also creates a multitude of actors with whom a president must deal in order to assure passage of his or her proposals. There was a time when a president could make deals or communicate with relatively few members of the congressional leadership and accomplish his[10] goals. Each committee or subcommittee (and at times there has been assignment of a bill to more than one committee for consideration) means one more point of contact for the president.

The party system in Congress is more of a double-edged sword. It can work to a president's advantage (but not always) if he or she is from the majority party in the chamber. It can work to his or her disadvantage in a number of ways. First and most obviously, if the president's party is in the minority, he or she is greatly disadvantaged in that the hill to climb to a majority vote for passage of a proposal is much higher and steeper. Second, if the president is from the chamber's minority party he or she has less control over the agenda and the processes. It is the president's opposition that controls how and when bills get to the floor and how debate will proceed.

The "housekeeping" of Congress is done by the political parties. The party organization makes member assignments to committees, decides the leadership, committee chairs, sets the agenda, and doles out those perks of office that do not come simply by virtue of membership.[11] However, for many decades the party system in the House and Senate has been characterized by rather lax discipline. This may not necessarily be the fault of the parties themselves, but more a function of our electoral system and the parties adopting coping mechanisms to survive. We elect our representatives in what is best known as a single member, first past the post system, or a single member, simple plurality (SMSP) system, where, quite simply, the candidate with the most votes wins. Though recent history has indicated that there are fewer and fewer "marginal" seats in the House of Representatives, parties still allow members a great deal of leeway in representing the interests of their districts as opposed to the interests of the party. In practice, the only vote on which the parties would require complete discipline would be on the vote for Speaker of the House. True, the parties will work harder and enforce some measure of discipline on other important votes. If, however, a party is in the majority and has sufficient votes, it will allow some members to "vote their districts." The same is true if the party is in the minority and the outcome is a foregone conclusion. It will then allow members to deviate from the party line. There have been instances of parties enforcing discipline on members over issues of votes, but even that sometimes doesn't work out for the best. For example, in the 1980s, Phil Gramm was a Democrat representing part of Texas, just south of Dallas, who was voting quite consistently with the Republicans on Reagan's tax and budget proposals. As a consequence, the Democrats stripped Gramm of his seniority and committee assignments. Gramm responded by resigning, returning to Texas, changing his party enrollment to Republican, and running in the special election to fill the vacancy he created by resigning. Gramm later ran for and won a seat in the US Senate, where he became a leading voice of the Republican Party for many years to follow.

In addition to committees and parties, the respective timeframes make the ability to see eye-to-eye more difficult. Congress tends to act more slowly than a president might desire. Congress is, after all, a deliberative body and is by design supposed to take time to consider legislation carefully. Also, it is common for a member of Congress to serve a rather long time, even 20- to 30-year careers. Presidents, on the other hand, can serve up to a maximum of ten years and more typically eight or less.[12] Members of Congress, therefore, can afford to wait out a president if the incumbent is threatening to block a member's pet project. Presidents tend to be in a hurry, especially as their political capital or time runs out, on their ability to leave behind a legacy.[13]

Members of Congress are more naturally concerned with issues impacting their constituents, which is tied directly to their reelectoral prospects, where presidents deal with a larger national constituency. Often, what is good for the country might not have as direct or positive an impact on a single congressional district or state. For example, the cancellation of a major defense contract for a futuristic bomber might be in the country's best financial interests, but the workers in a particular state or congressional district might suffer serious job losses. This different focus of attention is often a cause for friction between the president and members of Congress.

A few other considerations bring us back to the shared powers mentioned in chapter 1. Though Congress has the ultimate authority over the budget, the practice has evolved into one where it waits for the president's initiative. Once again, member concerns over reelection, whether with respect to benefits for the voters back home or playing to their party's base across the country, often put members into conflict with the president, sometimes even if they are of the same party. Congress also has the authority to oversee the executive branch, to ensure that money is being spent in the manner allocated, and that laws are being enforced as intended, none of which may be on the president's list of priorities. The constitutional role of the Senate in the confirmation of presidential appointees, formally known as the "advise and consent" power, creates yet another point at which contention between the president's wishes and the partisan or member goals of Congress may occur. In recent years, there has been a great deal of political conflict over the ideological viewpoint of presidential nominees to the federal court, from the Supreme Court down to the District Court level. The contention has been marked by threats of filibuster, threats to do away with the filibuster, and the holding up of consideration of nominees by the whole Senate or just an individual member.[14]

Presidential Tools for Handling Congress

The first obvious tool through which presidents may attempt to "handle" Congress, if they happen to be in the majority party, is partisanship. We have already seen that this can be a double-edged sword, but presidents in the majority naturally start out with an advantage their predecessors don't have. Many presidents, however, have had to deal with divided government, a situation where at least one chamber of Congress is controlled by the opposing party. As already discussed, the parties control the chamber agenda and the mechanisms by which proposals come to the floor. But, what other tools might be available to presidents in an attempt to manage their legislative package through Congress?

We can think of the president as we do any other interest before Congress, that he or she is also a "special interest." As such, the president has an entire office, within the Executive Office of the President, dedicated solely to moving the administration's policy proposals through Congress. The Office of Legislative Affairs (the name of the office under President Obama) is the president's lobbyist. This office has the most responsibility for dealing with Congress and managing the president's relationship with the other elected branch of government (Hess 2002; Kessel 2001).

By making use of the tools discussed in chapters 13 and 14, presidents can use their relationship with the media and the public in an attempt to influence Congress. Ronald Reagan would use televised addresses from the Oval Office to drum up public support to bring pressure on Congress prior to key votes on US aid to the Contra Rebels in Nicaragua. Bill Clinton used an address to a joint session of Congress, not so much to talk to Congress, but to speak directly to the American people about the need for health insurance reform.

In addition, presidents can "work" directly on the members through a number of techniques. First among these is a set of techniques focused on tangible rewards. These include offering support for the legislator's pet legislative project, regardless of the member's party. It also includes support on the campaign front for members from the president's own party, such as actively campaigning for the member or helping to raise funds for the member to campaign (Kessel 2001).

In a similar way, presidents can also make use of the trappings of their office in an attempt to persuade individual members of Congress. The use of the prestige or aura of the office can bear great fruit. Perhaps the height of this practice was when Bill Clinton was offering all sorts of opportunities to members of Congress for their support for the North American Free Trade Agreement (NAFTA).[15] Even members of the opposing party can be swayed by this technique. Being photographed meeting with the president gives the impression of importance, ripe for the consumption of voters back home, and thus can be a rather persuasive tool.

The Tool That Is the Political Weapon of Mass Destruction

The one last important tool in the president's belt, the most significant weapon in his or her arsenal, is the veto. Congressional Quarterly's *American Congressional*

Dictionary (Kravitz 1993) defines the veto as "the president's disapproval of a legislative measure passed by Congress. He [or she] returns the measure to the house in which it originated without his [or her] signature but with a veto message stating his [or her] objections to it" (298). Further, the president must do so within ten days[16] or the bill becomes law. The exception to this would be if the president did nothing, neither sign nor veto, and within the ten days the Congress adjourns for the year. This is referred to as the pocket veto, deriving from the idea that the president sticks the bill in his or her pocket.

Given that we have a system of checks and balances, the president's veto is not necessarily the end of the story. If Congress were so driven as to believe in the virtue of the legislation it passed and the president were to veto it, they could, in turn, override the president's action by a two-thirds vote of *both* chambers. Again, according to Congressional Quarterly's *American Congressional Dictionary* (Kravitz 1993), the motion to do this is put to each chamber as follows: "Shall the bill (or joint resolution) pass, the objections of the president to the contrary notwithstanding?" An override attempt is generally considered among the highest priority of business that Congress can consider.

Some political scientists have wondered if there were some pattern to vetoes and overrides, and still others have looked for explanations why some presidents veto more than others do, and why some Congresses override more than others do. Barbara Hinckley (1985) has provided a typology that helps us to place the patterns of behavior into logical categories. In her typology, there are two axes, one divided into low versus high vetoes by presidents, and one divided into low versus high overrides by Congress. This gives us the familiar 2 × 2 matrix and four categories (see table 15.1). The first is the Cooperative-Successful category, defined by low vetoes and low overrides. Examples of presidents in this category are Lincoln, McKinley, and Lyndon Johnson. The second is the Conflictual-Successful category, where there are high vetoes and low overrides. The examples Hinckley provides are Cleveland and Franklin Roosevelt. The third is the Cooperative-Unsuccessful category with low vetoes and high overrides. Presidents in this category include Arthur and Nixon. The last category is Conflictual-Unsuccessful where there are high vetoes and high overrides. Hinckley includes Pierce and Andrew Johnson in this category.

While Hinckley's categorization allows us to sort presidencies according to vetoes and success, it doesn't tell us much about why those presidents might veto a bill in

Table 15.1 Barbara Hinckely's veto patterns

	Cooperative	**Conflictual**
Successful	*Type 1* Low vetoes/Low overrides A. Lincoln, W. McKinley, L. B. Johnson	*Type 2* High vetoes/Low overrides G. Cleveland, F. D. Roosevelt
Unsuccessful	*Type 3* Low vetoes/High overrides C. A. Arthur, R. Nixon	*Type 4* High vetoes/High overrides F. Pierce, A. Johnson

Source: Table created by author from data in Barbara Hinckley (1985), *The Problems of the Presidency: A Text with Readings*.

the first place or what politics drives attempts to override those vetoes, let alone what makes those attempts successful. An early attempt at providing description and some explanation is Jong R. Lee's (1975) work. Among his findings is that, as one might expect, a president of the minority party is more likely to issue a veto than a president from the majority party. He also finds that more popular presidents, as measured by their Electoral College percentage in the last election, are more likely to issue vetoes. Former governors were more likely to veto than were presidents whose experience was in Congress. As a natural extension of these findings, Lee also found that there were certain circumstances where Congress was more likely to override a president's veto. These include cases where the president is from the legislative minority party or has little previous congressional experience, and following midterm elections. There was also a higher likelihood of an override during economic difficulty and less likelihood during military action.

Woolley (1991) divided vetoes into categories of "major" and "minor," where major bills contained subject matter of greater import such as establishing new programs, appropriations, and redefining the powers between the two branches, just to name a few areas. What Woolley found was that occurrences of major vetoes were more dependent on the president's strength, particularly as measured by his or her approval rating and the size of his or her party's contingent in Congress. Further, Woolley postulates that a weak president is more likely to exercise the veto on major legislation. This makes sense in that a stronger president, one with high public approval and/or a large majority in Congress, would not necessarily be presented with legislation he or she would oppose. While Rohde and Simon (1985) find similar foundations for vetoes, they go at least one step farther and argue that a president's status as a member of the congressional minority can be overcome with higher levels of public approval, making it less likely that Congress would challenge a veto or be successful in an override vote. Copeland (1983) adds to the mix of explanations the length of time president has served, and finds that presidents are least likely to veto legislation in their first year, and most likely to do so in their second year in office. Conley and Kreppel (2001) looked in more detail at the circumstances of the bill's passage, among other factors, and found that even when presidents are presented with a bill passed by what might be termed a "beyond veto proof"[17] majority, they may still veto legislation. Clearly, there is more at stake for such presidents than the mere legislative outcome—they are seeking to make a public statement. If a sufficient portion of the public agrees with them, Congress may concede the fight and fail to override the veto. In short, there are a great many factors structuring the circumstances of any veto, many considerations presidents make in deciding whether or not to veto, and many considerations for congressional leaders to undertake an override attempt.

Impeachment

In discussions of impeachment, I have often begun with a list of "seven heroes of the American presidency." These heroes are William Pitt Fessenden, Joseph S. Fowler,

James W. Grimes, John B. Henderson, Lyman Trumball, Peter G. Van Winkle, and Edmund Ross. The first question that usually comes up is "Who are these men?" They all were Republican Senators in the mid- to late 1860s. What, then, makes them heroes? They are the seven members of the Republican majority in the Senate in 1868 who voted "not guilty" in the impeachment trial of Andrew Johnson, a trial stemming from a predominantly political motivation.

Johnson, a Democrat from the border state of Tennessee, had been Lincoln's vice president and they had run on a unity ticket in an attempt to politically reunify the country as the Civil War wound down. The Republicans in Congress, with a two-thirds majority in the Senate, were of a mind to be relatively harsh on the Southern states as they sought reentry to the Union and Johnson was a bit more forgiving than they preferred. The difference in approach came to a head over the actions of the secretary of war, Edwin Stanton, the cabinet officer charged with the reconstruction effort throughout the recently rebellious states. It became clear that Johnson wanted to remove Stanton, much to the consternation of the Republicans in the House and Senate.

Seeking to prevent the Democrat, Johnson, from removing the Republican Stanton, Congress passed The Tenure of Office Act, which would prohibit the president from firing any officer of the government whose appointment had been approved by the Senate, without the further consent of the Senate. First, Johnson vetoed the bill and Congress passed it over his veto. Congress appeared to act here as though it didn't matter that Johnson would veto the bill and violate the law anyway—they appeared to be baiting him. Johnson continued to move ahead with his plans, though initially he merely "suspended" Stanton. When the Senate reconvened in January of 1868, they reinstated Stanton. In an attempt to avoid a major constitutional crisis, Civil War heroes, General Grant and General Sherman tried to convince Stanton that he should just step down, but Stanton stood firm. In spite of their efforts, a constitutional crisis did arise and on Friday, February 21st, Johnson fired Stanton.

The very next day, Saturday, February 22nd, 1868, a resolution of impeachment was read in the House of Representatives. The following Monday, the House voted to impeach President Andrew Johnson and appointed a committee to draw up specific charges against him.[18] On March 5th, the Senate began the formal trial process by swearing in the senators as jurors and drew up the rules to be used during the trial. The actual trial began on March 30th, 1868, and it became clear as things progressed that sentiment was beginning to turn against conviction. Yet, on May 16th when Article XI came to a vote, Johnson prevailed by a single vote, that of Edmund Ross of Kansas. The Senate did not consider any further articles of impeachment until May 26th. They recessed for the Republican National Convention at which the president pro tempore of the Senate—Benjamin Wade—was competing against Ulysses Grant for the party's nomination for president. At that time, the line of succession ran from the president, to the vice president, and then to the president pro tempore. If Article XI had passed, Wade would have gone to the convention as the incumbent president. Wade's loss to Grant seemed to take the wind out of the impeachment sails, as on May 26th two more articles met with the same fate as Article XI, and the Republican majority gave up and adjourned the trial (Milkis and Nelson 2012; McDonald 1994).

For all the political maneuvering there was a real constitutional issue involved, whether or not Congress could limit the presidential appointment power, albeit shared with Congress, any further. It took more than 50 years, but in the 1920s the Supreme Court struck down The Tenure of Office Act and proved Johnson correct. If the decision had been in place in May of 1868, the votes may never have taken place.

In strikingly similar circumstances, though the charges couldn't be more different, Bill Clinton underwent an impeachment trial in 1999. In the elections just prior to both the Clinton impeachment and the Johnson impeachment, the Republican Party suffered losses larger than one might normally expect. In both cases, the results of the elections (in Clinton's case it was his second midterm and in Johnson's case it was the odd year local elections), should have given Congress a caution sign. In fact, in Clinton's case it was one of those rare occasions where the incumbent president's party *gained* seats in a midterm election. The electoral outcomes in each case seemed to slow the zeal for impeachment a bit, but subsequent actions of each president fired the opposition back up. In Johnson's case, it was the actual firing of Stanton, and in Clinton's case it was his dismissive treatment of a questionnaire requested by the House Judiciary Committee. The outcome seemed more certain in Clinton's case in that the Republicans did not already have a two-thirds majority in the Senate. Clinton was more concerned, though he would get to stay in office, with the public relations problems that might stem from a simple majority vote to convict.

In the last several decades, we came close to a full impeachment trial one other time, during Richard Nixon's administration. Without getting into the lengthy details of the Watergate scandal that was his undoing, it is perhaps easier to say that the investigation by Congress was less political than in the Johnson or Clinton cases. With the decision of the Supreme Court in the case of *United States v. Nixon* (418 U.S. 683, 1974), the so-called smoking gun tape recording of Nixon's conversations with advisers where he instructed them to obstruct justice was released. Thus, strong evidence of Nixon's violation of preexisting law became public knowledge. While the House Judiciary Committee had already voted to send articles of impeachment to the full chamber, the vote to impeach by the House was averted by Nixon's resignation.

So, then, what is impeachment? Like the president's veto power, impeachment is much like a political weapon of mass destruction. It is the ultimate political tool for Congress to control a president and other officers of the national government, as it could result in removal of the officer. Most people seem to believe that impeachment is removal from office, but this is a misconception. While two presidents have been impeached, none has been convicted and thus removed from office. It might be convenient to think of impeachment as an indictment and that the vote in the Senate determines whether or not the indicted individual is guilty or not guilty. If guilt is determined, the automatic punishment is removal from office.

Once the House has drawn up its charges via the committee route and then had the full chamber vote to indict the president, the Senate establishes procedures for the conduct of the trial. During the trial, the chief justice of the Supreme Court presides over the Senate with the members of the Senate serving as jurors. In addition to the determination on guilt, the Senators also make many of the decisions that a judge in a regular criminal trial might make, deciding by majority vote what gets admitted into evidence and so forth. In the end, if two-thirds of the Senators find the president guilty, the president is deemed convicted and is immediately removed from office.

How Can a President Achieve a Successful Relationship with Congress?

After having read the last two sections, you may be thinking that most interactions between the president and Congress involve vetoes and impeachment. Certainly, that is not the case. The president and Congress interact regularly and get routine business done all the time. There are a number of things presidents can do to help ensure a successful relationship with Congress without the need for vetoes, veto threats, or for Congress to retaliate with impeachment.

Presidents need to set priorities, focus on a specific agenda, and not spread their policy attention too thinly. Presidents, like Jimmy Carter for example, who try to do too much, are bound to experience a bumpy road with lower levels of success. Ronald Reagan, on the other hand, kept his focus on his economic agenda and experienced a higher level of success during his first two years,[19] in spite of one chamber still being controlled by the opposing party. Presidents need also to maintain vigilance regarding their popularity and relations with the press. When they have successes, especially those that have a positive impact on their popularity, they should use that success to their advantage, like turning a foreign policy victory into a victory on passage of legislation they seek. They should be aware of the idea of the "two presidencies theory" (Wildavsky 1966) that suggests Congress will be more likely to cooperate on foreign and military ventures than they will on domestic policy.[20] Presidents also have at least one, and if they are lucky, two honeymoons—a period of time just after they have taken office when public approval is high, the media tend to give the benefit of the doubt, and Congress is just that little bit more cooperative. This honeymoon period usually lasts about three months—approximately the fabled one hundred days—but can be shortened or lengthened by events. Clinton's honeymoon was shorter due to his inability to find a trouble-free attorney general nominee and to avoid early controversy on issues like gays serving in the military. Reagan's honeymoon was extended somewhat—unfortunately—by the assassination attempt that left him seriously wounded.

There are a number of necessary conditions that make success possible. Presidents need a substantial majority to make success easier and a landslide with long coattails, that brings more members of Congress from his or her party into office with him or her. This often will result in a strong ideological coalition in Congress, though this can be achieved across party lines.[21] Occurring along with these circumstances, normally, would be strong public support. Making use of these conditions through skillful and aggressive leadership can also lead to success. Such was the case in Reagan's early years in office.

It is also true that it is easier to exert negative influence in Congress—to threaten or actually use the veto, to be stubborn in negotiations. Positive influence, moving Congress in the president's desired direction, particularly without members of Congress realizing they are being so influenced, is much harder to achieve.

We are left with some more philosophical questions to ponder. Intentions of the Framers aside, which branch of government is in the better position to exert itself and get its way? Which branch should be? Certainly, there are many who argue the supremacy of the legislature as a norm. Yet, others would argue that given our contemporary world with the possibility of near instantaneous war, the executive should dominate. If we sought to change the relationship, would instituting coterminus elections help one branch more than the other would? Would the institutionalization of communications in a fashion similar to the parliamentary question time[22] used in the United Kingdom hinder or facilitate the relationship? Perhaps thinking back to the categorization of presidents presented by Hargrove and Nelson (1984)[23] would help us to understand that we might not want to seek ongoing domination of the political process by one institution or the other. Perhaps, instead, we should seek a more fluid situation where the appropriate institution dominates at the right time.

In parts of the first, and early part of the second, decade of the twenty-first century cooperation appears much harder to achieve. It is not only a case of divided government as we have experienced many times in recent history, but is something like divided government on steroids. The political environment of this time period with very conservative House members threatening the leadership of the Republican Party and similar players in the Senate who use the filibuster much more frequently makes the ability of the president to accomplish anything more than the mere routine legislation nearly impossible. At the same time, more moderate members of both chambers, and in the two major parties at large, are leaving of their own choice or being forced out by much more vocal, well-organized, and well-funded challengers. This all leads to making compromise difficult and the need for future presidents to be ever more inventive.

Chapter 16

The President and the Judiciary

Where the president's relationships with Congress, the media, the public, and the bureaucracy all take daily nurturing, the relationship between the president and the judicial branch of government takes far less care and feeding. Of course, there are circumstances that influence the interactions of the two branches in either a positive or negative way. The most significant manner in which a president can influence his or her relationship with the judiciary is through the appointments process, where he or she attempts to fill a vacancy on a court with an individual who most represents the president's thinking on policy, the law, and the Constitution.

The President's Judicial Powers

The president is not without some judicial powers of his or her own. A president may grant pardons to individuals convicted of federal crimes. Pardons are releases from punishment. A president may also make use of a grant of amnesty, which is an act of forgiving, especially for what some might consider more "political" offenses. Presidents may also issue clemency, which is a demonstration of leniency, perhaps commuting a sentence for a very sick or older prisoner. All of these powers are, as stated, limited to those convicted of violations of federal law and generally have only short-term effects.

The use of such power is generally not very controversial and elaborate screening mechanisms have been established to review the requests of "worthy applicants." Occasionally, however, a president might get into some trouble through his or her exercise of the power. Such was the case when Gerald Ford pardoned Richard Nixon, even before a trial could take place. So too, Bill Clinton got into a bit of trouble over his pardon of Mark Rich as Clinton was leaving office. There were allegations that Rich's family had made substantial contributions to Clinton endeavors—campaign contributions and donations to the Clinton Library and Foundation.[1]

The pardon, though used in a broad sense in everyday language and media coverage, is a rather specific forgiveness of a crime and a restoration of the convicted individual's rights. It is often used to also include the granting of clemency, which is more generally the commutation of a convict's sentence. Both are generally considered the sole purview of the executive granting the pardon and are not subject to review or reversal by any other authority.

Long-Term Effects

The only way that presidents can have long-term impacts on the outcomes of the judicial process, absent a constitutional amendment or major structural change, is through appointments. Obviously, to do so requires that there be vacancies. Of most concern here is the Supreme Court, since its word is law and lasts until another Supreme Court changes its mind. Presidents do, however, get to make appointments to district courts, appellate courts, and specialized courts in addition to the Supreme Court. It is in these lower courts where the more day-to-day rulings occur that affect ordinary citizens more directly. Such lower court appointments also create a pool of potential nominees to the higher-level courts. If one party has been out of the White House for a number of years and the other party has had numerous appointments to the lower court benches, it restricts the pool of potential nominees by ensuring that the pool is dominated by justices of the opposing party's judicial perspective. In other words, a Democrat coming into the presidency after eight or more years of a Republican president would have his or her pool of choices greatly restricted because there are many more Republican judges available than Democratic judges (Hinckley 1985).

Some presidents are more fortunate in getting vacancies on the Supreme Court to fill during their tenure in office. Jimmy Carter, serving four years, had no vacancies to fill, made no appointments, and thus had no long-lasting direct impact on the decisions of the Supreme Court. Gerald Ford, on the other hand, served from August of 1974 until January of 1977, just short of two and a half years, and made one appointment, John Paul Stevens, who served until 2010. Barack Obama, through his first three years as president, has appointed two justices. Bill Clinton, having completed a full two-term presidency, only made two appointments to the Court. There is no set pattern, and in terms of a president's ability to have an impact in this manner, it is all really the luck of the draw.

At least one president attempted to create opportunities to make appointments to overcome a Court that refused to give him the slightest leeway in implementing his agenda. As we discussed in chapter 2, Franklin Roosevelt ran headlong into a Supreme Court with a fairly solid five (or more depending on the case) votes against any of his New Deal programs. The Court opposed his programs either as an overreach of congressional authority to delegate or as an overreach of Congress's power to regulate interstate commerce. Given that many of the judges were older, Roosevelt sought to augment the older justices with new appointments. The numbers would be sufficient to give Roosevelt an outright majority on the Court. In the end, there was no need to implement the scheme as Justice Owen Roberts (not be confused with the current chief justice—John Roberts) switched his vote to support a more aggressive regulatory approach, becoming the supposed "switch in time that saved nine."[2]

Ronald Reagan and George H. W. Bush employed a strategy of appointing younger justices to the Court. This had a twofold benefit. First, the nominees would have little record for the Senate Judiciary Committee to scrutinize, thus easing the advise and consent process. Second, and perhaps more important, once confirmed these justices should, theoretically, serve for a very long time, increasing the length of time a president gets to have an impact on constitutional interpretation and law. In fact, some of their appointees are likely to still be on the Court in 2020 and perhaps in 2030 (Biskupic 2008). A similar argument could be made about George W. Bush's appointment of Chief Justice John Roberts, another fairly young nominee. In contrast, only one of Obama's nominees to the Court could be categorized in this manner—Elena Kagan.

Lower Court Appointments

For appointments to the lower federal courts, the process is a bit less formal than that with which we are all familiar, including televised confirmation hearings. For the lower courts, the practice of senatorial courtesy is used. This is an unwritten tradition followed by presidents and the Senate, mostly to expedite the process (see Sollenberger 2008). Nominations made by presidents are not confirmed by the Senate (usually the president will withdraw the name or the nominee will ask to be withdrawn) when the nominee is opposed by a senator from the state in which the nominee would serve. For the higher-level appeals court appointments, the same practice is used, but the senator with the veto is from the nominee's state of residence.

Some attempts have been made over the course of the nation's history to make all of the appointments process more like the merit system in the civil service. Sollenberger (2008) points out that Jimmy Carter campaigned on a platform of reform in this regard. Carter sought to make use of a commission that would make nominations to judicial positions based on merit and diversity and be free of political considerations. Carter, his nominee to be attorney general, Griffin Bell, and the chair of the Senate Judiciary Committee, James Eastland met to make the arrangements. Citing a *Washington Post* story from February of 1978, which referenced the remarks of a Justice Department spokesman Marvin Wall, who indicated that while Carter and Bell may have thought they had won some great victory for reform, had merely been told by Eastland "what the Senate would sit still for" (Sollenberger 2008, 147). Apparently, as far as Eastland, the Judiciary Committee, and the rest of the Senate were concerned, no prenomination screening process that did not include some form of consultation with the Senate would be acceptable. Some senators dubbed themselves one-person merit commissions.

Reagan moved in another direction, eliminating Carter's commissions and using a mechanism where senators would submit the names of their personal preferred nominees. "Instead of permitting pluralistic commissions to choose the federal judges, Reagan placed the selection power back into the hands of home-state senators" (Sollenberger 2008, 150). The ascendency of George H. W. Bush changed little in the nomination of lower court judges. Bill Clinton openly embraced the senatorial courtesy and consultation norm and had Justice Department personnel actively seeking out senators for suggested nominations. Still, with a Congress in the hands of the opposing party and during a time of heightened levels of partisanship, Clinton's nominees faced rough going and many lower vacancies remained in place for Clinton's successor, George W. Bush to fill. The partisan divide over judicial appointments seems to have only deepened, with whichever party has been in the minority in Congress exerting whatever power it had, including the use of "holds" and the threat of filibusters in the Senate to prevent presidents George W. Bush and Barack Obama from getting many of their nominees approved, thus creating a backlogged federal court system due to the continued vacancies.

Factors in Making Nominations (Especially the Supreme Court)

Presidents look to a number of different characteristics in choosing whom they nominate to the courts, especially the Supreme Court. While purists would argue that the only thing that should matter is competence, there are other important considerations presidents need to take into account, primarily for political reasons. Generally speaking, however, the characteristic of competence ranks highest and is the chief limiting factor regarding Supreme Court nominees. What does it mean for nominees to be competent? While the Constitution does not require that justices of the Supreme Court be lawyers or have law degrees, a nominee would have to exhibit some other evidence of understanding of law, the Constitution, and legal theory. The "safe" indicators of competence beyond the simple one of having a law degree and/or admission to the bar to practice law include being a judge, a law professor, or an elected or appointed official. Recent practice has more heavily favored judges from lower courts as appointees.[3] Many justices of the Supreme Court also have had experience being a law clerk for another justice earlier in their careers.

Ranking just as high as competence on the list of attributes required of judicial nominees is the attribute of ethical behavior. Scandalous behavior of nominees to the Court would be disastrous, not just for the nominee's chances of confirmation, but also for the reputation of the appointing president. There was not sufficient evidence at the time, and in the eyes of the Senate Judiciary (and the Senate) to vote down George H. W. Bush's nomination of Clarence Thomas to the Court. However, the controversy over Thomas's alleged behavior, particularly with regard to his onetime clerk—Anita Hill[4]—certainly made the nomination ambiguous until the last minute and helped to advance Bush's falling approval rating.

The reality of politics over the course of our history has also made it necessary for presidents to consider issues of "balance" on the Court. Today we might think of ethnic, religious, gender, and, to some extent, ideological balance. Initially, the concern was more about geographic balance, to ensure that various regions of the country were represented on the Court. We have come back to that thinking somewhat, today. Some have grown concerned as we enter the second decade of the twenty-first century that the Court has too many members from the northeast, and the New York metropolitan area, in particular, to the virtual exclusion of other regions of the country. Generally speaking, however, this is of less concern in a mobile nation where people rarely stay as close to their birth location as they did much earlier in our history (Toobin 2009).[5]

Today, perhaps the most important factor in considering the balance on the Court is ethnicity/race. Presidents may talk about not considering such issues, but there is often great pressure on a president to make sure that certain ethnic or racial groups are represented, at least symbolically, on the Court. When George H. W. Bush was presented with the opportunity to replace Thurgood Marshall, the first black justice on the Court, he sought to avoid the controversy that would have ensued if he had chosen someone of another race. Instead, a great effort was made to find a conservative black nominee (Onwuachi-Willig 2005). There have been seats claimed by other ethnic and religious groups throughout our history, Italian Americans, the Irish, Catholics, Jews, and so on. In recent nomination discussions, other ethnic groups have been considered and we now have representation for Latinos (Associate Justice Sonya Sotomayor). There have also been Native Americans and Asian Americans who have been on the short list for recent vacancies, and it is possible that a member of one of those groups could be nominated to fill a vacancy in the near future (Schwartz 2011).

A most significant development in terms of this form of representational balance on the Court is with respect to gender. Since the women's rights movement of the late 1960s and 1970s, concern for the representation of women in all aspects of government has been a constant issue of discussion. A major breakthrough was made in the 1980s with Ronald Reagan's appointment of Sandra Day O'Connor as the first female associate justice in the Court's history. Following O'Connor's appointment there have been three subsequent nominations and confirmations of women to the Supreme Court—Ruth Bader Ginsburg, Sonya Sotomayor, and Elena Kagan (all of whom are serving on the Court as of this writing).[6]

Presidents rarely nominate someone to serve on the Court who does not share their political outlook. Most often, they nominate someone from their own party and usually of the same or similar ideological outlook. Occasionally, the outcome is a surprise for a president. Certainly, Eisenhower might not have nominated Earl Warren if he had known that Warren would end up presiding over what was, perhaps, the most liberal Court in our history. Similarly, Kennedy would likely have been surprised by the votes of Byron White, especially later in his career, as he moved fairly far to the ideological right on the Court. Sometimes it is the hidden ideology of the individual that causes the apparent change, but other times it is the application of the legal doctrine of *stare decisis* that makes justices of one ideological perspective appear quite different. For example, William Rehnquist had, for years, opposed the reading of rights to the accused and had, early in his career, advocated the overturning of the famous Miranda decision.[7] Yet, when presented with an opportunity to overturn the ruling, he voted to sustain it. He explained it with the logic that the rights had become so ingrained in our society and an integral part of our criminal procedure that to strike them down would create great havoc. Without an otherwise compelling reason to do so, Rehnquist felt that the Court's decision, though he felt it was wrong originally, should stand—the very essence of *stare decisis* (Toobin 2008).

Confirmation Process

All nominations by the president to the courts must be confirmed by the Senate. According to the US Senate website, 124[8] nominations to the Supreme Court have been confirmed by the Senate out of 160 made by the president. Only 12 of those 160 nominees were rejected outright by the Senate, with 10 other nominations having no action taken by the Senate. The president does not make nominations in a vacuum; he or she seeks out advice. The Department of Justice reviews the records of sitting judges in lower federal courts and in the higher-level state courts. They may also look to acknowledged constitutional scholars as potential nominees and thus add their names to the pool of those being considered.

Once the president's staff and the Justice Department have vetted the potential nominees and the president selects one, the name is forwarded to the Senate. The Senate has developed the practice of interviewing the nominees before its Judiciary Committee. The nominee is first interviewed informally by leaders of both parties in the Senate and then by the full-time staff of the Judiciary Committee. The staff interviews are used to develop questions for the members of the committee to ask the nominee once he or she appears for formal testimony. Usually these committee hearings are fairly routine and do not garner much of a viewing audience at all. Since the latter part of the twentieth century, there have been at least three occasions where the nominee and his history were controversial enough to warrant more media attention than usual. In the 1980s, Ronald Reagan's nomination of Robert Bork to the Supreme Court caused a stir because of Bork's controversial views on the law and constitutional theory. His nomination was eventually defeated by the Senate.

It took Reagan three tries to get it right. With his nomination of Bork having failed, some would argue that it was more a form of political payback.[9] Reagan then nominated Douglas Ginsburg (no relation to future Justice Ruth Bader Ginsburg) who seemed to be a more mainstream legal thinker and apparently acceptable to the Democratically controlled Senate. It soon became evident, however, that Ginsburg had his own problems. National Public Radio (NPR) Legal Correspondent, Nina Totenberg was among the first to uncover that Ginsburg had smoked marijuana as a college student and law student. Initial reaction was for a number of Washington insiders to step up and say that this was not a cause for concern or grounds to deny him the seat on the Court. After all, they said many of them had experimented with the drug while students. A bit later, it was revealed that he had smoked pot while he was a law professor. Many of the same Washington insiders went further and said that while this was not behavior that should be condoned, it still did not rise to the level of denying Ginsburg the seat. However, when it came out that he had *provided* pot to others at parties, members of the Senate thought it inappropriate to put a "drug dealer" on the highest Court. Ginsburg maintained his seat on the US Court of Appeals for the District of Columbia (Lauter and Healey 1987). The Supreme Court vacancy was eventually filled by Justice Anthony Kennedy.

Just a few years later, George H. W. Bush nominated Clarence Thomas to fill the vacancy created by the retirement of the first African American associate justice of the Supreme Court—Thurgood Marshall.[10] As mentioned earlier, Thomas's nomination, as distasteful as it was for many on the political left and those in the Civil Rights movement, seemed ready to sail through the Judiciary Committee. It was after the committee had seemingly wrapped up its work that details emerged of the staff investigation that had uncovered the allegations made against Thomas by Anita Hill. The committee reopened the hearings, after much public outcry, and what ensued was an embarrassing circus of events for all involved. In addition to prime-time televised hearings, others were seen first thing Saturday morning during the time usually dedicated to children's programming. Horrified parents had children exposed to graphic descriptions by Hill of many of the things Thomas was supposed to have said to her. Even after all of that, the committee voted to send the nomination to the floor, where by a very narrow margin Thomas was confirmed. The Bush White House supposedly rushed the swearing in of the newly confirmed justice to avoid the Senate being able to take back its advice and consent, so that if new evidence came about to change their minds, senators would have to initiate a more difficult impeachment proceeding against Thomas (Toobin 2008).

These controversies aside, evidence demonstrates that presidents most often get the nominee they wish. After the usually pro forma investigation and hearings, the Senate votes to grant its advice and consent to the nomination and the nominee, sworn in, becomes a justice of the Supreme Court.

Other Roles for Justices

Historically, presidents have put justices to work doing things other than merely interpreting the Constitution through the cases before them. In the very earliest days of our republic, George Washington would seek the advice of the justices on policy proposals and legislation to determine their constitutionality. That was a very short-lived practice as the Court soon saw it as having two basic flaws. First, it could be construed as a violation of the separation of powers. Second, and more importantly, the justices felt that they should not be prejudicing decisions they may have to make and thus should limit their rendering of an opinion to real cases and controversies. This would occur where there were two distinct parties to the case and at least one of them would have suffered, or be in imminent danger of suffering, harm. In addition, Washington made use of justices as high-ranking diplomats. Remember that in the earliest days of our nation's history, the Supreme Court met infrequently and thus the justices had much more free time than today.

More recently, after the assassination of John Kennedy, Lyndon Johnson asked Chief Justice Earl Warren to head a commission to investigate the circumstances of the assassination. The commission later came to be known by the name of its chair, the Warren Commission. When the commission concluded its investigation it issued a report—the Warren Commission Report—that found that John Kennedy's assassin, Lee Harvey Oswald, acted alone.

During the Nixon years, his appointee as chief justice, Warren Burger, was said to have regular informal conversations with the president about constitutional and legal matters. In fact, it was at Burger's urging that Nixon nominated Burger's fellow Minnesotan—Harold Blackmun. While not formal in any way, some saw this as an infringement on ethics (Woodward and Armstrong 1979).

The Court Decides Own Agenda

At the level of the Supreme Court, the justices set their own agenda and pick and choose among the cases that come before them. Most of the time cases come to the Court via a writ of certiorari, a request by a party to a case that a lower court be ordered to forward all of the documents for the case to the Supreme Court for review. In order that a writ of certiorari be granted, four of the nine justices must agree that the issues in the case are worthy of their scrutiny. This is commonly known as "The Rule of Four" (Epstein and Walker 2012).

The Court also has the authority to review the cases it chooses, particularly if the case involves acts of the other two branches of government. The case that is most often associated with the Court's assertion of the authority is *Marbury v. Madison* (1 Cranch 137, 1803), but it actually asserted the authority in a case seven years earlier in *Hylton v. U.S.* (3 Dall. 171, 1796). We remember *Marbury* more readily because though the Court asserted in its decision in *Hylton* that it had the power to review and declare unconstitutional the acts of the other branches, it did not exercise that power until *Marbury*.

At stake in *Marbury* was the status of several last-minute or eleventh-hour appointments to various positions in the federal government by Federalist Party president John Adams. In particular, Marbury had been appointed by Adams to the position of District of Columbia Justice of the Peace. The commission did not get delivered while Adams remained in office, the Secretary of State John Marshall having not completed the task of delivering the commissions. Two years later, with Marshall now the chief justice of the Supreme Court and Democratic-Republican James Madison in the position of secretary of state, the commissions were never delivered. Marshall was in a bit of a quandary since the case arose from his inability to deliver the commissions on time. Rather than rule in a way that would blame him, he got the Court to rule that the law Congress had passed granting the authority to make these appointments was unconstitutional. The outcome not only avoided embarrassment for Marshall, but also established even more firmly the assertion of judicial review the Court had made in *Hylton* (Epstein and Walker 2012).

An Independent Court?

The Supreme Court, and most of the federal judiciary for that matter, stands uniquely independent of the other branches of government. Once the president has made a nomination, and the Senate has confirmed the nominee, there is little real day-to-day cooperation. The Court is a reactive institution, not proactive as the other branches can be. The only other time there would be formal interaction between either of the other two branches and the Court is if there is an attempt to impeach a justice by Congress or the chief justice is called to preside over the impeachment trial of a president (or of a vice president).[11]

This structural arrangement, coupled with the lifetime tenure of all federal judges, makes for a rather independent judiciary. Certainly, presidents may publicly chastise the Court as Obama did at the 2011 State of the Union Address for their opinion in the *Citizens United v. Federal Elections Commission* (558 U.S. 310, 2010) case or Congress can, under its constitutional authority, limit the appellate jurisdiction of the Court, but both are rare circumstances indeed. Is the Court completely independent of the people? Many have argued that its unelected nature and the lifetime service of the justices make the judiciary a very undemocratic branch of the government.[12] The fact of this independence and lack of a democratic character, in theory, makes the justices answerable only to the law and the constitution, or at least their view of it.

Studies show mixed results (Segal, Timpone, and Howard 2000),[13] but the court is generally independent of direct influence, even from the people. Do the justices completely ignore public opinion? Not usually, unless public opinion is wildly out of sync with constitutional theory. Justices are as much a part of our society as any ordinary citizen and thus get a sense of what other citizens are thinking and feeling. If the Court is too often out of tune with society, it would negatively impact the public's support of the Court, and thus negatively impacting the prestige the Court has and uses to "enforce" its decisions. The public doesn't quite understand the nuances of constitutional law and jurisprudence, and as such, has little to say about most nominees, unless they end up as controversial as some we have already discussed. Later on however, the public often has an opinion about the nominees as more is revealed in the confirmation process, and much later as the justice's positions on issues of concern to the public become clearer. What kinds of appointments a president has made and which seats may be opening up are sometimes the subject of scrutiny by the punditry, but most often, the impact on electoral outcomes is relatively small.

What Power Does the Court Have on Its Own?

Left to its own devices, the Court has no army, no police, and no ability to physically enforce its own opinions. So, while the Court is independent in its ability to reach legal decisions, it must depend upon the president and Congress to provide the muscle for its enforcement capability. Andrew Jackson famously remarked on this, "[Chief Justice] John Marshall has made his decision, now let him enforce it."[14] The attitude of Jackson demonstrates rather keenly the lack of enforceability of the Court's actions without the assistance of the elected branches, particularly the executive branch. It is, after all, the executive branch that is charged with enforcing the law.

Think of occasions throughout our history when if presidents had not moved to enforce a decision of the Supreme Court, the outcome might have been quite different. If Eisenhower had not used US Marshalls and the federalized National Guard to enforce *Brown v. Board of Education* (347 U.S. 483, 1954) in Little Rock, Arkansas, or if Kennedy had not used US Marshalls to ensure the registration of James Meredith as the first black student at the University of Mississippi, would the Civil Rights Movement have taken a different course? Or in other cases, if presidents had not obeyed the order of the Court, what would have resulted if Truman had not returned the steel mills to private control?[15] What if Nixon had refused to follow the Court's instructions for him to turn over his recorded conversations with advisers during the Watergate investigation, what kind and magnitude of constitutional crises might we have had?

The Court and Presidential Power

Though a "coequal" branch of the government, in some ways the Court appears more powerful than the other two branches. That is, except under extreme circumstances, the Court has the final say over the interpretation of the law and the actions of the other two branches. Certainly, Congress may check the Court's power in the future by limiting its appellate jurisdiction and the president may change future decision making on the Court by appointment (remember the president needs vacancies to make this work). Those are post hoc powers, however, and cannot be used to change the course of the impact of the Court's decisions in real time. If you are Franklin Roosevelt, you might consider an attempt at packing the Court, but suffer the political fallout. The same is true of a blatantly political move by Congress to alter the Court or its jurisdiction—there will be political consequences. In this way, the Court at least appears to be more powerful. It is, as we have already seen, limited by its inability to enforce its decisions and must rely on the adherence to tradition and precedent by the other branches to exert any real power.

With this power, the Court has helped to define the boundaries of presidential power over the course of our history. Often, the Court will be more deferential to the president and an exertion by him or her of extra powers when we are in a time of war. Sometimes the tricky part is what the definition of war actually is. For example, we recall from our history, or watching reruns of *M.A.S.H.* on TV, the involvement of the United States in what is commonly referred to as the Korean War. During that conflict, there was a threat of a strike by the United Steel Workers against some of the most important steel mills in the country. A lengthy, widespread strike would have had a great negative impact on our ability to produce weapons for use in Korea.

In order to prevent the disruption of the production of steel, President Truman as commander in chief, seized the steel mills and ordered the workers to stay at their jobs. Youngstown Sheet and Tube Company sued, arguing that Truman, or any president, had no such power. Making a distinction between *de facto war* (what Korea was) and *de jure war* (a law declared by Congress under its constitutional power to do so), the Supreme Court ruled that the commander in chief power under a de facto war did not extend to seizing the steel mills (*Youngstown Sheet and Tube v. Sawyer*, 343 U.S. 579, 1952).

Many decisions of the Court have helped define the gray areas of presidential power. Among the most significant of these gray areas is that of "executive privilege." Roughly defined, it is the ability of a president to keep secret his or her interactions and conversations with advisers. It is argued that if the president's advisers must be concerned with how certain bits of advice, strategy, or speculation would look if made public in real time, they may restrict what they tell the president and thus deprive him or her of necessary analysis and information. There is no clear reference to the concept in the Constitution, the original document or any of the amendments.

The clearest delineation of the power comes from the Supreme Court's decision in *United States v. Nixon* (418 U.S. 683, 1974). In this crime-related proceeding, Nixon was asserting executive privilege with respect to compliance with a *subpoena duces tecum*—a subpoena to produce all relevant documents—that would require public disclosure of the recordings of all relevant communications between Nixon and his most senior advisers. Nixon claimed that these discussions related to national security matters and were, therefore, protected by executive privilege, but the political concern for him was that once in the public domain, these conversations might be used in any impeachment proceeding begun by the House of Representatives. The Court agreed with Nixon, in principle, but not on the specifics. While stating that it is necessary for presidents to be able to receive unedited, uncensored input from their advisers, such a right should not be construed to override other constitutionally protected rights, like those belonging to the accused in a criminal trial. The Court also argued that the judicial branch alone would be the final arbiter in determining what conversations—written or oral—between a president and his or her advisers could and should be protected from public scrutiny. As a result, the judge in the trial court, John J. Sirica, was given the authority to conduct an *in camera* inspection of the tapes of the conversations and to determine which ones might be relevant to the trial at hand. The result was the release of many incriminating conversations between Nixon and his most senior staff, including the infamous "smoking gun"[16] tape, which contained the recording of a conversation where Nixon ordered his two closest advisers to violate the law and use the Central Intelligence Agency (CIA) to thwart the Federal Bureau of Investigation (FBI) investigation into the break-in and cover up.

The Court has also played a role in determining how lower courts can be used to distract the president or limit his or her ability to perform official duties. The ability of ordinary citizens to sue the president has been a question that has arisen from time to time and has been addressed by the Court in recent decades. In *Nixon v. Fitzgerald* (457 U.S. 731, 1982), the Supreme Court decided that, with respect to the president's official duties, he or she could not be sued while still in office. In a controversial decision that would ultimately lead to an impeachment and trial of Bill Clinton, the Court ruled that while in office a president could be sued for actions committed prior to taking office. In this case, *Clinton v. Jones* (520 U.S. 681, 1997), the question was whether or not Paula Jones, an Arkansas state employee could sue the president for sexual harassment based on actions while Clinton was governor of Arkansas and *before* he was president of the United States. The Court ruled that the president could be sued for such actions, and that distractions created by defending himself were sufficiently small that they would not interfere with the performance of presidential duties.

During the presidency of George W. Bush, the Court further limited the ability of the president to act in an unchecked fashion. After the attacks on September 11th, 2001, much power accrued to the office of president, some by unilateral presidential action, and some by act of Congress. Bush came to power in a period where the power of the presidency had been in decline, so much so that after the Republican victories in the midterm elections of 1994, Bill Clinton at one point had to declare that he was still relevant (Kurtz 2010). The attacks, as horrific as they were, handed Bush (and anyone who might have been in office at the time) and his successors a huge bounty of new or renewed powers. Within a week of the attacks, in a rare showing of bipartisan patriotism, Congress passed one of two key pieces of legislation that would lead to greatly enhanced powers for an institution severely imperiled by both the domestic and international political environment. The Authorization for Use of Military Force (AUMF) provided that the president could "use all necessary and appropriate force against those nations, organizations, or persons" (AUMF in Epstein and Walker 2012) involved in the attacks.

With this power, President George W. Bush ordered US troops into Afghanistan to seek out and destroy the al Qaeda network and its Taliban supporters. Soon after US forces arrived, Afghan sympathizers captured American citizen (by birth) Yaser Hamdi. Hamdi was moved from one US military installation to another, denied access to legal counsel, and was charged as an "enemy combatant," a loosely defined legal category that carried no formal charges and thus none of the usual rights guaranteed to American citizens. Hamdi's father filed for a writ of *habeas corpus* against US secretary of Defense, Donald Rumsfeld. Hamdi's case hinged on the argument that the "necessary and appropriate force" authorized by the AUMF did not include suspension of *habeas corpus* and indefinite detention. A majority of the Court agreed with Hamdi and argued that the AUMF did not allow the executive to exercise powers that denied the accused the right to due process (*Hamdi v. Rumsfeld*, 542 U.S. 507, 2004). On the same day as the ruling in *Hamdi*, the Court handed down its ruling in *Rasul v. Bush* (542 U.S. 466, 2004), in which it rejected the administration's claims that the US courts had no jurisdiction over actions by US officials on foreign soil, namely the Guantanamo Naval Base in Cuba. Basing their reasoning on existing US statutes, a six-member majority reversed lower court rulings and agreed with the petitioners (Rasul and hundreds of other prisoners) that they had every right to access the courts for relief, particularly when agents of the government are in violation of US statutes or the Constitution. The day these two cases were decided by the court, June 28th, 2004, was neither a good day for the Bush administration nor for the expansion of executive power.

Having taken the ruling in *Hamdi* in stride and adapting to its requirement of providing even enemy combatants with due process, the Bush administration implemented a system of military tribunals, but did so by presidential edict. In a subsequent case, *Hamdan v. Rumsfeld* (548 U.S. 557, 2006), Hamdan, another enemy combatant, argued that the military tribunals created by executive order violated his constitutional right to due process. Once again, the Court narrowed the scope of executive authority and ruled that the particular military tribunals employed by the military at the direction of the Bush administration were unconstitutional in that the executive exceeded its authority. Tribunals could be used; it was just that they had to be authorized by Congress (Epstein and Walker 2012).

A Bulwark against Ambition

The relationship between the president and the judiciary, especially the Supreme Court, is not unlike an elaborate dance. The president appoints the judges/justices, with the advice and consent of the Senate, and hopes the appointee behaves in a more or less predictable manner. Generally, this predictable manner is to vote in ways consistent with the president's outlook on the interpretation of the Constitution. At the same time, the Court seeks to avoid the wrath of presidents bent on structural change to achieve their goals (Franklin Roosevelt's pack the Court scheme) or public admonishment (Obama's shaming of the Court at a State of the Union Address).

The Court remains however, the one bulwark against an overambitious executive. True, the Court sometimes allows questionable actions to slide while the country is at war or in a state of unrest, but generally will come back to scold the offending president once circumstances have settled. If not for a "vigilant" Court, Truman might have nationalized the steel mills; Nixon may have successfully covered up his involvement in the Watergate cover-up and survived the impeachment process; and George W. Bush may have extended executive authority such that it diminished the constitutional rights of the accused.

Chapter 17

The President and Policymaking: Domestic, Economic, and Foreign

"The term *public policy* always refers to the actions of government and the intentions that determine those actions. Making policy requires choosing among goals and alternatives, and choice always involved intention" (Cochran et al. 2006, 1). For our purposes, public policy and the making of it, is about the intentions of the president and about his or her choices among goals and alternatives. It's about decision making, but it's more than decision making; it's also about the follow-through. In the preceding chapters we have discussed the electorate's choice between candidates—an alternate way of saying a choice between one set of preferences and another—the character or personality of presidents, how they get advice, how they interact with other political actors, and the tools available to them. In other words, we have discussed how presidents make decisions—how they go about making policy.

Public policy, regardless of its location in the arena of domestic policy, economics, or foreign policy, involves making decisions about the formation of policy and how that policy gets implemented. It is the president's relationship with his or her advisers and Congress that determines what policy decisions are made and how they are made. It is the president's relationship with the judiciary and the bureaucracy that determines how policy gets implemented.

We have already seen how Franklin Roosevelt created the presidential bureaucracy that we know today as the Executive Office of the President (EOP) to manage the larger federal bureaucracy created to implement his regulatory and relief policies in response to the Great Depression. Some have argued that Richard Nixon's creation of a formal office of domestic policy in the EOP institutionalized much of the work begun by Roosevelt and every president since Nixon has had some formal office with similar responsibilities (Warshaw 1997). The same could be said of the impact of the creation of the Council of Economic Advisers and the National Economic Council in the area of economic policy, which has led to the current mechanism for economic policy making in the White House. It is also true of the usurpation of many aspects of foreign policy by the National Security Council (NSC) to avoid the slower mechanistic approach of the Foreign Service in the State Department.

This is all part of a trend to bring policy making—formation—more closely under the control of those most loyal to the president. It coincides with the overall growth of the presidency at least as far back as Franklin Roosevelt. Certainly, earlier in history, policy making, such as it was, was kept much closer to the president. Recall Lincoln's cabinet and the descriptions of a rather tight-knit group of decision makers during the conduct of the Civil War (Goodwin 2006). One would be hard pressed to imagine that Thomas Jefferson had a vast bureaucracy or an open process while deciding whether or not to make the Louisiana Purchase. As the country grew, and the government's mission along with it, it is easy to imagine presidents feeling as though they were at the controls of an ever-increasingly large ship, but the controls no longer functioned. Franklin Roosevelt took the steps necessary to repair the existing controls and create new ones where needed.

This is the crux of the individualized aspect of the presidency. Each president, with his or her unique combination of worldview, character, politics, and place in time changes the office he or she inhabits, no matter how subtle or grand, for all those who will follow.

Domestic Policy

Through both law and practice, and for good or bad, the president has become the nation's principal domestic policy maker. There is an old saying, usually used in relation to the budget that "the president *pro*poses and the Congress *dis*poses."[1] This pithy quote encapsulates the essence of budgetary politics and much of domestic policy as well. Our society has come to expect that most major policy initiatives, like the budget, will begin as proposals by the president and that Congress will then deal with those proposals in its own fashion. It will add to, subtract from, or outright dismiss the initiative made by the president. Naturally, because the president is not a member of either chamber of the legislature he cannot actually introduce his proposals and must have the cooperation of at least one member of Congress in order to get presidential initiatives any kind of hearing at all.

Presidents have not always been this assertive. In fact, throughout our history presidents often merely made judgments about the actions of Congress. At first presidents would make use of the veto power to prevent acts of Congress they believed were unconstitutional from becoming law. In a more reactive mode, presidents would later judge acts of Congress, not just on their constitutionality, but also on whether or not they thought the acts to be good policy.

The more aggressive, initiator role is much more a twentieth-century phenomenon, but as we saw in the discussion in chapter 2 of the history of the presidency, there are always exceptions to the rule. Certainly, some early presidents provide such exceptions. Jefferson's purchase of the Louisiana Territory from France and Lincoln's Emancipation Proclamation are but two such examples. It is far harder to come up with a pre-twentieth century example of domestic policy initiative by presidents than it is to find a more passive, reactive president since 1900. To be sure, some presidents since 1900 have taken on the more traditional role; Coolidge, Hoover, Eisenhower, Ford, and (it could be argued) Obama are the exceptions.

While developing as early as the administration of Teddy Roosevelt, this domestic policy making role was a consequence of social, economic, and political problems requiring federal solutions. These forces or problems converged under the administration of Teddy's cousin, Franklin Roosevelt. It was Franklin Roosevelt's response to the Great Depression that firmly established this leadership role on domestic policy for himself and all future presidents. It was under Truman, however, that the process truly became institutionalized such that Congress came to expect fully drafted legislation from the White House whenever the president would make a policy proposal.

Changes in the Political System Make the Task More Difficult

A more assertive Congress and media in the aftermath of Vietnam, Watergate, and the many scandals that followed have made this role both more necessary and difficult. The president is the center of the media spotlight and the American political stage. As a result, there are higher expectations of him or her. At the same time, Congress has asserted itself far more than in the past in opposing presidential initiatives, especially those aimed at domestic issues. In more recent days, a highly charged partisan political environment has exacerbated this assertion and opposition.

As a result of these changes, presidents need to employ all of the strategies and skills we've been discussing thus far. A president, to be successful in the domestic policy arena, will need to assure the public that there is a constitutional basis for the proposed initiative. This can be a problem, as it was for Obama during the health care debate in 2009 and 2010. Many critics of the proposed reform to health insurance argued that there was no constitutional foundation for the government to regulate the health insurance industry in the manner proposed and that mandating the purchase of insurance was not within the constitutional grant of power under the commerce clause.[2] Certainly, the president has the constitutional grant of authority to recommend legislation to Congress and this is the overall foundation of his or her right to take a leading role in domestic policy, if not the lead role. Of more concern to the president's opposition and some of the public, however, is whether or not the proposed legislation would have a strong constitutional footing.[3]

Constitutionality aside, to get the program approved by Congress and to get Congress to allocate money to fund the implementation of the program, the president must be a political actor. He or she will have to mobilize the appropriate policy coalitions, in other words, to reach out to the lobbyists and the relevant members of the public for support. In order to accomplish this, the program must be properly packaged to be appealing to as many as possible and to blunt the opposition to it. Often this entails making use of opinion polling and other market research techniques (e.g., focus groups) to determine the right kind of wording to make the proposal the most appealing and to avoid the opposition being able to define the proposal in the most negative light. Regardless of what you as the reader might think about the health care reform legislation and the debate that preceded its passage, it should be easy to see that the "package" was not skillfully crafted enough to avoid its redefinition by the opposition. We recall the debate now as one about health care reform, which allowed its opponents to argue that this was a government intrusion into the relationship between patients and providers. What the proposal was mostly concerned with, however, was the provision of insurance for those who did not already have it and with making health care more affordable and accessible. Perhaps much of the most heated opposition to the proposal could have been defused if it had been more appropriately packaged as health *insurance* reform instead of health *care* reform.

In the overall scheme of things, for the larger view of his or her policies or legislative agenda, a president needs to do two things. First, he or she must establish a long-term national perspective. A set of policies that stem from a particular ideological perspective could be helpful here, especially with respect to mobilizing support. Second, a president needs to set priorities among his or her favored programs. The question to be asked by a new administration is "which of these goals do we seek to accomplish first?" Immediately after that, the administration would need to ask themselves what obstacles there might be to achieving their policy objectives. Once again, when Barack Obama came into office in January 2009, the nation's priorities had changed dramatically. While most of the discussion during the Democratic primary season had been about health care, the economy crashed in the fall of 2008 changing the focus of the fall campaign and the necessities of governing come January 2009. Economic recovery had moved to the top of the agenda for both parties, though they differed with regard to how it might be achieved. Obama's priority of reforming health insurance had to wait for another year and a half, and even then, he was criticized for not paying attention to the need to create jobs.

In setting out priorities, presidents often use two mechanisms to establish their agendas in the press, the Congress, and in the minds of the people. The first mechanism is the opportunity every elected president has to set forth the overall goals for his or her administration through the use of the inaugural address. When delivering this speech, presidents need to find the right mix of "lists" of objectives and soaring rhetoric. Too much in the way of lists and the speech is boring and gets little attention. Too much soaring language and the speech has no real substance. The second mechanism available to presidents is the annual State of the Union Address to Congress. Between the presidencies of John Adams and Woodrow Wilson, presidents didn't really take advantage of the opportunity presented by the State of the Union Address. Wilson was the first since Adams to truly use the State of the Union Address to lay out his agenda.

One of the early efforts to provide the president with help in taming the bureaucracy (see chapter 11) was the creation of the EOP and the movement of the Bureau of the Budget (BOB) from the Treasury Department to the White House. With this move, BOB took on a much broader range of responsibilities. Rather than just coordinating the budget requests of other executive branch agencies and fitting them into the president's overall policy agenda, BOB now also had responsibility for ensuring that bills under consideration in Congress would have some measure of whether or not the administration found the legislation to comport with its views. One could argue that BOB was now playing the role of the legislative clearinghouse for the White House. Even Congress seemed to find this role useful, for it enabled members of Congress to know with ease whether or not the president supported a particular piece of legislation. BOB was also able to provide recommendations to the president about the "fit" of proposals coming from Congress with the president's priorities.

Certainly, this clearinghouse role was useful to both presidents and Congress. A bill that was given "the presidential seal of approval" could more easily garner support in Congress from members of the president's party. BOB's more expanded role helped *within* the executive branch as well. Even before it moved to the EOP, BOB was able to facilitate communication between executive branch agencies and provide a potential forum for dispute resolution. Those roles were further enhanced by the Bureau's new location and by the fact that it now reported directly to the president.

Today, these functions are performed by BOB's successor agency, the Office of Management and Budget (OMB). The function of providing the president advice on supporting bills has been more firmly established and an OMB recommendation to support a bill is accepted by the president most of the time. This is understandable, given that vetoes are more highly politicized and the president's most senior advisers need to take many more factors into account. For example, OMB may look more exclusively at the merits of the bill, but the political environment and the likelihood of an override in Congress, may play a larger role in the president's decision to veto or not to veto.

Recent Attempts at Organizing Domestic Advice

Just as Franklin Roosevelt sought to bring some order to the organizational chaos of the executive branch, many more presidents who have followed him have sought to do so as well. The institution these more recent presidents inherited, while certainly not as unwieldy as the one Roosevelt inherited, has grown even more since Roosevelt's time. It is not just that presidents need to organize the executive branch for the purposes of controlling the output, but that the process by which presidents are advised and information flows needs to be structured such that the president is getting all the appropriate advice necessary for carrying out his or her duties.

In chapter 11 we discussed Nixon's attempts to create a "super cabinet" in order to gain more control over the executive branch. In addition to that attempt, which failed before Congress, Nixon made use of what he called a "Domestic Council," which was a group of relevant cabinet officers who would in theory coordinate administration domestic policy. The council was run by Nixon's chief domestic policy adviser, John Ehrlichman. Carter took a different approach by creating an office of Domestic Policy, staffed completely by EOP employees. Reagan continued Carter's approach of keeping the process of domestic policy advising within the EOP with the creation of the Office of Policy Development. No matter what form of organization a president chooses, it can be seen as a reflection of his or her personality and the politics of the times. For example, Carter as an outsider to the Washington political scene and perhaps unsure of himself in dealing with those who had been around Washington for a long time, chose to keep domestic policy advice closer to home.

Move Quickly, Stay Focused

In developing and implementing domestic policy, presidents need to take an approach similar to that which they take with Congress. Naturally, this makes sense in that the president would need congressional cooperation in order to gain passage of any legislative package stemming from decisions about domestic policy. As in dealing successfully with Congress, presidents need to focus by limiting the number of policy items dealt with at one time. Reagan was successful in this respect. Presidents also need to move quickly, taking advantage of the honeymoon period soon after their inauguration or of any boost in their approval ratings. Jimmy Carter was a bit unfocused, was looking to accomplish too much and as a result did not take full advantage of the opportunity presented to him early on in his administration.

Similarly, as in dealing with Congress, the media, and the public, presidents need to develop a long-range view, determining how this will impact the public in a few years and in generations to come. They also need to ensure that their approach contains a national perspective and that their domestic program does not appear to favor too narrow a slice of the American people. Presidents, in presenting their domestic programs also must strike a balance between too much and too little detail. If they provide too much detail, their proposals could be subject to lengthy nit-picking. If they provide too little detail, criticism will be focused on the lack of substance in their program. If more detail is necessary to "sell" the proposal, the delivery should be left to subordinates so that the president can take the higher ground, to demonstrate the long-range view and the national perspective. Last but not least, presidents should avoid the appearance of asking for too much and avoid the "laundry list" of things they'd like to accomplish. In the end, presidents have what is their equivalent to Congress's elastic clause, their "faithful execution" of the laws clause.[4] This provides them with some wiggle room in the interpretation of the laws passed by Congress to make minor "corrections" in the direction of their originally intended policy.

Economic Policy Making—It's Still the Economy, Stupid[5]

Closely related to the area of domestic policy is that of economic policy. Some may see economic policy as one part of overall domestic policy or as more closely tied to foreign policy. Certainly, in a global society as we live in today, economic policy is intertwined with foreign policy. At the same time, however, economic policy is a major component of domestic policy that deals with unemployment, inflation, the debt, tax policy, and so forth. With this straddling of both domestic and foreign policy, it is appropriate, therefore, that a separate section be devoted to it and that section be located between those dealing with domestic policy and foreign policy, respectively.

The president's role in economic policy is both substantive and symbolic. Yes, the president can have an impact on the economy; it just might not be easily perceived by voters. The symbolic role is centered on what the public does, in fact, perceive about the president's impact on the economy. Voters hold the president responsible for the health of the economy, but as we saw earlier with our discussion of presidential approval, there is an asymmetric effect. We hold the president accountable for the poorly performing economy, but take our time in rewarding him or her for the economy's recovery. This, recall, was the congratulation/rationalization effect where we blame the president if we lose our job, but give credit to ourselves if we suddenly find ourselves back to work. We also tend to hold the president's party responsible for the actions of the president. We saw this evidence in our earlier discussion of the performance of the president's party in midterm elections.

How Is the Economy Managed?

There are two major tools available for the "management of the economy." *Fiscal policy* deals with the relationship between revenues and expenditures. This was the focus of the debate over the raising of the debt limit throughout much of 2011. The two parties differed about the economic impacts of tax hikes as opposed to cuts in spending. *Monetary policy* is primarily under the purview of the Federal Reserve Board (the Fed) and deals with the supply and price of money. Similar to the debt limit debate, monetary policy has also been an integral part of the debate over how to climb out of the economic recession that began in late 2008. While the elected branches of the government haggled over the correct fiscal approach to ending the crisis *and* to lowering the nation's debt, the Fed took steps to control inflation. This is sometimes the result of other efforts to get an economy moving again. The Fed also engaged in a practice more recently referred to as quantitative easing (QE) or adding to the money supply. Some have criticized these efforts by the Fed, but it is what the body has done for decades. QE is accomplished by the Fed buying back notes that represent consumer investment in the government, and by doing so adding more money back into the economic system.

Fiscal policy is really a more recent tool for the federal government to apply in attempts to manage the economy. It is, in essence, the application of budgetary policy to attempt to influence the performance of the economy. Prior to the 1930s and without the coordination and massive government intervention newly available to President Franklin Roosevelt,[6] revenue and expenditure decisions were made without much relation to one another and the budget was too small to have much of an impact on the economy. Much of the information available to the government about the economy was not very reliable and tended more toward theoretical thinking rather than concrete application. Since the 1930s, the federal budget has run around 25 percent of GDP (and was near 50% during World War II) and we adopted a more Keynesian approach to our economic policy where we generally spend more money during economic downturns. The problem has been that we have only very infrequently applied the other side of Keynesian economics and run surpluses during prosperity.

Monetary policy, however, as noted above deals with the supply and price of money. Economists have many definitions of the word "money," but for our purposes, it will be that which is readily available for spending. This means money that is liquid, and can be used for purchases. Monetary policy is a very old issue and is often at the root of why governments exist. Governments have always controlled the supply of money, both in terms of the amount of money available for use and the cost of obtaining more. What is this cost of money? Generally speaking, it is the interest you pay to borrow money.

In the United States, much of the supply and cost of money is controlled by the Fed. "The Fed" is responsible for the buying and selling of bonds, setting the required reserves that member banks must have on hand to meet customer demands, and for setting the interest rate paid by member banks for money borrowed to meet short-term obligations. The first two of these responsibilities help to regulate the supply of money. If the Fed sells bonds to consumers, it has taken that money consumers had in their pockets and, for the time being, has removed it from circulation, thus decreasing the supply of money available. If the Fed buys bonds back from consumers it puts more money back into the pockets of those consumers, which could then be used to purchase goods and services in the marketplace. Similarly, if the Fed increases the amount of money member banks must have on hand (figuratively sitting in their vaults) to meet potential customer demand that money is out of circulation and thus decreases the money supply. The interest member banks pay to borrow from the Federal Reserve System, known as the discount rate, is set by the Fed's Open Market Committee and in turn establishes the rates its member banks charge consumers for loans. The initial impact is on the prime rate, which is the rate banks charge their biggest and best customers, with a trickle-down effect on mortgages, car loans, and credit cards.

The Federal Reserve System

The Fed is a seven-member board with each member appointed for a 14-year term so that one member is appointed every two years. As is the case with most other presidential appointments, the Senate must confirm the appointment. The appointment is nonrenewable except if the appointment is to fill an unexpired term. The chair and the vice chair of the board are selected by the president from among the members of the board and serve a renewable term of four years (Federal Reserve Board of Governors n.d.).

With 12 Federal Reserve Banks and twice that many branch offices (Federal Reserve Board of Governors 2005),[7] the Fed operates in much the same way as many independent regulatory commissions and does not need the approval of either elected branch for it to take action. It is still, however, subject to the oversight of Congress. The Fed was created with the passage of the Federal Reserve Act of 1913, which was signed into law by Woodrow Wilson in December of 1913. In addition to the powers already mentioned, the Fed is at least partly responsible for regulating the nation's banking system and for regulating the actions of the banks that are members of the Federal Reserve System.

One of the main purposes of the Federal Reserve System is to ensure that member banks are safe from failure. Near the end of the nineteenth century and in the early twentieth century, a number of banks failed when they were unable to meet demands on their deposits made by wary customers seeking to get hold of their money during economic downturns. All banks chartered by the Office of the Comptroller of the Currency in the Treasury Department are considered national banks and are automatically members of the Federal Reserve System. A fairly large number of state chartered banks may, and do choose, to join the system.

A Third Tool

A third tool available to presidents, but seldom used, is direct wage and price controls. Throughout history, governments have experimented with the use of wage and price controls as a means of checking inflation while dealing with another economic or social problem, the solution to which might set off a round of inflation at an undesirable time. In the United States, wage and price controls have been used in times of war to ensure that short supplies created by the focus of manufacturing on war-related good do not force prices on necessities too high. Richard Nixon was the first president to employ wage and price controls during peacetime and did it to keep inflation under control while his administration dealt with rising unemployment.

The debate over the utility of wage and price controls, or any government regulation of economic activity, is at least as old as governments themselves. Some scholars have made the argument that the most legitimate reason for the existence of government is when private markets fail. Others might argue that governments exist only as referees in disputes arising from markets. Either way, government regulation of economic activity is a virtual given, the real argument being about the scope of the jurisdiction and the strength of the regulator. Even those who would take a looser approach to the scope issue might debate the utility of wage and price controls.

Wage and price controls generally consist of some government rule or law that freezes wages and prices or caps the growth of wages and prices, thus setting in effect, an artificial rate of inflation. Here, in the United States, Congress often passes a law granting the president the power to issue wage and price controls within statutorily established boundaries, which could include an outright freeze on wages and prices. As consumers, the public may love the fact that the government has limited the ability of prices to rise too quickly. As workers, however, the public probably is not quite as supportive of the government's actions since it does not generally allow wages to rise any faster than prices.

"Jawboning"[8]

Presidents may also make use of what Teddy Roosevelt called "the Bully Pulpit" to try to bring about more desirable economic behavior without the need for outright government intervention. This would be where a president, rather than seek extra economic powers from Congress or use what powers currently exist, would talk to the American people and ask union members to accept less in the way of pay hikes or ask business to keep prices as low as possible. Gerald Ford took this path in the mid-1970s with his Whip Inflation Now (WIN) campaign. The government set targets for wages and prices and asked workers and businesses not to exceed those targets. The unsuccessful campaign included lapel buttons and a campaign song, much like a campaign for a candidate might (Miller Center 2012).

Fearing that the attacks of 9/11 would spread fear and Americans would stay home, thus creating an economic crisis on top of the security crisis, George W. Bush urged Americans to go about their daily lives and participate in the economy, which some interpreted as "go shopping." Whether poorly interpreted or delivered, the comment had some merit. If consumers stay home, nothing gets purchased, inventory remains in storage, workers get laid off, and the economy spins into recession. Though nowhere near the level of tragedy, one can see a similar if smaller effect of bad winter weather on the holiday shopping season.[9]

The Role of the President

Naturally, presidents will emphasize different things in attempting to manage the economy based on their particular, partisan outlook. Democratic presidents will tend to focus on maintaining lower levels of unemployment and Republican presidents will tend to focus on keeping inflation lower. These differing emphases stem from their respective support coalitions; the Democrats generally supported by organized labor and the working class and Republicans generally supported by the more affluent and the investment class.

So too, the president's advisers will tend to be from a similar perspective. A Democratic president for example, will likely appoint to key positions on his economic team individuals who agree with him or her and have job creation (perhaps through government stimulus of the economy) as a key concern. Republican presidents, being more concerned with their supporters being able to invest are going to surround themselves with individuals who agree that keeping the cost of money low (interest rates) so that it may be invested and return a much higher profit is a priority. The individuals who sit on the Council of Economic Advisors and the National Economic Council will generally share the president's economic outlook.[10]

These perspectives generally fall into two main economic schools of thought: Keynesians and Monetarists. Keynesians tend to be what we think of when we think in terms of contemporary liberals. Risking oversimplification, it could be said that Keynesians tend to emphasize fiscal policy and are willing to go into deficit spending during times of economic downturn in order to stimulate the economy.[11] At the same time, however, they would tend to argue that during prosperity the government should run surpluses as a hedge against future downturns or to pay off debt from the last one.[12]

Monetarists tend to be more politically conservative and follow the general principles advanced by Milton Friedman. In recent debates, however, many more polarized conservatives would take to citing the many works of Ayn Rand over that of Friedman. These individuals are more generally skeptical of social welfare programs of any kind. They advocate smaller government and, by extension, less government spending, seeing it as a contributing factor to inflation. Any government intervention in the money supply should be based on strict rules and not left to the discretion of the central bank—The Fed—as the tendency might be to misuse the discretion or misinterpret conditions, either of which would be further injurious to the economy. Monetarists believe in the sanctity of the free market and seek to limit the government's role in the market. For monetarists, during the economic downturn that began in 2008, the Fed would not have been able to make what they would consider arbitrary guesses about how much money to inject into the marketplace, but the Fed would have had preexisting rules by which their actions would have been regulated. This would create greater predictability of government behavior, one of the leading goals of monetarists.

In addition to these two main schools of economic thought, the 1980s brought about another brand of policy—supply side economics. During the Reagan years, the policies that resulted from this theoretical approach were derisively referred to as "trickle-down economics." What this implied was that as those at the top of the economic hierarchy benefitted from government economic policy, the benefits would trickle down the pyramid to benefit even those in lower economic classes.[13] One of the early proponents of supply side economics was economist Arthur Laffer, who argued that the relationship between government revenue and marginal tax rates[14] could be described by an inverted parabola, where once a theorized optimal tax rate was achieved every subsequent increase in taxes would actually result in a decrease in government revenue. The underlying argument here was that beyond that point of marginal tax rates, the incentive to produce—create supply—would diminish because the suppliers would see a decreasing return on their investment. Thus, with tax rates lowered to a point lower than the optimal tax rate, government revenues would increase. The graphic image of this parabolic relationship came to be known as the "Laffer Curve." This approach is also based on the concept that supply will create its own demand[15] (Laffer 2004).

Can the President Control the Economy?

One could think of the ability of the president to control the economy—regardless of his or her theoretical perspective—as similar to trying to push a large glob of Jell-O up a greased incline. There's almost no telling which way it will go, but you *might* eventually get it to the top. Why would this be the case? First and foremost, economists cannot and do not agree on what makes an economy move in which direction. Second, it is very hard to predict economic events for any number of reasons. Economic activity is tied to human events and nature, neither of which is easily predicted. It is hard to tell what products and services might be in demand in the future. It is also hard to tell what natural event might impact on supplies of natural resources or interrupt delivery routes. Sometimes the two types of events come together to create an even greater impact on the economy. For example, during Hurricane Katrina and its immediate aftermath in 2005, the price of gasoline jumped considerably. Part of this increase was due to the closing of oil wells in the Gulf of Mexico and the subsequent disruption of distribution of the product, but a substantial part of the increase was human in construct, created by speculation about what the supply of crude oil was, and might be in the near future.

Supplies of gasoline could be limited by much more external factors than domestic speculators. Actions of other countries, whether in collusion to raise prices—by the Organization of Petroleum Exporting Countries (OPEC), for example—or to engage in war, might disrupt distribution. Certainly, these are beyond the normal activity in open markets and are hard to predict and, thus, include in a predictive model of economic performance.

So too, politics plays an important role in the lack of long-term predictability and control of the economy. Change in political outlook from a party that advocates Keynesian principles to one advocating monetarist principles has an impact on the economy, both through direct change in policy and in terms of the human element of speculation and investment. Naturally, each president will seek to move economic policy in the direction advocated by his or her party. Monetarists will tend to concentrate their efforts at control through the appointments process and fill vacancies both in agencies that report directly to the president and those with a more independent mandate with individuals of like mind.[16] Keynesians may be more likely to seek overall policy changes that achieve their goal involving government investment in infrastructure and social welfare policies.

Which school of thought is correct? Individuals, both those trained as economists and members of the public, have their own view. Politicians advocate for policies from a particular school of economic thought based on the constituencies they serve and how the policies generated by those theories impact those constituencies. The last presidents to have accomplished a balanced budget, and actually run a surplus, are Eisenhower, Johnson,[17] and Clinton. Does this say anything about whether Keynesian economics is superior to monetarism or supply side economics? Certainly, the three presidents served during a time when Keynesian theory was a bit more dominant than monetarism,[18] but Clinton was balanced by a more monetarist Congress. Certainly, fiscal policy (Keynesian tools) is generally easier and quicker to use, budgetary politics notwithstanding. Aside from lengthy debates over various parts of the budget, presidents can do a number of other things that have small but important impacts on the economy. The chief executive can put some money back into the economy by paying the government's bills early or can speed up or slow down payments to certain entitlement recipients (Tufte 1978).

The President and Foreign Policy: A New World Order?

Foreign policy is the area of presidential power that one would think would give the president the most latitude and be subject to the least restriction on his or her power. The Constitution after all, says that the president shall be the commander in chief of the armed forces, shall have the power to make treaties, and appoint and receive ambassadors. In other words, the president shall have all powers necessary to conduct the foreign affairs of the United States. Yet, as we have seen (and will see further in this chapter), these powers are often limited by some joint power of Congress. Also, as we will see, Congress, while on occasion limiting the scope of presidential power, is generally more respectful of the president's power in this area of policy than in economic or domestic policy.

Sources of and Limits on Presidential Power in Foreign Policy

As indicated above, the source of presidential power in foreign policy is firmly rooted in the Constitution. He or she is the commander in chief, appoints and receives ambassadors, and negotiates treaties. It is also true that the president is the one individual, supposedly, with the greatest access to information necessary to the conduct of foreign and military affairs. Foreign policy is one area of government activity where there is something of an agreement, and perception, that there is a need for greater central direction and control. It has often been said, "politics ends at the water's edge."[19]

Compared to domestic and economic policy issues, foreign policy involves much less in the way of interest group activity. Certainly, military budgets and contracts do involve a high level of such activity, but most of what constitutes interest group activity in this area is based more on ethnic ties. US policy in the Middle East, particularly with regard to Israel, for example, does have important domestic consequences. The American Israeli Political Action Committee (AIPAC) watches the actions of elected officials carefully and influences its members to support or oppose politicians based on their votes regarding US–Israeli relations. Campaign contributions from members of this group are vitally important to many who seek election or reelection to the House or the Senate.

Additionally, there is a more natural role for the president here as he or she is seen as the living symbol of the nation, the embodiment of our government. To use an old science fiction-like example, if an alien craft from a distant planet were to land in the middle of your street and the occupants emerged asking to be taken to your leader, you'd likely direct them to 1600 Pennsylvania Ave, Washington, DC—the residence of the president of the United States. It is the president we all think of first as our leader, and it is the president to whom foreign powers look as our leader.

Naturally, Congress is empowered by the Constitution with certain powers that overlap with those of the president and thus limit his or her ability to conduct foreign affairs in an unfettered fashion. First among these shared powers is the advise and consent power, which applies to appointments and treaties alike. Congress also has the power of the purse in approving expenditures to fund the president's foreign policy initiatives. Members of Congress may be more motivated if the issues have a greater impact on domestic politics, as indicated above or involving trade issues or immigration policy.

Perhaps a more significant limitation on presidential power in the area of foreign policy is one that is rather controversial and now somewhat questionable.

In 1973, in response to what Congress saw as presidential overreaching in the use of military force in Southeast Asia, the War Powers Act (or Resolution)[20] was passed over Nixon's veto in an attempt to limit the president's ability to use troops without checks and balances. The Act requires that a president notify Congress within 48 hours of the engagement of US troops in hostilities. With no further action by Congress, the use of troops must stop in 60 days, but the president has 30 more days to conduct an orderly withdrawal of the troops. So, without congressional action to extend the time, troops may be engaged in foreign hostile action for a total of 92 days (don't forget to count the 48 hours up front).

The problem with the War Powers Act is that it may, in fact, be unconstitutional. In the case of *INS v. Chadha* (462 U.S. 919, 1983), the Supreme Court ruled that laws that include what amounts to a veto of executive action by a single chamber of the legislature violates the presentment clause of the Constitution. The presentment clause requires that all bills passed by the House and the Senate must be presented to the president for his or her signature or rejection. A single chamber veto clearly violates that process. The Court did not directly address the issue of those laws that contained vetoes of executive action by both chambers, but did cast doubt on the legitimacy of those vetoes as well. It could be argued that neither the executive branch nor Congress wishes to really challenge the constitutionality of the War Powers Act because they are afraid of a Washington political environment without it as a guide. The Act has never formally been invoked by either branch of the government, but presidents have frequently sought approval from Congress (either before or after) for military action. In 2011, President Barack Obama took a great deal of heat for not seeking more formal congressional approval for the use of air power in aid of the rebels in Libya.

One other tool that gives presidents much latitude in the foreign policy arena is the ability to negotiate so-called executive agreements. These are similar to treaties, but do not require congressional advice and consent. On the down side for the president, executive agreements also do not carry the force of law as treaties do. Naturally, executive agreements cannot be law because they do not pass through a legislative process of any kind as treaties do. Technically, such agreements expire with the terms of office of the national leaders who negotiated the agreements. However, some leaders will continue to honor some executive agreements negotiated by their predecessors in order to maintain continuity in foreign policy. After the tension between the branches generated by the Vietnam War and Watergate in the early 1970s, Congress passed legislation requiring the president to *notify* the legislature of any agreements entered into.

The Two Presidencies

Political scientist Aaron Wildavsky (1966) was among the first political scientists to note the existence of the "two presidencies" phenomenon. As explained earlier, this is a circumstance where the president tends to get more support in Congress on votes related to foreign policy than he or she does on votes in the domestic policy area. Wildavsky studied votes in Congress between 1948 and 1964 in examining the phenomenon, and found that during that time the president won about 70 percent of the time in Congress.

As we discussed in chapter 15, the overall impact of the two presidencies has diminished somewhat over time and the president is less successful today than 40 years ago. Two factors contribute to this decline. First, Congress by way of reforms during the 1970s and the following decades has been restructured to be far more decentralized than in the past. Because there are more committees and subcommittees, chairs of those committees would naturally have a greater stake in any legislation. There are more caucuses of members to reflect areas of member interest and perhaps contact points for interest groups. Second, since the Vietnam and Watergate era, Congress has been more assertive and more frequently sought to limit presidential exercise of power across the board, including foreign policy. Since that time, Congress has passed the War Powers Act, many pieces of legislation attempting to regain control of the budgetary process, and attempted to impeach one president and did impeach (but did not remove) another. This assertiveness backslid a bit during the years George W. Bush was president and a Congress controlled by his party was less combative with their own president.

Importance of Foreign Policy

Since World War II, every president has been deeply concerned with foreign policy. Certainly, failures in the conduct of foreign policy have the ultimate possibility of resulting in war, whereas domestic policy does not. It is in this area of politics where most presidents seem to seek to make their mark on history. Carter will, regardless of his other shortcomings, always be remembered for starting the Middle East peace process with the Camp David Accords. Both Bushes will be remembered for their foreign policy ventures, particularly in the Persian Gulf, but the elder Bush is more likely to be remembered more favorably in this regard. Ronald Reagan has gone down in history as winning the Cold War. Even the much-maligned Nixon will be remembered for his opening of relations with China.

Yet, John Kennedy's reflection about the electoral impacts of the two different policy areas shows up even in our selection process. In recent history, only George H. W. Bush came to the race for president with a strong résumé in foreign affairs. The elder Bush had been vice president under Reagan and as such, had travelled extensively as Reagan's personal emissary to the funerals of foreign leaders.[21] Additionally, he had served as US ambassador to China and to the United Nations and had been the director of the Central Intelligence Agency (CIA). Other presidents may have had some experience in foreign affairs, but it was their domestic policy résumés that were most carefully scrutinized during the campaign. Carter, Reagan, Clinton, and the younger Bush had all been governors for varying lengths of time and had little real foreign policy experience. Barack Obama had even less such experience than any of the governors who preceded him to the Oval Office, himself having served just one-third of his first term as a US senator from Illinois and as a state senator prior to that. All of this lack of experience makes the president's support system and the personnel selected to staff it all the more important.

Support Structure

As discussed earlier in chapter 10, the area of foreign policy, particularly national security, is one of the areas of large and rapid growth in presidential advising and support. Traditionally, the State Department and the Foreign Service are the pillars the public thinks of as being the support structure for the president. We might also add to that image the military, via first the Departments of War and Navy and then the Defense Department. These more traditional support mechanisms have also been occasionally fraught with difficulty, based in part on what could be termed behavioral conservatism combined with the typical slow movement of diplomacy. These are two conditions that might not fit well with a president's desire to see some foreign policy actions move faster or in a more bold direction.

As a result of these inadequacies and cross-purposes, the State Department for a number of decades, has played a much smaller role than in the past. The rise of intelligence gathering capabilities outside the direct purview of the State Department in agencies like the CIA and the NSC—two agencies that have been under more direct presidential control and free of the traditions of the Foreign Service—has been a major contributing factor in this decline. When Nixon took steps to open US relations with China, many of the initial forays were made, not by the State Department or other Foreign Service officers, but by his National Security Advisor Henry Kissinger, who like Condeleezza Rice under George W. Bush, later became secretary of state. Other National Security personnel have engaged in not just the development of foreign policy, but the implementation of it as well.

Often other agencies one might not readily think of as foreign policy in nature contribute to the development of foreign policy. For example, cabinet departments such as the Treasury Department will weigh in on international economic policy or the Justice Department will on matters of international law. The same is true of the Commerce Department with respect to business matters that cross oceans and borders, as would the Environmental Protection Agency on environmental matters. By now, we are all well aware of our cooperative ventures in space with Russia and other countries conducted under the auspices of the National Aeronautics and Space Administration (NASA).

Of course, Congress is a player that could be seen as either a competitor to the president or as part of the support structure. This is dependent upon the relationship the president has with Congress, which is determined by the partisan makeup of the two branches. Here is where we would most notably see the influence of any interest group in the area of foreign policy, but as noted earlier the activity is generally much less intense than with domestic policy.

No Sitting Idly in the Stands

As with all of the other interactions we have discussed in the most recent chapter, presidential action, even in an area that would seem to be more exclusively his or hers (like foreign policy), is limited by the institution's and the individual's interactions with the other branches and with other political players, both domestic and foreign. Yet, in keeping with theme of our overall discussion, it is the manner by which those interactions occur that is significant for the president's success. The manner of interactions is most determined by the president's partisan or ideological viewpoint and his or her personality.

Every president since Franklin Roosevelt has had to be considerably concerned about the conduct of our foreign policy. World War II, and the status of world politics since, has made it impossible for presidents to be too isolationist. The advent of nuclear weapons, the Cold War, and the spread of terrorism have made it impossible for the United States to sit on the sidelines and watch as the game of world politics plays out before us. If we use the analogy of a baseball game, the concept might be a bit clearer. If you were playing the game and were injured by the action, you at least had some impact on the outcome of the game. If, however, you were simply sitting in the stands and got struck by a foul ball or a bat that had slipped out of the hands of the hitter, you'd still be injured but would not have had any impact on the outcome of the game. For nations in a world of terrorists and nuclear, biological, or chemical weapons, it is impossible for their leaders to be still waiting for the foul ball to hit.

Overall Conclusions Drawn from Presidential Policy Making

What should now be clear is that regardless of the particular area of public policy involved, the common thread of concern is the reliability of advice given to the president. Political scientist Hugh Heclo (1975) argued that the last thing presidents needed, and for that matter what US citizens needed, was an advisory structure that was neutrally competent. Such impartiality as is implied by this concept, Heclo argued, could bring about lengthy debates throughout government that stymied executive branch reaction to problems. Further, if such debates continued beyond the point of a decision having been made, it could lead to a perception of disunity within the executive and undermine the confidence of the people in the government's ability to respond to circumstances.

Rather than neutral competence, Terry Moe (1985) suggested that we should desire, and presidents should seek, responsive competence. This would be an advisory system where the individuals who populate it have the requisite background, training, and experience to do the job, but make no pretense about the fact that they support the president. Moe and others have pointed out that ensuring responsive competence among the president's advisers and ensuring that each president gets to bring in his or her own team allows for new ideas, sometimes in counterweight to the advice given by career civil servants, is a good thing. Certainly, this does not mean that presidents should surround themselves with "yes men," but should emphasize the role of being a team player. As an adviser, make your dissent known within the administration, but support the ultimate decision. Presidents do need to strike a balance so that the advice they receive from the more political advisers is not perceived by the permanent civil service, Congress, or the media as purely political.

In other words, presidents should by all means appoint individuals who, at base, agree with them on policy questions, but may want to ensure that a few advisers have opposing viewpoints. While restricted in making appointments to the Council of Economic Advisers to those who support the concept of a market economy, a president can assuredly appoint individuals who favor regulation of economic activity or those who support little to no regulation, depending on his or her own economic perspective. Similarly, while historically there has been much bipartisan agreement on foreign policy, there are certainly divergent views, often defined by partisan perspectives, which allow presidents to appoint those with whom they agree. It is, however, in the area of domestic policy where presidents have the greatest latitude in appointing advisers (and by extension make policy) who are closer to their personal political preferences.

Part VI

Conclusion

Chapter 18

Hope and Change and the Future of the Presidency

In the 2008 presidential selection process, Barack Obama came from virtual political oblivion with a Messianic message and image to defeat the odds on favorite in the Democratic contest—Hillary Clinton—to become his party's nominee for president. His message of "hope and change" resonated once the economic crisis hit hard in the fall and allowed him to easily paint his Republican opponent—John McCain—as more of the same. Only two years before his election, Obama was a member of the Illinois State Senate.

Obama did, in fact, give many voters a feeling of hope. As a newcomer to the Washington scene, Obama was able to both state what was wrong with our government and that only someone who had not yet been tainted by the process could fix it. Ultimately, Obama's success or failure will be left up to individual readers of this work, voters, and historians to judge. Even then, we must ask ourselves how we can judge the success or failure of any one individual in the office. If, as we've been discussing throughout this work, the individual helps to shape the office for all who follow, how do we deem those subtle (or not so subtle) changes to the office as successes or as failures?

The Ups and Downs of Presidents and Presidential Power in the Late Twentieth Century

As we have been addressing throughout this discussion, each president leaves an indelible mark, a lasting change, of one sort or another on the institution he or she occupies. This can be through intentional expansion of the scope and powers of the office or the unintentional frittering away of that power. It can also be through the creation of new institutional structure, the passage of landmark legislation, the appointment of justices of the Supreme Court whose impact will be felt long after the president has left office, or simply by their very election. John Kennedy as the first Catholic president or Barack Obama as the first black president have forever changed the way voters will look at future potential presidents with "different" demographic characteristics.[1]

Obama entered the office of president in historic fashion, not just as America's first black president, but also in the midst of the worst economic downturn since the Great Depression and in the middle of two wars. He inherited a presidency that had gone through a great many ups and downs over the half century or so before he took the oath of office. The presidency had been weakened considerably by the mistakes of presidents, the activism of the press, and the assertiveness of both Congress and the Court. Nixon's actions regarding Vietnam and Watergate and the reactions to those actions by Congress and the Court broke down many of the walls of the imperial presidency. Ford's pardon of Nixon, his weak response to an economic crisis, his apparent lack of physical grace,[2] and having to wear the legacy of Nixon put him in a category, in the minds of voters, not unlike a caretaker. Jimmy Carter's apparent mild manner, his inability to reign in the economic woes he inherited from Ford, his style that included delivering a major speech on the American sense of "malaise," and his inability to secure the release of the Americans held hostage in Tehran made him seem ineffectual and weak.

Ronald Reagan was elected at a time when the American people were looking for a renewed strength in the president. Reagan's use of whatever tools were available, including his ability to speak directly to the people, began the rebuilding of the institution of the presidency. He, and his staff, found ways to achieve the administration's goals, even if sometimes those ways were on the edge of what was legal. The Iran-Contra Scandal demonstrated to the American people that once again presidential administrations could go too far.

George H. W. Bush succeeded Reagan and with his impressive résumé, including time served as ambassador to China and director of the Central Intelligence Agency (CIA), it would appear that he would have the skills necessary to restore power to the presidency and prevent the institution from becoming imperiled. Certainly, the elder Bush's approval rating after the Persian Gulf War seemed to be evidence of the potential for a resurgent presidency. His inability to convert that strength into tangible domestic policy, however, led to his defeat and an apparent further weakening of the institution.

Bill Clinton's presidency was, in a sense, a microcosm of this whole up and down phenomenon. He entered office at a time when the public had high hopes and high expectations. Right out of the gate, he appeared to fumble the ball. With two attorney general nominees having to withdraw because of ethical issues,[3] the then divisive issue of gays in the military moving to the top spot on the agenda, and the tragedy at Waco, Texas,[4] it appeared as though the institution was in for a tough time under Bill Clinton. For Clinton and the presidency, it had to get much worse before it got better. The premier legislative item—health care reform—took too long to get before Congress, and when it did, it died a slow death and never even made it to the floor of either chamber. Partly as a result of that failure, Clinton's party suffered a historic defeat in the 1994-midterm elections and the Republicans took control of both chambers of Congress for the first time in over 40 years. It was not until the 1995–1996 budget dispute with Congress that Clinton would begin to turn things around. Using a combination of interpersonal skill, TV advertising, and some fortunate twists of fate, Clinton was able to reassert the power of the institution. His personal problems, however, would upend all that progress. Certainly, one could not say that the institution was strengthened by its occupant being impeached by the House of Representatives. In the end, though the institution might have become a bit worse for wear, Clinton left office with highest approval rating of any departing president.

The presidency of George W. Bush saw a slim Republican majority (51–50, counting the vice president's vote) switch to a 51–49 Democratic majority in the Senate. This of course followed the brutal 37-day long election night with recounts and legal challenges, which culminated in the Supreme Court's decision in *Bush v. Gore* (531 U.S. 426, 2000) to end the recounting of votes and declare Bush the winner of the 2000 presidential election. The outcome resulted in the fourth time in our history where the winner of the popular vote did not win the election. Such circumstances might lead to the conclusion that the Bush presidency would be a weak one and that the institution would, at best, get no stronger than it had been at the end of Clinton's second term. Instead, as a result of many factors we have already discussed, including the "rally 'round the flag" effect (which occurred a number of times during George W. Bush's tenure, most significantly after September 11th, 2001), Bush became a rather popular president though he finished his tenure as rather unpopular. He was eventually able to assert executive power where it had been absent in the 30 or more years prior to his election. Bush left his successor a stronger institution—for good or ill—than the one he had inherited. What Barack Obama would do with it would be controversial, to say the least.

What Did Barack Obama Bring to the Presidency?

Hope and change was the major theme of the Obama 2008 presidential campaign. The theme attracted the normally disenfranchised, the frustrated, and the optimistic. Eight years with the fear of terrorists and difficult wars, coupled with a sense that a president we trusted may have gone too far with that trust, motivated Obama's supporters and his message had a vaguely religious aspect to it. For many, the Obama campaign was about making the government better, more responsive, and more democratic (emphasis on the lower case "d"). For these voters, perhaps the tone of Washington politics would change, special interests would have less influence, the wars would end, and we'd get universal health care. In looking back, some voters have been disappointed by what they saw as a less than adequate health care reform policy, the wars that took too long to end, and the apparent lack of leadership. Presidential scholars and historians will wonder if it was something about the timing—Obama being elected just after the onset of the economic crisis in 2008—or was it something about Obama's personality or character that seemed to divert his attention.

With less than four years in office, biographies and analyses of Barack Obama already abound. It is beyond the scope of this discussion to do a comprehensive review of all that material. What we can do is to use a snapshot of some of it to get an idea of what the forty-fourth president brought to the office with him in terms of skills, experience, and character. Obviously, Obama meets the minimum requirements to qualify for president—those laid out in the US Constitution (see chapter 1). Birther Conspiracy Theories notwithstanding, Barack Obama is a natural born citizen of the United States, is at least 35 years old, and meets the residency requirements. The more legitimate question for many was whether or not his level of experience was sufficient to qualify him for the job he sought. In other words, many questioned whether or not his service in the Illinois State Senate and what would be two years in the US Senate would be sufficient experience to prepare him for the rigors of the presidency.

Still others wondered about the psychological makeup, the ethics, and the value system of this relative unknown. Who was Barack Obama? What did he believe—not in terms of politics (that would be become fairly clear during the campaign), but in terms of faith, values, and a simple sense of what was right and what was wrong?

We now have several years of evidence to see that in terms of basic human values; Barack Obama is not that different from most Americans. He appears to have a stable, loving relationship with his wife, Michelle, and they both seem intent on providing some sense of a normal life for their two daughters in spite of them growing up so close to the media spotlight and surrounded by folks in dark suits, wearing sunglasses and earpieces. Though during the 2008 campaign the beliefs of his minister caused a bit of controversy, for most Americans, Obama appears to have relatively run-of-the-mill religious beliefs—though there are some who still believe him to be a "closet Muslim." It is not the intention here to address all of the conspiracies; rather, we will take what information is available at face value and try to get some idea, as we said back in chapter 9, about what makes him tick.

Some might make the argument that Obama's abandonment by both his mother and father might create a weak self-esteem and drive him to pursuits where he could easily find a substitute for the esteem he lacked.[5] Others might argue that ending up as successful as he has indicates that he learned to cope with any possible abandonment issues and instead has a rather healthy self-esteem.

Psychiatrist Justin Frank (2011) has undertaken an attempt at performing psychoanalysis on Obama in his work *Obama on the Couch: Inside the Mind of the President*. Frank points out that much of what drives Obama, psychologically, is a desire to fix or "synthesize his broken self" (229). It could be argued then that Obama's first book, *Dreams from My Father* (1995), and later his exploration of the Irish heritage from his mother's side was a part of his search for synthesis. This, seemingly, is reflected in political scientist Stephen Wayne's (2011) assertion that Obama is a conciliator, attempting to reconcile diverse demography and interests and, yes, to be bipartisan. Wayne argues that Obama's practice of conciliation politics is not just a demonstration of what Obama sees as a tool he wields well, but "has become a personal philosophy" (Frank 2011, 65). For Frank, this conciliation is manifested in what he calls "obsessive bipartisan disorder" (2011).

Certainly, right-wing critics of Obama have argued that he is the least bipartisan president in history. I would argue that it may be that even though obsessed with the concept of bipartisanship, he may not have been successful at it. By contrast, there are critics on the left who would argue that Obama has been far too accommodating of the opposition. These critics on the left point to the wasted opportunity of fairly large Democratic majorities in the two houses of Congress during the first two years of his tenure as evidence that Obama took too much time seeking the bipartisan solution, the conciliated solution, rather than just the solution. Frank argues that such behavior was the "outward manifestation of a fundamental organizing principle of his psyche, which he must protect from challenge in order to maintain his sense of calm and self" (Frank 2011, 85).

For the most part, Obama handed the health care ball off to Congress and allowed a deliberative committee process, with many committees involved to arrive at something close to a consensus program. In the end, the program that emerged was far from a consensus and appeared to be more like the proverbial horse designed by a committee—a camel. In part, because the bill that emerged from this process was a series of compromises, the Obama administration had a difficult time defining it and owning it. The opposition seemed to be creating the definition of the package better and faster than the administration. "Death panels" and rationing became the mantras from the right and the positives—supported by large majorities in polls—such as banning denial of coverage for preexisting conditions, extension of the coverage of children to 26 from 23 years of age, among other provisions got buried in the noise. It could be argued that this approach was a reflection of Obama's desire for consensus on the legislation. In this case, that desire may have come at the cost of the program he really would have preferred and one that, if passed solely with Democratic votes a year earlier, would have avoided the summer of Town Hall protests.[6]

Wayne put it best as, "Consensus is the end game for Obama, not winning the debate or achieving a particular policy outcome" (2011, 39). Naturally, this can be seen as strength, but in American style democracy, it may not be possible to achieve such consensus. This would have been difficult even before partisan rancor reached the levels it has since the earliest days of Obama's presidency. In our system, it might be easier to achieve some measure of conciliation once strength has been shown. British journalist Walter Bagehot, perhaps, put it best when writing about the English Constitution that "no man can argue on his knees" (Bagehot 1864). Perhaps things would have been a bit different for Obama had he made use of his partisan advantage, one of the tools available to the president for dealing with Congress (see chapter 15), and pushed for a larger stimulus, called the opposition's bluff on threatened filibusters, and moved health care reform much earlier.

Thus far, I have steadfastly avoided using Barber's framework to analyze Obama. In part, that is due to one of the weaknesses of Barber's construction, the inability to account for variation over the course of an individual's life and how the office might change him or her. Given that we spent a great deal of time on the subject in chapter 9, it might be worth some attempt to link Obama's character with Barber's categorizations. It appears clear that Obama is active in politics, especially once he got a taste of the national political spotlight during his 2004 campaign for the US

Senate from Illinois. Using the attention he garnered from his keynote address to the Democratic National Convention in 2004, he quickly moved into consideration as a potential future presidential candidate. Few expected, however, that it would be just two years later that he would jump into the 2008 race.[7]

For a Barber style analysis though, we need more information than what motivates someone to run for president. We know Obama spent a good deal of his adult life trying to figure out who he was and how to reconcile the white and black aspects of his heritage. Commentary has abounded about Obama's coolness—not in a "hey, that's cool" manner—but rather his calm, and apparent detachment. This commentary has come from both ends of the political spectrum, so it appears to lack a partisan component. Obama is also often referred to as analytical, calculated, and driven. Wayne (2011) notes that his one loss in politics, before his contest against Hillary Clinton, did not sit well with Obama. Wayne quotes Obama's *Audacity of Hope* (2006) where Obama says that his loss in a 2000 primary for Congress "still burn[s]."

In the end we should ask the question, but understand we may not yet be able to answer it, "Is Barack Obama an Active-Positive, an Active-Negative, a Passive-Positive, or a Passive-Negative?" Many have argued that it is not possible for a contemporary presidential candidate to be passive. The process of selection in place today requires candidates to actively pursue the office. Might it be possible, however, that a generally passive personality could "fake it" long enough to get elected? Maybe. Wayne (2011) provides little help with our larger question, but offers a great insight. He writes, "Obama needs to be recognized. He wants to make a difference. Politics provides a salve for his ego, a direction for his restlessness, a channel through which he can achieve desirable social goals" (23). To me, this sounds a bit like the negative character that uses politics as a substitute for psychological shortcomings, the need for an external boost to one's low self-esteem. At the same time, there is a hint of the positive character who seeks to use politics for good. It is entirely possible that Obama is in Barber's most dangerous category, the Active-Negative, using politics to fix "his broken self," to use Justin Frank's words.

Barack Obama: Presidency Imperiled or Imperial Presidency?

Even though we may not be sure about Obama's location in Barber's 2 x 2 matrix, we can examine what he inherited, what he did with it, and what he will leave his inevitable successor. As indicated earlier, the presidency had gone through a rather tumultuous period in the latter portion of the twentieth century, but had regained a great deal of its institutional strength, perhaps at the expense of George W. Bush's popularity. The institution that Barack Obama inherited then was one far stronger than the one Bush had inherited from Bill Clinton.

Naturally, a great deal of the resurgence in the strength of the institution is due to a perception of necessity following the events of 9/11. This includes the wars in Afghanistan and Iraq and the fears at home of increased terror potential. In a sense, for the presidency, the confluence of these events plus the presence of Richard Cheney as George W. Bush's vice president and key adviser, was something of a perfect storm.

Cheney had been around the Washington political scene for many decades dating back to the Nixon/Ford years. It was under Gerald Ford that Cheney rose to the position of chief of staff. He later served in Congress and then as Defense secretary before being chosen by George W. Bush to run for vice president. It was in the Nixon/Ford administration that Cheney began to form many of his beliefs about the power of the executive branch. In part, the formulation of these beliefs was in reaction to the slippage of power caused by reaction to Watergate and administration overreach in Vietnam.

A theory that would come to be known as the "unitary executive" began to take shape in the Ford White House (where Cheney would eventually serve as chief of staff) in the Office of Legal Counsel (headed by future Supreme Court Justice Antonin Scalia[8]). This theory was based on two parts of the Constitution, "the 'Oath' and 'Take Care' clauses of Article II" (Montgomery 2009, 57). According to Montgomery, these aspects of "the Constitution gave the president exclusive authority over everything in the executive branch, and any infringement on these powers was unconstitutional" (58). Out of a job after Ford was defeated by Carter in 1976, Cheney decided to run for a seat in the House of Representatives from Wyoming. Once in the House, Cheney became a legislative advocate of the unitary executive theory and remained perhaps its chief legislative proponent until he left Congress in 1989 to serve as George H. W. Bush's secretary of Defense.

Calabresi and Yoo (2008) note that this conception of the unitary executive dates back to the debates at the Constitutional Convention in 1787, where as we have discussed earlier, there was much debate over the structure and power of the executive. Calabresi and Yoo argue that the Vesting Clause of the Constitution[9] is the basis of the theory. It could be argued that between the Vesting Clause and the Oath and Take Care clauses, we have what amounts to the executive equivalent of the necessary and proper clause that has been used as a theoretical/legal justification for expansion of legislative powers into areas not specifically enumerated in the Constitution. A similar argument about the Constitution empowering a strong president comes from well-known conservative commentator and publisher of *The Weekly Standard*, Terry Eastland (1993). Where political scientist Richard Neustadt has told us that our conception of our government as a system with a separation of powers, while a nice legal construct, is in reality misconceived and is a system of "separated institutions *sharing* powers" (Neustadt 1990, 29, emphasis in original), Eastland argues that Neustadt is wrong. He asserts that the Constitution created separated institutions with separated powers.

The (George W.) Bush administration used this theory as a foundation to push the constitutional envelope to reassert and expand executive power during a time of national crisis. The use of domestic surveillance, rendition, enhanced interrogation techniques, and many other practices during these Bush years were the implementation of the unitary executive theory. Some would argue that Congress was complicit in this implementation by passing vaguely worded measures and not exerting its powers of legislative oversight. This complicity occurred regardless of which party controlled either chamber of Congress, so it wasn't simply partisan support by Republicans of a Republican president.

Perhaps even more important was that this assertion and expansion of powers was not limited to the fight against terror. George W. Bush used the power of executive orders, signing statements,[10] and claims of executive privilege to expand executive power on the domestic front. According to this theory, these actions by the president are unchallengeable by Congress or in the courts. Yet, it was the Supreme Court that eventually did tame some of the powers claimed by the Bush administration. As with most limits on executive power the Court has established over the years, it acknowledged the power existed, but that it was used improperly or needed a legislative approval or grant of authority. While primarily a normative theory—about what ought to be—and virtually untestable with respect to the Framers' wishes (Morris 2010), its use or assertion by a president can have great consequence for that president and those who follow. Successful assertion of the unitary executive theory could go a long way toward restoring a withered executive institution.

In other words, George W. Bush, regardless of anyone's perception of him and his policies or style of governing, left Barack Obama a much stronger presidency than Clinton had left him. In what shape is the presidency now that Obama has occupied it for some time? Once again, regardless of anyone's opinions of Obama, his policies, or his approach, Obama has at least maintained much of the power left to him by George W. Bush. To this point, he has exhibited more limited use of executive privilege and signing statements, but he has left Guantanamo Bay Prison open, in spite of an executive order to close it. He has used executive power to act in areas where congressional stalemate has prevented action, including implementing aspects of an immigration policy that allows the children who came here illegally with their parents to find a pathway to legitimacy.

Unless some serious challenge to Obama's use of unitary power comes along before he finishes his time in office, he should be leaving to his successor an institution at much the same strength—newly restrengthened—as the one he inherited. Is that all there is to preventing an imperiled presidency or creating an imperial one? Certainly, the assertion of unitary power goes a long way in creating an imperial presidency and, for a time, preventing imperilment. However, there the more intangible aspects to presidential power, those that rest not on clear grants of authority either in the Constitution or through congressional delegation of authority, but rest on the president's personal characteristics and abilities.

The Real Power of the Presidency

Richard Neustadt (1990) has argued that the true power of the presidency lies not in law, but in his or her ability to persuade. As we have gone through this discussion, we have demonstrated on a number of occasions and in many circumstances where the president must use persuasion to accomplish what he or she needs. All of what we have touched upon thus far in this discussion can be summarized here in this concept.

John Kennedy used the first edition of Neustadt's book as a sort of "handbook" for organizing and running his administration. In our earlier discussion of the Cuban Missile Crisis, we saw that actual command by the alleged "commander in chief" is often elusive, at best. Neustadt begins his treatment of presidential power from the premise that command does, in fact, have a limited role in presidential leadership. For Neustadt, command has to meet three criteria: clarity of the command, the ability of the recipient to carry it out, and the legitimacy of the command and the commander. In American politics, clarity is often hard to discern and many mistakes in leadership and governance occur when the "commands" issued are not absolutely clear. We also often hear the expression "that's above my pay grade" or from a 1970s TV show, "not my job."[11] Such statements are an expression of an individual's desire not to take the risk of failing, particularly when their responsibility may not be wholly clear to that individual. Legitimacy of the commander rarely comes into play in discussions of presidential power, though it can surface as an issue if the issuer of the commands is perceived as an illegitimate holder of the office. Early vice presidents who took office upon the death of their predecessor, and presidents who won the election with an Electoral College majority, but not the popular vote, have also been subjected to criticism as illegitimate.[12] Presidents with naturalized parents, with one parent who was not a citizen, or presidents born in territory outside the United States may also have their legitimacy questioned.[13]

Neustadt asks three questions in analyzing the application of presidential skill in attempting to persuade. The three questions are simple one-word questions: Who? What? How? The targets for the "who" question are many. As we have seen in previous chapters, presidents must have the cooperation of Congress in order to advance their agendas, and they need to convince bureaucrats of the legitimacy of their agenda. Outside of the federal government, presidents may need to gain the cooperation of other officials at the state- and local-government levels or they may need to garner support from interest groups. Ultimately, presidents may also need to seek, gain, and hold the support of the voters. All of these we have discussed directly or indirectly in earlier chapters.[14]

With respect to the "what" question, the answer is heavily dependent upon which target is the subject of the discussion. For example, if the president needs support from members of Congress he or she may make use of any of the tools laid out in chapter 15, but if necessary may also go public and seek the assistance of the voters to convince Congress for him. This is the route we discussed regarding Reagan seeking public support for his program on aide to the Contras in Nicaragua in the mid-1980s. It is also the choice Obama made when all other attempts at negotiations with Congress over the debt ceiling in the summer of 2011 failed. And still, Obama was not successful in achieving his goals.

The answer to the "how" question depends highly on the subject of the "who" and "what" questions. What the question addresses is what tools the president can or may apply to process of persuasion. If the target of persuasion is Congress, the president may make use of a number of tools (see chapter 15 for more detail) including, but not limited to, support for public works projects in the districts of members, support in campaigns (for members of his or her own party), and public pressure. If the target is the bureaucracy, the tools include the possibility of career enhancement through elevation to the senior (political) ranks of public service, the use of the prestige of the office, and the president's approval among the public as a lever to convince the reluctant bureaucrat. For interest groups and the public, the tools focus more on explication of the president's positions on the issues and using the media to "teach" the target about the righteousness of the president's position.

"No man can argue on his knees"

We return then to the English journalist and essayist, Walter Bagehot, who made the case that it is rather difficult for anyone to succeed in arguing, persuading, or bargaining when in a position of disadvantage. Naturally, one could think of this in terms of physical combat and have the image of a warrior who has lost the battle and is on his knees before his opponent attempting to negotiate a victory. It just doesn't work, unless the victor is extremely magnanimous.

Generally speaking, combatants of any kind need to be in a position of relative strength in order to have anything with which to bargain. From such a position, presidents, or anyone for that matter, can make appeals to the self-interest of the target of persuasion. A simple cost-benefit analysis could be used to demonstrate that the president's position is actually in the best interests of the target. Sometimes it is the simple prestige of the office of president that may be employed to impress or intimidate the target. It could also be that a president is held in high personal regard by the target of persuasion and can make use of that regard to cash in a personal favor. Presidents, if in the majority, can also make appeals to partisanship or ideology to help gain support for their proposals.

In the end, for contemporary presidents and those in the decades to follow, it is and will be evermore difficult to accomplish their goals. It may be more difficult to even survive their term in office, certainly with their dignity and self-esteem intact. This does not mean, however, that it is hopeless for the president to display and assert leadership and to achieve his or her goals. The presidency, as a player in contemporary politics, has the most all-encompassing array of tools in the American political system. It is the skilled application of the right set of tools, at the right time, and on the correct target of persuasion that allows presidents to be successful. This is where the individuality, the personality, and the internal makeup of the person sitting in the Oval Office separates that individual, for good or bad, from all those who came before or will come after.

Notes

1 Introduction

1. Approximately 1.4 million active troops according to Department of Defense projections for FY 2012, United States Department of Defense Budget Request FY 2012, Overview.
2. Generally speaking, to veto something means to reject it or to prevent an action from taking place. More specifically and with respect to our concerns, to veto means that the president may reject an Act of Congress even though a majority of both houses have agreed to the legislation. Thus, a single individual may stop something from becoming law that has been passed by Congress by an overwhelming majority. Naturally, Congress has the power to override the veto by a two-thirds vote of both chambers.
3. The actual wording in the Constitution is, "He shall from time to time give to the Congress Information on the State of the Union."
4. Presidents may also enter into other agreements with foreign leaders that do not have the same force of law as do treaties. These arrangements are called "executive agreements" and are generally enforceable only while the two leaders who are party to the agreement are still in office.
5. Among others, the most controversial was perhaps that of Marc Rich, convicted of 51 counts of tax fraud and evading $48 million in taxes, there was the appearance that the pardon could have been in return for political contributions made by Rich's wife (Reaves 2001).
6. Explicit powers are defined as those powers granted by the Constitution in explicit language or, in other words, those that are quite clearly written in the document either by the founders or by later amendment. The elastic clause creates, for Congress, a broad array of implicit or implied powers. The same is true of the other two branches and all are subject to the interpretation of the courts. In fact, the Supreme Court's application of the power of judicial review in the case of *Marbury v. Madison* 5 U.S. (1 Cranch) 137 (1803) is one example of the application of implied powers.
7. Once again, see *Marbury v. Madison*.
8. See the Twenty-Second Amendment to the US Constitution.
9. While the president's travel for official business is paid for with public funds, travel for political purposes must be reimbursed to the government.
10. Approximately $590,000 in 2006 dollars, according to the calculator at measuringworth.com and using the Consumer Price Index (CPI) as the index.
11. Many of the numbers here come from http://www.lib.umich.edu/node/11736/ and 3 U.S.C., Chapter 2, § 102.

12. Author's personal observation from visits to the Kennedy, Ford, Carter, Reagan, and Clinton libraries.
13. Carter wrote, "From the beginning, our differences were obvious, even in personal habits. Prime Minister Begin was the soul of propriety. He preferred to wear a tie and coat and *strictly observed protocol*, always reminding President Sadat and me that he was not a head of state and therefore did not rank as an equal with us. When I wanted to see him, he insisted that he come to my cottage and not the other way around" (1982, 331, emphasis added).

2 The Historical Context: How We View the Presidency

1. Milkis and Nelson in summarizing Jackson's view actually use the expression "a president should reject any bill that he felt would injure the nation" (1994, 127).
2. The commission was appointed by Roosevelt in 1936 to make recommendations about more efficient governance of the executive branch. For more detail and a brief memoir, see James Fesler's "The Brownlow Committee Fifty Years Later" (1987, 291–296).
3. While popular accounts have Roberts changing his mind soon after Roosevelt's announcement of the Court Reform Plan, evidence seems to indicate that Roberts had actually decided to support the Washington State law just after oral argument in December of 1935. The Court was awaiting the return of the ailing Harlan Fiske Stone before issuing its opinion about three weeks after Roosevelt laid out his plan in a Fireside Chat on March 9th, 1936. See, for example, Marian C. McKenna's (2002) *Franklin Roosevelt and the Great Constitutional War: The Court-packing Crisis of 1937*.
4. See, WhiteHouse.gov "Executive Office of the President, Fiscal Year 2011, Congressional Budget Submission," retrieved on July 2nd, 2012, from http://www.whitehouse.gov/sites/default/files/2011-eop-budget.pdf.
5. See, for example, H. R. Haldeman's (1978) memoir of his time as Nixon's chief of staff, *The Ends of Power*.

3 Introduction: The Process in General

1. Some noted examples include George Wallace in 1968, John Anderson in 1980, Ross Perot in both 1992 and 1996, and Ralph Nader in 2000. In particular, Nader's candidacy is thought to have had an impact on the outcome of the election in 2000 in that his margins in New Hampshire and Florida would have provided Gore with sufficient votes to be the winner in those states, either one of which would have changed the outcome of the election. In New Hampshire, Nader received 22,198 votes and the difference between George W. Bush and Gore was a 7,200-vote margin for Bush. In Florida, where the difference between the two candidates, officially, was just over 500 votes, Nader received more than 97,000 votes (source: http://www.fec.gov/pubrec/2000presgeresults.htm).
2. See CNN.com (2008) "Election Center 2008," retrieved on June 25th, 2010, from http://www.cnn.com/ELECTION/2008/candidates/.

3. Most recently, California joined Louisiana in adopting a primary where all candidates from all parties face each other in a single contest and the top vote getters face each other in a general election regardless of party affiliation.
4. Ragsdale (1993) uses a similar scheme. She delineates four periods: the Congressional Caucus (1800–1824), the Brokered Convention (1828–1912), the Emergent Primary (1912–1968), and the Media Primary (1972–present). The major difference is my argument that the brokered convention still dominated the political environment through 1968.
5. According to the website Dictionary.com, the expression dates back to the period between 1910 and 1915.
6. This was the system of distributing political jobs often credited to the presidency of Andrew Jackson that abandoned the government of "gentlemen" approach of the Jeffersonian Era, but before the Civil Service system that would come decades later.
7. Herring (1979) is among those who point to exaggerated media coverage of North Vietnamese/Viet Cong success. In fact, he says, "Early reports of a smashing enemy victory went largely uncorrected" (197). In addition, Stanley Karnow (1983) provides a thorough narrative of how the media turned on Johnson and his policies regarding the war.
8. The reference here is to the riots following the assassination of Dr. Martin Luther King in April of 1968.
9. Chicago, Illinois, was the site of the Democratic Convention that year.
10. It is generally believed that Senator Strom Thurmond from South Carolina defected from the Democratic Party to the Republican Party—thus supporting Goldwater for president in 1964—as a result of the Johnson administration's support for the Civil Rights Act of 1964.

4 The System Changes Forever

1. Formally known as the Commission on Party Structure and Delegate Selection, the commission is most often and popularly referred to as the McGovern-Fraser Commission, named for its successive chairs.
2. My interpretation here is that "open" refers to a public and accessible process where the party's rank and file could participate, thus limiting the ability of party leaders to control the process. One could also interpret "open" to refer to the later opening of the delegate selection contests in some states to include nonparty members.
3. McGovern's speech began at 3 a.m. (EDT) and with Hawaii 6 hours behind Eastern Time, the speech would have begun there at 9 p.m., which is usually considered prime time. The delay was attributed to a number of factors such as demonstrations in support of candidates and 39 challengers to McGovern's vice-presidential selection of Senator Thomas Eagleton.
4. Technically, it was the Commission on Presidential Nomination (DNC 2005), chaired by Governor James Hunt of North Carolina.
5. The 2005 DNC report noted that at least in one case—South Dakota—the state legislature, being controlled by the opposing party, seemed to want to instigate mischief by creating a conflict with the rules.
6. See, for example, "It Could All be Over after Super Duper Tuesday" by Bill Schneider (2008) on CNN.com. The story can be accessed at http://articles.cnn.com/2007-02-05

/politics/schneider.superduper.tuesday_1_new-hampshire-south-carolina-democrats-diverse-states?_s=PM:POLITICS.
7. In the end, both delegations were seated.
8. A federal system of government is one where there is shared responsibility and some measure of independence for the lower level of government. To use this analogy would be to argue that Republican state party organizations would be somewhat independent from the national party.
9. In a similar way, in a unitary form of government, where all the sovereignty lies at the central level, this analogy would argue that the DNC would allow less autonomy for its respective state party organizations than the more federally organized Republicans.
10. To make it easier to understand some of the more difficult detail in this discussion, it might be useful to think in terms of the reforms. As such, Wigoda's group were the "bad guys," trying to keep things the same and the Cousins group were the "good guys," trying to reform the system and beat the evil political machine.
11. A request for a writ of certiorari is a request by an appellant of the Supreme Court to order a lower court to produce the entire record of a case so that the parties to the case may make arguments to the Court. A successful request requires that four of the nine justices agree that a case is important enough for the Court to hear the arguments.
12. US Senator Lowell Weicker, a liberal to independent leaning Republican, proposed the idea, some thought as a way to bolster his own chances in future internal party contests, in 1983.
13. The state constitutional officer charged with the oversight of elections.
14. Of course, part of the problem for the party in 2008 was that it was attempting to enforce a penalty it had made harsher after the violation of the rule was committed. Their case might have been clearer and less controversial if they had stuck to the penalty as delineated in the rules—a reduction of voting power to the elected delegations by one-half—instead of stripping the states of all delegates elected in violation of the rules.
15. Indeed, by as early as 1988, the event seems to have gotten away from its creators and a significant enough number of nonsouthern states were holding contests on the same day to diminish any real regional impact.
16. The 7 Republican victories were Nixon twice, Reagan twice, Bush I, and Bush II twice. The 5 Democratic victories were Carter, Clinton twice, and Obama twice.

5   Campaign Finance

1. This point is based on my personal experience observing candidates for offices ranging from local government (myself included) to state legislative office, Congress, and statewide office.
2. This provision, while the dollar amount was raised briefly, was later eliminated.
3. This was just one of many vetoes overridden by Congress in the post-Watergate era of Nixon and Ford.
4. The "others" included former senator Eugene McCarthy, thus this was a lawsuit that spanned the ideological spectrum with Buckley a well-known conservative and McCarty an antiwar liberal.

5. The Court held that this was a violation of the separation of powers doctrine.
6. Independent expenditures were defined as those made by any supporter without coordination with the candidate's campaign or those by a candidate on his or her behalf.
7. According to Whitaker (2004), "the term 'soft money' generally referred to unregulated funds, perceived as resulting from loopholes in the Federal Election Campaign Act" (Summary).
8. Money laundering is a mechanism, usually illegal, that takes questionable funds or funds from questionable sources and makes them appear "clean." This was one of the many reasons why organized crime, for example, would often have a legitimate business enterprise as its "front" operation.
9. The specified times are within 30 days of a primary and within 60 days of a general election.
10. Individuals may contribute up to $1,000, but in order to demonstrate broad-based support, the candidate must raise the money in smaller contributions in order to qualify for the matching funds.
11. For a detailed description of the requirements, readers should visit the FEC website and http://www.fec.gov/info/chone.htm in particular.
12. This contribution does not impact the taxpayer's liability—it does not increase the amount of taxes owed or reduce the amount of any refund the taxpayer might be due.

6 The National Nominating Conventions: Are They Worth It and What's Next?

1. Reagan's hope was to demonstrate that Ford's vice-presidential pick would not be as unifying a selection as his own—Richard Schweiker of Pennsylvania. Schweiker was more moderate than Reagan was and balanced the ticket not only in ideological terms, but in geographic as well with the running mates being from different coasts.
2. Some mystery did occur with respect to Obama's pick, mostly with pundits and voters wondering if he might pick Hillary Clinton. The mystery disappeared the weekend before the convention when Obama announced, initially via the Internet, that his pick was Joe Biden.
3. This is the way the story was reported in the "mythology" of American politics for quite some time. However, in an uncredited story in the *New York Times Magazine* (1987), Frank Mankiewicz—the aide alleged to have asked the question—said what he actually asked was, "Have you done anything that you think could give us trouble?"
4. My personal observation and experience as a guest at both the 2004 and 2008 Democratic Conventions.
5. Some might argue that it was done to take Hillary Clinton's name being placed in nomination and her later motion to declare Obama the nominee by acclamation out of the limelight.
6. Credentials committees determine the legitimacy of delegates to be seated at the convention. Among the many things examined by credentials committees is whether or not the delegate was selected according to the party's rules.
7. In the end, the DNC Rules Committee voted, by large margins, to seat both the Florida and Michigan delegates as elected in the rogue primaries of those states, but with only one-half the votes and some debate over a small number of delegates being awarded to Obama that the Clinton camp felt were theirs (Adam Smith 2008).

8. This also marked the first departure from the tradition that candidates should not attend the party convention. In order to make his point, Roosevelt actually led protests and demonstrations in support of his argument about the 72 contested delegates from Arizona, California, Texas, and Washington.
9. An editorial in *The Harvard Crimson* from June 3rd, 1952 (retrieved on July 14th, 2010, from http://www.thecrimson.com/article/1952/6/3/the-eyes-of-texas-psenator-tafts/), cites the expulsion of pro-Eisenhower delegates from the Texas State Republican Convention by Taft supporters because they could not determine if the delegates had been elected by "Republicans of long standing and protracted loyalty."
10. This was a reference to the fact that Bush was originally from Connecticut, had a summer home in Maine, and now claimed Texas as his primary residence.
11. The seven were: Mondale, Senator Edmund Muskie from Maine (the 1968 vice-presidential nominee), Senator John Glenn from Ohio (the former astronaut), Senator Church from Idaho, Senator Adlai Stevenson III from Illinois (the son of the former Democratic presidential candidate in 1952 and 1956), and Representative Peter Rodino from New Jersey (well known for his role as chair of the House Judiciary Committee during the Nixon Impeachment hearings).
12. Carter was well known as the "Peanut Farmer from Georgia," having taken over his family business when his father passed away.
13. Some would say that the magnanimous effort on the part of the Clintons was rewarded by Obama's appointment of Hillary to be secretary of state.
14. It was at the 1992 Republican convention that Buchanan declared a culture war and attacked the Democrats for their positions on important social issues. In particular, he attacked the Clintons, Bill for his draft evasion and Hillary for her more left positions on issues. In fact, he used the words "speak for yourself, Hillary" to point out that she did not speak for mainstream America.
15. A great many of these proposals, predating the 2000 conventions are nicely summarized in "A Review of the Republican Process: Nominating Future Presidents" published in May of 2000 by the Republican National Committee Advisory Commission on the Presidential Nominating Process, chaired by former RNC chair, Bill Brock. The report was accessed for this work on July 15th, 2010, from http://pweb.jps.net/~md-r/ps/brock report.pdf.
16. Though apparently first presented by Cronin and Loevy in 1983, the plan was presented to the RNC by Stephen J. Wayne.
17. As is the case with the Republican approach to rules, this plan if it had been considered and approved by the full convention would have been for the 2004 cycle. Though the RNC employed a commission—The Advisory Commission on the Presidential Nominating Process—it was to make recommendations for the next cycle as opposed to the way the Democrats employed commissions for the upcoming cycle.
18. This is the more one-on-one campaign style that can only be adequately achieved in small state environments as opposed to wholesale politics that employs a broader, more media oriented approach.
19. State secretaries of state are usually the chief officer responsible for the conduct of elections in the states.
20. The states and territories could hold their contests at any time within the 30 days, but not before or after.
21. The Democrats preferring centralized solutions that address problems in a way that attempts to make the least waves and the Republicans preferring solutions of a more federalist nature with only suggestions from the national party structure to the state organizations.

22. Yes, I am suggesting that the process be limited to party members (perhaps independents) because it is after all about a party's selection; the general public gets to select in November.

7 The General Election: So You've Got the Nomination, Now What?

1. The "base" is one's key supporters, the party diehards, and often the most ideologically extreme members of the party.
2. A constitutional amendment requires the agreement of three-quarters of the states and there are a sufficient number of states with a small number of electoral votes that would likely not vote to ratify an amendment that would diminish their role in the general election. There are some states, however, that are considering adopting legislation that would effectively nullify the impact of state-by-state counting of votes and allocate their states' Electoral College votes in accordance with the national popular vote.
3. This election was also one of the occasions on which the popular vote winner lost.
4. According to at least one account (Farhi 2004), MSNBC pundit/host, the Late Tim Russert, gets the credit for the current designations of red for the Republicans and blue for the Democrats. At times in the past, different media outlets used the reverse designations. There does seem to be some agreement, including Russert, that the current arrangement was reached by tacit agreement of most of the media during the coverage of the 37-day recount of the 2000 presidential vote in Florida.
5. The Green Party is a small third or minor party that embraces a pro-environmental platform and becomes most controversial in close elections such as in 2000. There still some less radical liberals who blame their more radical brothers and sisters who voted for Nader for their suffering for eight years under President George W. Bush.
6. This is, of course, a reference to the 37-day-long recount and court cases culminating in the US Supreme Court decision in Bush v. Gore (531 U.S. 426, 2000) that effectively shut down the recounts and awarded Florida's 25 electoral votes to George W. Bush, giving him the requisite number of votes to win.
7. At that time, the presidents were sworn in on March 4th following their election.
8. For an interesting fictional account of just such a scenario, see Jeff Greenfield's *The People's Choice* (1996).
9. Author's calculation.
10. By contrast, in other notable landslides the percentages were much higher. Franklin Roosevelt's landslide win over Alf Landon in 1936 was with 60.8 percent of the vote, Lyndon Johnson's victory over Goldwater was with 61.1 percent, and Richard Nixon's 1972 landslide was with 60.7 percent, all clearly substantially larger than Reagan's 50.7 percent (Longley and Peirce 1996, Appendix A).
11. This is sometimes referred to as the "Federalism Bonus" (see Adkins and Kirwan 2002).
12. Naturally, this scenario would likely lead to one candidate winning the small states by larger margins and thus overwhelm the popular vote totals of the candidate who won the Electoral College by winning the large states.
13. See earlier reference to Greenfield's novel (1996) in endnote number 8.
14. Vincy Fon (2004) goes further and differentiates two other forms (both based on voting within that state) of proportional allocation. First, the perfect proportion system would

allocate electoral votes based on fractional proportions of the popular vote and award electoral votes in fractional amounts. Thus, it would be the most accurate representation of the popular votes within the state. Second, the integral proportion system would preserve much of the popular vote, but would "round up" to the nearest whole vote for the winner of the majority vote.

15. Some have also suggested the use of approval voting where in a larger field of candidates, voters would simply vote "yes" for every candidate of whom they approved and the candidate with the most "yes" votes would win.
16. According to the National Council of State Legislatures, as of April of 2011 (NCSL 2011), seven states (DC, HI, IL, MD, MA, NJ, and WA) have passed bills by both chambers of their state legislatures and then signed into law. Several other states have had bills passed by one chamber.
17. For example, in U.S. Term Limits v. Thornton, 514 U.S. 779 (1995), the Supreme Court ruled that mechanisms, as clever as they may be, that seek to "effect a fundamental change in the constitutional framework" without benefit of a constitutional amendment are unconstitutional. It seems that the National Popular Vote Compact may be an attempt to do the same thing as the Arkansas law in question in *U.S. Term Limits v. Thornton*.
18. Gallup shows a brief surge pushing Republican identifiers ahead of Democratic identifiers around 1991 and again briefly in 2002 (Jones 2012a). The Pew Research Center (2010) shows party identification (PID) about even right around the time of the 1994-midterm elections.
19. According to Smithsonian Magazine (Smithsonian.com 2008), it was the 1940 Republican Convention that was *the* first one to be televised.
20. Perot's 30-minute ads are sometimes recalled for their quaint use of old-style cardboard graphs on easels in an era of high tech graphics.
21. Some might argue that with the overabundance of debates during the primary season in 2008 that we may have reached the saturation point.
22. Johnson's exact words were, "These are the stakes—to make a world in which all of God's children can live, or to go into the dark. We must either love each other, or we must die" (in Westen 2007, 56). There are copies of the video of the ad available on numerous websites including YouTube and at the website for the Johnson Presidential Library.
23. Additional material comes from what appears to be a well-documented website, Conelrad: All Things Atomic (Conelrad.com n.d.), cofounded by Bill Geerhart.
24. The campaign of 1972 saw fairly extensive use of negative ads aimed at McGovern.
25. As one might expect, McClure and Patterson (1976) also found that voters who read newspaper coverage had the most extensive knowledge of the issues of the campaign.
26. Early on there was also the development of a 30-minute format headline news service, which eventually became Headline News Network (an offshoot of CNN) and then later HLN (which now offers more than the original headline format). Since then NBC and FOX have developed specialized channels dealing with financial news and their original channels have specialized in opinion content filling much of their schedule from the left and right, respectively.
27. Certainly, President Obama hopes that release of his "official long-form" birth certificate will put persistent rumors as to the location of his birth to rest.
28. A great nonpolitical example of the ability to build crowds with this new technology was the massive public snowball fight in Washington, DC, during "snowpocalypse" or "snowmaggedon" (both terms coming from the creativity of users of social networking technology) organized via Facebook and Twitter in the winter of 2009–2010.
29. One treatment of the early application of such technology is available in *Mousepads, Shoe Leather, and Hope* by Teachout and Streeter et al. (2008).

8 You've Been Elected, Why Is This Guy Asking How You Feel All the Time? The Vice President and Succession

1. Through 2010.
2. The actual quote is, "In this I am nothing. But I may be everything" (quoted in Schlesinger 1965, *A Thousand Days: John F. Kennedy in the White House*).
3. The closest we come to a firm source on this quote is the account, by Theodore White (1961), of advice given to Lyndon Johnson by Garner while Johnson was contemplating accepting an offer from John F. Kennedy to be vice president. It is also alleged that the reference to "spit" is the cleaned up version used by Garner in polite company, but the actual reference was to another bodily fluid at the opposite end of the digestive tract.
4. While the institution was debated early on, many of the points of contention over the institution, including whether or not there should be a vice presidency and what it should look like, were postponed and then dealt with months later in the final days of the convention.
5. The "title," according to David McCullough (2001), was first bestowed by Ralph Izard, of South Carolina, and quickly caught on among members of Congress. According to Milkis and Nelson (2012), Ben Franklin referred to the office as "His Superfluous Excellency."
6. The Twelfth Amendment, passed in response to the 1800 election between Adams and Jefferson, changed this particular structural aspect to the animosity by entrenching political parties in the process of electing the president and vice president.
7. The only defined role for the vice president in the Senate is to preside—decide who gets the floor and to make decisions about procedure—and cast a tie-breaking vote.
8. This title refers to Tyler's being an "accidental" president, being the first vice president to have to assume the office following the death of the president.
9. At that time, and currently, a simultaneous vacancy in the presidency and vice presidency would be filled by the sitting Speaker of the House of Representatives.
10. Though the Twenty-Fifth Amendment *was not* invoked following the failed assassination attempt that resulted in a lengthy surgery with Reagan unconscious.
11. A few years later, President George H. W. Bush was set to do the same thing and devolve power to Vice President Quayle. A lack of confidence in Quayle's abilities within the Beltway, it was speculated, caused Bush to ask doctors for an alternative procedure that would require only a local anesthetic (Advertiser 1991; Bryant 1991; Rennert 1991; Savva 1991).
12. Similar to *The West Wing* example is the plot of the Harrison Ford movie, *Air Force One*. In this treatment, the president himself is a hostage (along with his family and much of his senior staff) and some members of the cabinet agree to invoke the disability clause. Among the most dramatic scenes in the movie is when the vice president, played by Glenn Close, refuses to sign the letter with the cabinet members.
13. The individual named by the Senate to preside in the absence of the vice president, usually the most senior member of the majority party.
14. An interesting twist on this is the scenario where a president declares (or the cabinet votes) his or her inability to carry out their duties under the disability clause of the Twenty-Fifth Amendment when there is no sitting vice president. The Speaker or the president pro tempore would have to give up their seat for the duration of the presidential disability and then, if they so desired, seek to replace themselves in their legislative position by special election (for the House everywhere and in some states for the Senate) or appointment (for the Senate only in some states). As mentioned earlier, this scenario

was dealt with in an interesting fashion in the fictional setting of a TV drama—*The West Wing*—in the early 2000s.
15. A reference to Cheney's accidental shooting of a hunting partner in the face with his shotgun, which, fortunately for his friend, was loaded with a lighter weight birdshot.

9 Presidential Character: Everybody Has One

1. Frye's routine depicting this transformation is entitled "The Trial" and is part of his 1973 comedy album *Richard Nixon: A Fantasy*. The entire album is dedicated to a fictional prediction of what might yet be revealed as the Watergate Scandal unravels. In "The Trial," Frye has TV lawyer Perry Mason question Nixon on the stand and gets him to break down in much the same way as the lawyer in the *Caine Mutiny* gets Queeg to break down and reveal his underlying psychological issues.
2. It could be argued that this is the image Hillary Clinton was going for in her TV ad during her battle against Barack Obama for the Democratic nomination in 2008. Many now know this ad, produced for the Ohio and Texas primaries in March of that year, as the "3 AM ad," where the voice over asks us, essentially, who we want answering that phone that rings in the middle of the night.
3. Marvick discusses Lasswell's reliance on the Freudian personality model and "aimless instinctual drives" (1980, 221).
4. Some might argue that the actual quote used "fortune" in place of "chance," either way the meaning is the same.
5. Recall the discussion of these events in chapter 6.
6. For those interested in the psychological literature on this point, Albert Bandura (2005) provides a nice summary of sociocognitive theory.
7. Political scientist Charles O. Jones has argued that, at least in his first term, Bill Clinton was an active-positive (Jones 1997).
8. Barber's other work on political mood and presidential electoral cycles, *The Pulse of Politics* (1977b), details a three-stage cycle of conflict, conscience, and conciliation. Each stage of this cycle calls for a different presidential character. For a thorough treatment and table, see also Michael Nelson (2003).
9. It should be noted that when Madison took office, the building was not referred to as the White House. In fact, it wouldn't even be white in color until after the War of 1812.
10. Patterson wrote, "Scratch Barber, and you will find a liberal Democratic partisan" (1973, 64).
11. For one, Patterson focuses on Barber's "more than ordinarily" selectivity and the potential for "lazy students to 'fit' presidents into neat little cubbyholes" (1973, 64).
12. Psychologists may be more skeptical of employing personality theories, despite their prevalence in popular culture. Further, readers should note that the usage throughout this chapter is predominantly that of political scientists, not psychologists and thus might not accurately reflect typical usage in the psychology literature or classroom.
13. Hargrove discusses this in the context of ego defense, a scheme also found in Greenstein (1969).
14. A more popular theory, but not well supported by empirical work.
15. For those interested in a more psychological treatment, see Kagan et al. (2007).
16. It is hard for me to imagine Nixon in this category where the foundation principle is the expectation of doing the right thing, but when one digs deeper and notes the focus on reward and punishment, sense of duty, and preservation of the institution it makes a bit more sense.

17. Some might also argue in favor of the "cocktail party value" of the typology. Certainly, I have experienced some interesting class discussions over the years about some of Barber's more controversial placements.
18. As is the case with Whicker and Moore's (1988) summary, which includes work from management and marketing.
19. Terms that refer to the camaraderie often present in political interactions.
20. Liberal and conservative are used here in their contemporary meanings in politics circa 2013. They can be confusing and mean very different things, depending on one's perspective. They are used as descriptors of ideology and not necessarily partisanship—Democratic or Republican.
21. See chapter 12 for a discussion of these events.
22. It might say something, as well, about the president's choice for chief of staff.

10 The Presidential Advisory System: For Good or Ill, There Really Is One

1. The War Department lasted until World War II, when it was replaced by the Department of Defense, which retained the seniority of its predecessor.
2. Using its power, primarily under the interstate commerce clause, Congress not only created a large, new bureaucracy, but also empowered that bureaucracy to create rules and regulations of a much more detailed nature than a law could cover that had the force of law behind them. These actions by Congress were taken in response to the need to create jobs and regulate the economy in the aftermath of the Great Depression.
3. Some have noted a different organizational form, which could be said to be collegial in nature. The more traditional view of this form is that it looks like the hub-and-spoke or competitive model, but assumes collective responsibility for decision making as opposed to competition for presidential attention. The alternative view employs an ad hoc system that could be hub-and-spoke, but may also makes use of committees and task forces (see California Regents 2006).
4. Clinton also held preinauguration summits on the economy, leading to the creation of the council.
5. HEW was created in 1953, DOT in 1966, and HUD in 1965.
6. For example, the Justice Department had overall responsibility for enforcement of new civil rights laws, but other agencies like HUD with regard to fair housing also had primary responsibility for enforcing the new laws under their jurisdiction.
7. This behavior is often referred to as "capture." One might think of this as working for the special interests and as a good thing, but the perspective here is from the White House and the representation is seen as a bad thing for good government or good policy development (Berman 1986).
8. For a wonderful treatment of Lincoln's cabinet as a decision-making body see, Doris Kearns Goodwin's (2006) *Team of Rivals: The Political Genius of Abraham Lincoln*.
9. Hamilton was serving at the time as Washington's secretary of the Treasury.
10. Nixon also did not want Romney outside the administration in a position where he might make use of his growing constituency, independent of Nixon's, to challenge Nixon for the Republican nomination in 1972.
11. The metaphor of the "Iron Triangle" has been used in political science to demonstrate the strength of the relationship among the organizations depicted. Iron is a strong metal and a triangle is the strongest geometric shape.

222 NOTES

12. These would include his rivals for the Republican Party nomination: William Seward, Salmon Chase, Simon Cameron, and Edward Bates. This inclusion prompted the title of Doris KearnsGoodwin's book about the Lincoln administration, *Team of Rivals*.

11   The President and the Bureaucracy

1. This simple definition comes from breaking the word into its component roots—bureau and kratia—roughly translating to department rule.
2. I realize that another usage here is to say "in line," but the region in which I grew up and the time before the Internet the common usage was "on line."
3. Some scholars have interpreted Weber's ideal to have as few as four and as many as ten characteristics. These comprise my particular spin on Weber. Milakovich and Gordon (2001) also layout six characteristics as they derive from the work of Gerth and Mills (1946).
4. Freund (1968) provides eight principles derived from Weber's work. They are (I summarize and closely paraphrase here): specific areas of competence defined by law; protection of officials in the performance of their duties, including life tenure; a hierarchy; merit qualification; regular remuneration and retirement benefits; work subject to regulation by a superior; merit promotion using objective criteria; and separation from politics (234–235).
5. For examples of good reviews of the concept and the literature on it, see Demir (2009) and Garofalo (2008).
6. This was the "street" story. A number of news stories made reference to low levels of compliance or enforcement. For examples from the policy discussions in New York State, see Fisher (1995), Stuart (1986), and Yates (1988).
7. Certainly, politics of the early twenty-first century has led to massive cuts in the NASA budget, delaying or canceling a planned trip to Mars by human beings or even a return to the Moon.
8. For more on the legend of Smokey the Bear, there are a number of web sources available, among which is the website for the National Forest where the injured bear cub that became the icon for the ad campaign was found (United States Forest Service "Story of Smokey Bear"). It is notable that "Smokey Bear" was first named "Hot Foot Teddy" for his fire-singed feet.
9. As indicated earlier, in the next chapter, we will see a rather well researched instance of such lack of control.
10. Meier (1993) provides a very good review of the literature up to that point in time.
11. Charles Perrow (2006) provides a detailed account and an analysis of the options available.

12   Presidential Decision Making

1. Janis details his thought process in the preface to *Victims of Groupthink* (1972).
2. Fiasco is defined by *Webster's New World Dictionary* (1990) as "a complete, ridiculous failure."
3. Janis (1972) asserts that this reinforcement is often the side effect of a leader's style. For this fiasco, he argues, it was often the way Kennedy ran meetings. Subtle manipulation

of the agenda, unintentional, and his domination of the questioning of the CIA presentations led the other members of the group to a more docile state that reinforced their desire, collective or individually, to not rock the boat (43–46).
4. According to Janis, these are individuals who are "self-appointed" members of the group who come forward to protect "the leader and the members from unwelcome ideas that might set them to thinking about the unfavorable consequences of their preferred course of action and that might lead to dissension instead of a comfortable consensus" (1972, 42).
5. Bowles was later "promoted" to a different foreign policy position as a way of easing him out of the State Department for his failure to be a team player. Bowles was later returned to a position he had held earlier in his career, US ambassador to India. He is also supposed to have been the Wikileaks of his time, releasing information to the press about the Bay of Pigs operation; this was perfectly in keeping with his liberal approach to government—having been defeated for reelection as governor of Connecticut for being ahead of his time on civil rights issues.
6. Janis asserts that Dulles and Bissell were viewed as "valuable new members of the team" unlike the Joint Chiefs who were seen as more loyal to their respective services than to the president. However, acknowledging that these valuable new members might feel a bit uncomfortable as part of an inner circle of men they had not previously worked with and thus the group was careful not to make them feel defensive.
7. As we will see in the chapter on the president and Congress (chapter 15), in midterm elections—those held in the even years between presidential elections—the president's party tends to lose seats in Congress, especially in the House of Representatives. As of the 2010-midterm elections, only three times has this not occurred—1934, 1998, and 2002.
8. "ExComm" was a shorthand reference to Executive Committee.
9. A reference to the Japanese emperor who ordered the surprise Sunday morning attack on US forces at Pearl Harbor in 1941.
10. Green and Shapiro (1994) provide an extensive critique of the application of the rational actor model in political science.
11. Utility maximization is a standard assumption about what humans seek in the solution to problems, with the decision maker receiving the most benefit for the least cost. The distinction between the two terms is that optimization would more broadly cover those circumstances where the goal was the minimization of costs as opposed to the maximization of benefits. For the purposes of this discussion, the terms may be used interchangeably.
12. During the time of the Kennedy administration, the close-knit decision making body in the Soviet Union was actually the Presidium of the Central Committee of the Communist Party, but the old name—used back in the days of Stalin—seemed to stick even though it did not formally return to use until 1966 after Khrushchev had been removed from office.

13   The President and the Media

1. Individuals whose job it is to place a partisan interpretation of news events into the mix of coverage. Such practices seem to be more prevalent following debates, but can happen at any time. They are usually not the same as "talking heads" who are more likely to be in the employ of the media, where spin-doctors are employed by or allied with politicians or political organizations, though in recent years the line has been blurred a bit.

2. A "backgrounder" is an opportunity to meet with a source that has information that might flesh out a story for a reporter, provide him or her with important details that other reporters might not have. This could be done prior to the press conference to help shape the kinds of questions that might be asked or it could be done after the fact to help influence a follow-up story.
3. Nixon (and his staff) was known to have accumulated a "list" of enemies who were targeted for investigation by the Internal Revenue Service. According to *Washington Post* publisher Katharine Graham, the Nixon administration may have also had a role in the challenging of broadcast licenses for two of *The Post*'s TV stations in Florida as retaliation for *The Post*'s coverage of Watergate (Graham 1997).
4. At this point in history, the reference is primarily to broadcast networks, only CNN was up and running as a cable news organization.
5. Rare exceptions might be if there is a need for a direct address from the president while he or she is traveling. For example, George W. Bush stopped on his way back to Washington to deliver some reassuring words from Barksdale Air Force Base in Louisiana on September 11th, 2001.
6. This was Carter's attempt to mimic the famous addresses given by Franklin Roosevelt during the Depression.
7. Though initially receiving a positive response from the American people and some commentators (Safire 1977), after being roundly criticized by the media and political pundits, these "FDR-like" chats were considered less than presidential and thus a failure.
8. Reagan's handlers sought to avoid these circumstances and even resorted to having Marine One's engines start up as the president exited the White House so he could not hear the questions being asked by the Press Corps.
9. We will deal with this power in greater detail in the conclusion to this text in chapter 18.

14 Presidential Popularity: How Do I Approve of Thee? Let Gallup Count the Ways

1. In recent history, it has only been men.
2. In the 2004 election, it was said that more people would prefer to have a beer with President George W. Bush than with Senator John Kerry (his opponent in the general election). Some thought this was a bit ironic considering Bush's status as a recovering alcoholic who could not have a beer (Benedetto 2004).
3. During the Reagan presidency, House Speaker Tip O'Neill would often make reference to his warm personal relationship with the president, but how that did not change his mind about his opposition to Reagan's policies (Matthews 2011).
4. In part, this was the public perception of his "malaise" speech. While later thought of by historians and pundits as perhaps an excellent philosophical exposition of the nation's state of mind, at the time it was seen as "preachy" and too intellectual. Perhaps this stemmed from Carter's background as a Sunday school teacher.
5. This was diminished significantly with the first post-Clinton poll that showed the impact of the controversy over a number of Clinton's granting of pardons and clemency. This is a practice often done near the end of a year, but the most controversial are usually held until a president is about to leave office.
6. See more detailed discussion in chapter 4.
7. He had served as Reagan's vice president.

8. While Gronke and Newman (2003) provide a very good review of the literature, some of the classics in this field include work by Brace and Hinckley (1993), Kernell (1978), MacKuen (1983), Mueller (1970, 1973), and Ostrom and Simon (1985).
9. As has been the case with most presidents, including the most recent—Barack Obama—even though he inherited much of the economic problem causing the unemployment.
10. See the discussion of the "rally 'round the flag" effect further on.
11. One exception is said to be the previously mentioned bombing of Marine Headquarters in Beirut, Lebanon, in October of 1983. Instead of rallying 'round the president in this case, the public blamed him for the Marines being there in the first place.
12. The scandal involving Senator John Ensign of Nevada comes to mind with its marital infidelities, job placements, and monetary payoffs, which finally resulted in the Senator's resignation—in an effort to thwart an ethics investigation in the Senate—after an extended period of time and media coverage.
13. For example, a politician who promotes family values and has engaged in marital infidelity or opposes gay rights and is found to have had homosexual relationships. The most vivid example in recent history is that of New York Governor Eliot Spitzer. Having built his career on an image of integrity, and in particular made something of a name for himself in the prosecution of prostitution rings (when serving as assistant district attorney for Manhattan), only to be brought down by the discovery of his patronage of such establishments, later when he was governor of New York.
14. It is also the case that Clinton presided over a rather lengthy economic boom and most voters were more concerned with the fact that they had more money in their pocket than whether or not the president was being unfaithful to his wife. So too, once he had admitted his indiscretions, the public saw the impeachment proceedings brought by the Republicans in Congress as more overtly partisan and the offenses as not rising to the level of impeachable actions. True, few parents wanted their daughters to be White House interns, but they were not willing to say that the actions justified impeachment.
15. Clearly, without resigning Nixon would have been the second president to be impeached (at that time). Impeachment is similar to a criminal indictment and if the impeached individual is found guilty the punishment is immediate removal from office. In all, two presidents—Andrew Johnson and Bill Clinton—have been impeached (while the Judiciary Committee voted to impeach Nixon, the vote never got to the floor of the House) and none have been convicted and removed. Nixon short-circuited the process by resigning soon after a meeting with leading Republicans from Congress who allegedly informed him that he lacked sufficient support to avoid conviction.
16. The difference was the public's acceptance of Kennedy's open admission of responsibility for the failure, rather than trying to blame others. It is often the case that such an admission of responsibility for errors, not scandals, will result in a positive impact on approval ratings.
17. In a rather timely coincidence, the movie was out right around the time Clinton had been forced to reveal to his wife, Hillary, that he had been inappropriately involved with Lewinsky. He returned from a family retreat at Martha's Vineyard to order cruise missile attacks on al Qaeda leadership, including bin Laden, in retaliation for terrorist attacks on US embassies in Africa.

15 The President and Congress

1. Recall that while this amendment limits a president to two full terms, the actual limit in terms of the number of years is ten. He or she is allowed two terms in his or her own right if he or she ascended to the office through a vacancy created by his or her predecessor.

2. The term "lame duck" refers to an elected official who is serving out the remainder of his or her term. This could occur through a number of mechanisms, defeat in a general, or primary, election, a decision not to run for reelection, or being prohibited from running by a statutory or constitutional limit on the office. The length of the lame duck period would depend on the length of the term of the office and the method by which the member would be leaving office.
3. The social sciences have sometimes been referred to as "soft science" to distinguish them from the "harder" physical and biological sciences.
4. Information about politics is much easier to find and it seems to flood into the living rooms of voters via TV and other technologies more readily in presidential election years.
5. House member rates are often above 95 percent and the Senate tends to run a bit lower between 85 and 90 percent.
6. Some don't even wait to "retire" by not seeking reelection and resign outright. Recent examples of this include Senator John Ensign of Nevada, Representatives Eric Massa, Chris Collins, and Anthony Weiner (all of New York).
7. A filibuster is a parliamentary tactic employed by a minority of the members of a legislative body to slow down the legislative process or to stop the majority from getting its way. The minority could be as small as a single member. For fans of old movies, the best portrayal of a filibuster in a fictional setting is the climax of *Mr. Smith Goes to Washington*.
8. These are individuals with resources to bring to the aid of members seeking reelection. Such resources can include votes, volunteers, and money.
9. Resources here is a nonpejorative term referring to the more commonly understood: bacon, pork, and earmarks.
10. The use of the male pronoun here is historically speaking.
11. These often include items such as fund raising help, campaign assistance, staff, and choice office space.
12. Franklin Roosevelt was the notable exception winning four terms as president, but serving just over 12 years when he passed away early in his fourth term.
13. Typically "leaving a legacy" is a greater concern for a second term.
14. Under Senate rules, members may place "holds" on chamber consideration of various legislative actions, including presidential appointments.
15. It was said that Clinton had even offered helicopter tours of the Capital area among other less tangible rewards in attempt to gain support.
16. The ten-day count starts at midnight on the day following the president's receipt of the bill. In other words, if it is received at 1 p.m. on Tuesday, the clock starts at 12 a.m. Wednesday. The ten days do not include Sundays.
17. I would define "veto proof" as above two-thirds or 67 percent, but Conley and Kreppel (2001) look at what they call a "supermajority veto" of 75 percent or better.
18. A bit different from the way we have done this in the most recent past, with Clinton and Nixon, respectively. In those more recent cases, the charges came first and then the House Judiciary Committee considered whether or not there was sufficient evidence to bring those charges to the full House. In 1868, the process was almost the complete reverse.
19. The average success for Carter in his first two years was 76.8 percent with both houses controlled by his party and for Reagan's first two years; his success was 77.35 percent with one chamber controlled by the opposition. This is author's calculation from *Vital Statistics on American Politics* by Stanley and Niemi (1988).
20. Some scholars have found the effect to be waning over time, perhaps due to a more assertive Congress since the mid-1970s and Fleisher and Bond (1988) have found that perhaps the effect only exists for Republican presidents.

21. In the contemporary political environment with very high levels of partisanship, this is much less likely.
22. Question time is a regularly scheduled opportunity for members of the legislature to ask questions of cabinet ministers, especially the prime minister.
23. Recall that Hargove and Nelson's categorization looks at the strength of the institution of the executive and whether or not that strength is good or bad for the country.

16 The President and the Judiciary

1. It has also been alleged that it was pressure from the Israeli government, which "owed" Rich a favor. In return for the pardon, supposedly, the Israelis reopened peace talks in Egypt (Conason 2009).
2. Recall from the discussion in chapter 2 that Owen Roberts may have actually changed his vote *before* Roosevelt's "court packing scheme" had been announced.
3. The three recent exceptions have been Chief Justice Earl Warren, Associate and Chief Justice William Rehnquist, and Associate Justice Elena Kagan, all other recent nominees have, at one time or another, been a judge.
4. The allegations involved sexual harassment while Hill was employed by Thomas at the Equal Employment Opportunity Commission.
5. At least one news account/analysis from 2010, after Justice Stevens had announced his retirement, indicates a concern with intellectual diversity on the Court. Shailagh Murray and Paul Kane (2010) of *The Washington Post* detailed the dominance of Ivy League legal training among the sitting justices. They went on to list some of the backgrounds of potential nominees and emphasized their *lack* of Ivy League training.
6. George W. Bush's White House Counsel Harriet Miers had been nominated, but the nomination was withdrawn after a public outcry regarding her apparent lack of experience.
7. These are the rights familiar to anyone who watches "cop" shows on TV or sees the occasional policy drama (or comedy) in theaters. The reading of these rights in these fictional settings often begins, "You are under arrest. You have the right to remain silent."
8. Seven of this 124 declined to serve *after* having been confirmed.
9. Bork, as acting attorney general in October of 1973, fired the Watergate special prosecutor—Archibald Cox (a Kennedy family friend)—in what later became known as the Saturday Night Massacre, during which Nixon not only fired Cox, but also accepted the resignations of the Justice Department's top two officials who refused to fire Cox.
10. Marshall was best known, prior to his nomination by Johnson, as the attorney for the National Association for the Advancement of Colored People (NAACP) who argued for Brown in the landmark Supreme Court case Brown v. Board of Education, Topeka, Kansas.
11. The Constitution requires this for the president, but the Senate included trials of vice presidents with a change to the chamber's rules in 1986.
12. This is an argument cited often when there is a public outcry over a particularly unpopular decision of the Court.
13. In addition to their work, Segal, Timpone, and Howard (2000) provide a very good review of the other literature in this particular field.
14. In reference to Worcester v. Georgia (31 U.S. (6 Pet.) 515, 1832).
15. Truman had seized them in the name of national security to avoid a United Steelworkers Strike that could have hindered our efforts in the Korean War. See the discussion further on in the text.

16. This was the recording of conversations between the president and his closest advisers that made it next impossible for Republicans in the House and Senate to continue their support of him. Writer William Safire (2003) traces the origin of the term to a Sherlock Holmes story by Sir Arthur Conan Doyle, but that two House Republicans used it in reference to evidence in the Watergate investigations. "On July 31 [1974], Representative Jack Brooks of Texas told the impeachment panel that he thought Nixon was guilty of income-tax evasion: 'Millions of Americans will view this evidence as a so-called smoking gun.' With insufficient proof, that charge did not stick" (Safire 2003). Republican Representative Barber Conable of New York, after hearing the tape, reportedly said, "That looked like a smoking gun."

17 The President and Policymaking: Domestic, Economic, and Foreign

1. According to BrainyQuote.com, the actual quote comes from Franklin Roosevelt, who said, "It is the duty of the President to propose and it is the privilege of the Congress to dispose." There is also some discussion that Roosevelt was making a play on words from the religious arena where the reference is supposedly, "Man proposes but God disposes."
2. The commerce clause is that section of Article I of the Constitution that grants Congress the power to regulate interstate commerce.
3. Naturally, this question was resolved by the Supreme Court's decision in *National Federation of Independent Business v. Sebelius* (132 S. Ct. 2566, 2012), where the power of Congress to mandate individual purchase of health insurance was permissible via the congressional power to tax.
4. See the discussion of the theory of the unitary executive in chapter 18 for more detail.
5. Paraphrasing Clinton campaign adviser James Carville's famous quote from 1992, "It's the economy, stupid."
6. And, some might add, the economic ideas of John Maynard Keynes, who argued that governments should run surpluses in times of economic prosperity and deficits to stimulate the economy during downturns.
7. Each of these banks and branches operates in a given geographic region of the country.
8. The term "Jawboning" comes from the concept of Samson's cudgel—the jawbone of an ass—from the Biblical story where Samson used only this weapon to defeat thousands of enemies. Its use as an economic weapon by presidents is explained by Thomas Donlan (2008) in an article in *Barron's*.
9. Naturally, the effects of weather on shopping tend to be more localized.
10. It may be true that some presidents seek to have dissenting voices in such advisory groups "to keep them honest."
11. It should also be noted that Keynesian economics most often advocates for such spending to be in the area of infrastructure, not only creating jobs very quickly but also creating conditions to help business and industry to prosper. That is, there is an assumption that road and rail repair and construction, building of airports and seaports, and, more recently, government investment in new technologies will make it easier for business to function and generate private profit, investment, and jobs.
12. The problem as I see it is that Keynesian policy hasn't worked to its full potential because our elected officials became electorally addicted to deficit spending.

13. To better imagine this concept, picture one of those pyramids of champagne glasses where after the pyramid is built all the glasses are empty, but a server begins pouring champagne into the glass at the very top of the pyramid of glasses until it begins to overflow. This overflow then begins to "trickle down" through the remaining glasses until the champagne reaches the bottom layer of glasses and fills them as well.
14. Marginal tax rates are defined as the rate of taxation on the last dollar earned.
15. Keynes rejected this notion in his well-known work, *The General Theory of Employment, Interest, and Money* (1936), and postulated that it was demand that created supply.
16. Naturally, presidents who are more Keynesian will also seek to make like-minded appointments, but they may also be more likely to use budgetary policy to achieve their ends.
17. Though the surplus was for Fiscal Year 1969, it was achieved by Johnson's last budget prior to Nixon taking office.
18. This is mostly true, except for the Reagan Era experiment with supply side economics. Even under Reagan, some have argued, the government used a combination of tax cuts and government spending, both of which are Keynesian prescriptions for ending a recession.
19. According to Richard Benedetto of *USA Today* (2005), the phrase comes from former Senator Arthur Vandenberg (R, MI) from the late 1940s.
20. The War Powers Act is sometimes called the War Powers Resolution by those who are not in power, or in opposition to the president, in an attempt to diminish its authority and scope.
21. Recall our earlier reference to Bush traveling the world, as he put it, "on the frequent *dier* plan."

18 Hope and Change and the Future of the Presidency

1. A recent Gallup Poll indicates that as long as individuals were otherwise qualified to be president, clear majorities could see themselves voting for individuals identifying as Gay or Lesbian, Muslim, or even Atheists—groups that would have had little political chance of winning a presidential election just a few years ago (Jones 2012b).
2. Recall the satire invoked weekly on NBC Television's *Saturday Night Live*, where Ford was portrayed by Chevy Chase as someone who would easily trip and fall, breaking the podium, or otherwise causing himself bodily harm.
3. His first two nominees—Kimba Wood and Zoe Baird—both withdrew their names when it was revealed that they had not paid appropriate payroll taxes for domestic help. As working mothers, they both had hired nannies to help care for young children. The "scandals" became known as nannygate.
4. This was the incident where the Federal Bureau of Investigation (FBI) raided a compound in Texas belonging to a religious cult headed by self-proclaimed messiah, David Koresh, after allegations of child abuse. The raid resulted in the compound burning to the ground killing many of the occupants.
5. His father returned to Kenya not long after Obama's birth and his mother took a very young Barack with her to locations associated with her work as a budding academic and then later left him to be raised by her parents back in her native Kansas.
6. These were protests by opponents of the legislation conducted at the regular "town hall" meetings of members of Congress with their constituents conducted while Congress is in

recess and the members are at home. Senator Arlen Specter (D, PA) was featured in photos as though he were under physical threat from an angry constituent and Representative Barney Frank (D, MA) famously compared an angry woman at one of his meetings to a dining room table.

7. I, personally, recall saying to the person sitting next to me at that convention in Boston after Obama finished his speech that we had probably just heard a speech from what would be the first African American president. Neither of us thought it would come just over four years later.
8. Interestingly or ironically, though Scalia appears to have been an early proponent of the unitary executive, he, along with Justice Stevens provided the dissent in *Hamdi v. Rumsfeld* (542 U.S. 507, 2004) arguing that the president did not have the right to suspend Hamdi's right to habeas corpus without congressional action.
9. The Vesting Clause states, "The executive Power shall be vested in a President of the United States of America" (Article II, section 1).
10. This is a controversial practice where when signing a bill into law the president makes some comment about the law. Bush went further and used these statements often to indicate what aspects of the law he would have his administration implement and which provisions would be ignored.
11. This expression comes from the 1970s hit TV show *Chico and the Man* starring Freddie Prinz, whose character would often shirk responsibility for something by making the claim "not my job."
12. In recent history, this was the case for George W. Bush's first term. A number of critics charged that, given the controversy over the election results and the Supreme Court's decision to terminate the recount in Florida, he was not a legitimately elected president.
13. Such was the case for Barack Obama, who was born of a mother who was a citizen and a father who was not and whose appropriate birth documents were questioned by the so-called Birther Movement.
14. We could also include the Supreme Court, but as we have seen, there is little direct action a president can take to influence the outcome of a Supreme Court decision.

Bibliography

Abramowitz, Alan, David J. Lanoue, and Subha Ramesh. 1988. "Economic Conditions, Causal Attributions, and Political Evaluations in the 1984 Presidential Election." *The Journal of Politics* Vol. 50, No. 4 (November 1988): 848–863.

Adams, John. 1793. Letter to Abigail Adams in John Adams, *The Works of John Adams, Second President of the United States: With a Life of the Author, Notes and Illustrations, by His Grandson Charles Francis Adams* (Boston: Little, Brown and Co., 1856). 10 volumes. Vol. 1, Chapter IX, "Organization of the New Government—Election and Services as Vice-President of the United States." Retrieved on August 31st, 2011, from http://oll.libertyfund.org/title/2099/159554/2817426.

Adkins v. Children's Hospital, 261 U.S. 525 (1923).

Adkins, Randall E., and Kent A. Kirwan. 2002. "What Role Does the 'Federalism Bonus' Play in Presidential Selection?" *Publius* Vol. 32, No. 4, The State of American Federalism, 2001–2002 (Autumn 2002): 71–90.

Advertiser, The. 1991. "No Heart Jolt for President." Nationwide News Pty Ltd., May 7th. Retrieved on September 1st, 2011, from LexisNexis Academic at http://www.lexisnexis.com.

Allison, Graham. 1971. *Essence of Decision: Explaining the Cuban Missile Crisis*. Boston: Little, Brown and Company.

Allison, Graham, and Phillip Zelikow. 1999. *Essence of Decision: Explaining the Cuban Missile Crisis*, 2nd Edn. New York: Addison Wesley Longman.

AllMusicals.com. n.d. Lyrics from *Camelot*. Retrieved on April 26th, 2011, from http://www.allmusicals.com/lyrics/camelot/camelot.htm.

Almond, Gabriel. 1987. "Harold Dwight Lasswell, 1902–1978: A Biographical Memoir." National Academy of Sciences. Washington, DC. Retrieved on June 6th, 2011, from http://www.nap.edu/html/biomems/hlasswell.pdf.

Amar, Akhil Reed. 2008. "The Constitution and the Candidates: What Would the Framers Say?" *Slate.com*, February 4th. Retrieved on July 8th, 2010, from http://www.slate.com/articles/news_and_politics/jurisprudence/2008/02/the_constitution_and_the_candidates.html.

Arrow, Kenneth. 1951. *Social Choice and Individual Values*. New Haven, CT: Yale University Press.

Bagehot, Walter. 1864. *The English Constitution*. ClassicAuthors.net. Retrieved on June 27th, 2012, from http://bagehot.classicauthors.net/EnglishConstitution/EnglishConstitution4.html.

Bailey, Jr., Harry. 1975. "Controlling the Runaway Presidency." A book review essay. *Public Administration Review* Vol. 35, No. 5 (September–October): 547–554.

Bandura, Albert. 2005. "The Evolution of Social Cognitive Theory." In K. G. Smith and M. A. Hitt, eds., *Great Minds in Management*. Oxford, UK: Oxford University Press, pp. 9–35.

Barber, James. 1965. *The Lawmakers: Recruitment and Adaptation to Legislative Life.* New Haven, CT: Yale University Press.
———. 1966. *Power in Committees: An Experiment in the Governmental Process.* Chicago: Rand McNally.
———. 1969. Quoted in Michael Nelson, "James David Barber and the Psychological Presidency." *Virginia Quarterly Review*, August 1980. Retrieved on May 12th, 2011, from http://www.vqronline.org/articles/1980/autumn/nelson-james-david-barber/.
———. 1977a. "The Nixon Brush with Tyranny." *Political Science Quarterly* Vol. 92, No. 4 (Winter 1977): 581–605. Retrieved on May 12th, 2011, from Article Stable URL: http://www.jstor.org/stable/2148845.
———. 1977b. *The Pulse of Politics: Electing Presidents in the Media Age.* New York: Transaction Publishers.
———. 1992. *The Presidential Character*, 4th Edn. Englewood Cliffs, NJ: Prentice Hall.
Barnes, Robert. 2010. "Alito's State of the Union Moment." In "44: Politics and Policy in Obama's Washington." *Washington Post*, January 27th. Retrieved on May 3rd, 2011, from http://voices.washingtonpost.com/44/2010/01/alito-mouths-not-true-at-obama.html.
Baum, Matthew A. 2002. "The Constituent Foundations of the Rally-Round-the-Flag Phenomenon." *International Studies Quarterly* Vol. 46, No. 2 (June 2002): 263–298.
Beard, Charles. 1913. *An Economic Interpretation of the Constitution of the United States.* New York: The MacMillan Company.
Benedetto, Richard. 2004. "Who's More Likable, Bush or Kerry?" *USA Today*, September 17th. Retrieved on June 14th, 2012, from http://www.usatoday.com/news/opinion/columnist/benedetto/2004-09-17-benedetto_x.htm.
———. 2005. "Remember When Partisan Politics Stopped at the Water's Edge?" *USA Today*, November 18th. Retrieved on June 25th, 2012, from http://www.usatoday.com/news/opinion/columnist/benedetto/2005-11-18-benedetto_x.htm.
Berman, Larry. 1986. *The New American Presidency.* Boston: Little, Brown and Company.
Billings Gazette. 2010. "Election May Get Record Turnout." May 10th. Retrieved on May 2nd, 2011, from http://billingsgazette.com/news/local/government-and-politics/elections/article_958ae74a-5c89-11df-b0f9-001cc4c03286.html.
Biskupic, Jane. 2008. "Reagan's Influence Lives on in U.S. Courts." *USA Today*, May 12th. Retrieved on June 18th, 2012, from http://www.usatoday.com/news/washington/judicial/2008-05-11-appellate-judges_N.htm.
Brace, Paul, and Barbara Hinckley. 1993. *Follow the Leader: Opinion Polls and the Modern Presidents.* New York: Basic Books.
BrainyQuote.com. n.d. "Dispose Quotations." Retrieved on June 28th, 2012, from http://www.brainyquote.com/words/di/dispose155716.html.
———. n.d. "Louis Pasteur Quotes." http://www.brainyquote.com/quotes/quotes/l/louispaste159478.html.
Brock, Bill. 2000. "A Review of the Republican Process: Nominating Future Presidents" published in May of 2000 by the Republican National Committee Advisory Commission on the Presidential Nominating Process, chaired by former RNC Chair, Bill Brock. Retrieved on July 15th, 2010, from http://pweb.jps.net/~md-r/ps/brockreport.pdf.
Brown v. Board of Education, 347 U.S. 483 (1954).
Bryant, Carleton. 1991. "Quayle Loses Chance to be President for a Day." *The Washington Times*, May 7th. Retrieved on September 1st, 2011, from LexisNexis Academic at http://www.lexisnexis.com.
Buchanan, James, and Gordon Tullock. 1962. *The Calculus of Consent.* Ann Arbor, MI: University of Michigan Press.
Buckley et al. v. Valeo, 424 U.S. 1 (1976).

Bibliography

Bush v. Gore, 531 U.S. 426 (2000).
Calabresi, Steven, and Christopher Yoo. 2008. *The Unitary Executive: Presidential Power from Washington to Bush*. New Haven, CT: Yale University Press.
California Democratic Party et al. v. Bill Jones, U.S. 567; 120 (2000).
California Regents. 2006. "AP US Government and Politics: Lesson 21—The White House." The Regents of the University of California and Monterey Institute for Technology and Education. Retrieved on September 8th, 2011, from http://www.hippocampus.org/homework-help/American-Government/The%20Executive%20Branch_Presidential%20Management%20Models.html.
Campbell, Angus, Gerald Gurin, and Warren Miller. 1954. *The Voter Decides*. White Plains, NY: Row, Peterson, and Company.
Campbell, Angus, Philip Converse, Warren Miller, and Donald Stokes. 1966. *Elections and the Political Order*. New York: John Wiley & Sons.
Campbell, James. 1987. "The Revised Theory of Surge and Decline." *American Journal of Political Science* Vol. 31, No. 4 (November 1987): 965–979.
Carpenter, Daniel. 1996. "Adaptive Signal Processing, Hierarchy, and Budgetary Control in Federal Regulation." *The American Political Science Review* Vol. 90, No. 2 (June 1996): 283–302.
Carter, Jimmy. 1982. *Keeping Faith: Memoirs of a President*. New York: Bantam Books.
CBS News. 2009. "Nixon Pardon Defined Ford Presidency." CBS News Politics, CBSNEWS.com. February 11th. Retrieved on June 14th, 2012, from http://www.cbsnews.com/2100-250_162-2299592.html.
Choiniere, Ray, and David Keirsey. 1992. *Presidential Temperament: The Unfolding of Character in the Forty Presidents of the United States*. Del Mar, CA: Prometheus Nemesis Book Company.
Citizens United, Appellant v. Federal Elections Commission (FEC), 558 U.S. 310 (2010).
Citizens United. n.d. Retrieved on July 7th, 2010, from http://www.citizensunited.org.
Clinton v. Jones, 520 U.S. 681 (1997).
Clinton, Bill. 1992. "I Still Believe in a Place Called Hope." Democratic Underground.com. Retrieved on May 4th, 2011, from http://www.democraticunderground.com/speeches/clinton.html.
———. 2004. *My Life*. New York: Knopf Doubleday Publishing Group.
CNN.com. 1996. "Democratic Rules: Some highlights of Recent Democratic Convention Rules Disputes." Retrieved on July 2nd, 2012, from http://www.cnn.com/ALLPOLITICS/1996/conventions/chicago/facts/rules/index.shtml.
———. 2008. "Election Center 2008." Retrieved on June 25th, 2010, from http://www.cnn.com/ELECTION/2008/candidates/.
Cochran, Clarke, Lawrence Mayer, T. R. Carr, and N. Joseph Cayer. 2006. *American Public Policy: An Introduction*. Belmont, CA: Thomson Higher Education.
Conason, Joe. 2009. "The Real Reason Bill Clinton Pardoned Marc Rich." Salon.com. January 16th. Retrieved on June 20th, 2012, from http://www.salon.com/2009/01/16/holder_4/.
Conelrad.com. n.d. "Daisy: The Complete History of an Infamous and Iconic Ad." Retrieved on July 2nd, 2012, from http://www.conelrad.com/daisy/index.php.
Conley, Richard, and Amie Kreppel. 2001. "Toward a New Typology of Vetoes and Overrides." *Political Research Quarterly* Vol. 54, No. 4 (December 2001): 831–852.
Copeland, Gary. 1983. "When Congress and the President Collide: Why Presidents Veto Legislation." *The Journal of Politics* Vol. 45, No. 3 (August 1983): 696–710.
Cornell University Law School Legal Information Institute. 2003. "Bipartisan Campaign Reform Act of 2002: An Overview." Retrieved on May 3rd, 2011, from http://topics.law.cornell.edu/wex/bcra.

Corrado, Anthony, Dan Ortiz, Frank Sorauf, Thomas E. Mann, and Trevor Potter, eds. 1997. *Campaign Finance Reform: A Sourcebook*. Washington, DC: Brookings Institution Press.

Cousins et al. v. Wigoda et al., 419 U.S. 477 (1975).

Covington and Lexington Turnpike Railroad Co. v. Sandford, 164 U.S. 578 (1896).

Cronin, Thomas, and Robert Loevy. 1983. "The Case for a National Pre-Primary Convention," *Public Opinion* Vol. 5 (December–January 1983): 50–53.

Davidson, Roger, Walter Oleszek, and Francis Lee. 2012. *Congress and Its Members*, 12th Edn. Washington, DC: Congressional Quarterly, Inc.

Demir, Tansu. 2009. "Politics and Administration: Three Schools, Three Approaches, and Three Suggestions." *Administrative Theory & Praxis* Vol. 31, No. 4 (December 2009): 503–532.

Democratic National Committee (DNC). 2005. *Report of the Commission on Presidential Nomination and Scheduling to Governor Howard Dean, Chairman, Democratic National Committee*. Washington, DC: DNC Office of Party Affairs and Delegate Selection.

Democratic Party of the United States et al. v. Wisconsin, Ex rel. LaFollette et al., 450 U.S. 107 (1981).

Donlan, Thomas. 2008. "The Cudgel of Samson: How the Government Once Used 'Jawboning' to Fight Inflation: The Fed Merely Talks the Talk on Inflation." *Barron's*, March 24th. Retrieved on June 27th, 2012, from http://online.barrons.com/article/SB120614228496656237.html#articleTabs_article%3D1.

Eastland, Terry. 1993. *Energy in the Executive*. New York: Simon and Schuster.

Epstein, Lee, and Thomas Walker. 2012. *Constitutional Law for a Changing America: A Short Course*, 5th Edn. Washington, DC: Sage / CQ Press.

Fairvote.org. n.d. "The Delaware Plan." Retrieved on July 15th, 2010, from http://archive.fairvote.org/?page=2064.

Farhi, Paul. 2004. "Elephants Are Red, Donkeys Are Blue, Color Is Sweet, So Their States We Hue." *Washington Post*, November 2nd. Retrieved on May 4th, 2011, from http://www.washingtonpost.com/wp-dyn/articles/A17079-2004Nov1.html.

Federal Elections Commission (FEC). n.d. "Appendix 4—The Federal Election Campaign Laws: A Short History." Retrieved on May 3rd, 2011, from http://www.fec.gov/info/appfour.htm.

Federal Election Commission, Appellant v. Wisconsin Right to Life, Inc.; Senator John McCain et al., Appellants v. Wisconsin Right to Life, Inc., 551 U.S. 449 (2007).

Federal Reserve, Board of Governors. n.d. "Who Are the Members of the Federal Reserve Board, and How Are They Selected?" Current FAQs: Informing the Public about the Federal Reserve. Retrieved on June 25th, 2012, from http://www.federalreserve.gov/faqs/about_12591.htm.

———. 2005. *The Federal Reserve System: Purposes & Functions*, 9th Edn. Washington, DC: Board of Governors of the Federal Reserve System.

Feibel, Caroline. 2008. "A Guide to Texas' Electoral Two-Step." *Houston Chronicle*, March 1st. Retrieved on February 21st, 2011, from http://www.chron.com/disp/story.mpl/politics/5583761.html.

Fenno, Richard. 1978. *Home Style: House Members in Their Districts*. Boston, MA: Little, Brown, and Company.

Ferling, John. 2005. *Adams vs. Jefferson: The Tumultuous Election of 1800*. New York: Oxford University Press.

Fesler, James. 1987. "The Brownlow Committee Fifty Years Later." *Public Administration Review* Vol. 47, No. 4 (July–August 1987): 291–296.

Fiorina, Morris. 1977. *Congress: Keystone of the Washington Establishment*. New Haven, CT: Yale University Press.

———. 1981. *Retrospective Voting in American National Elections*. New Haven, CT: Yale University Press.

Fisher, Ian. 1995. "Catching Up to Its Drivers, State Goes 65." *The New York Times*, April 12th.

FitzGerald, Frances. 1972. *Fire in the Lake*. Boston, MA: Little, Brown and Company.

Fleisher, Richard, and Jon Bond. 1988. "Are There Two Presidencies? Yes, But Only for Republicans." *The Journal of Politics* Vol. 50, No. 3 (August 1988): 747–767.

Fon, Vincy. 2004. "Electoral College Alternatives and US Presidential Elections." *Supreme Court Economic Review* Vol. 12 (2004): 41–73.

Fox, Margalit. 2004. "James D. Barber, Expert on Presidents, Dies at 74." *The New York Times*, September 15th. Retrieved on May 12th, 2011, from http://www.nytimes.com/2004/09/15/politics/15barber.html.

Frank, Justin. 2011. *Obama on the Couch: Inside the Mind of the President*. New York: Free Press.

Freund, Julien. 1968. *The Sociology of Max Weber*. Translated from French by Mary Ilford. New York: Pantheon Books.

Frye, David. 1973. "The Trial." *Richard Nixon: A Fantasy*. Buddah Records, 1600, LP.

Gangale, Thomas. 2007. *From the Primaries to the Polls: How to Repair America's Broken Presidential Nomination Process*. Santa Barbara, CA: ABC-CLIO Incorporated.

Garofalo, Charles. 2008. "With Deference to Woodrow Wilson: The Ethics-Administration Dichotomy in American Public Service." *Public Integrity* Vol. 10, No. 4 (Fall): 345–354.

George, Alexander, and Juliette George. 1988. *Presidential Personality and Performance*. Boulder, CO: Westview Press.

Gerth, H., and C. Wright Mills. 1946. *From Max Weber: Essays in Sociology*. New York: Oxford University Press.

Gittinger, Ted, and Allen Fisher. 2004. "LBJ Champions the Civil Rights Act of 1964, Part 2." *Prologue Magazine* Vol. 36, No. 2 (Summer 2004). Washington, DC: National Archives. Retrieved on May 4th, 2011, from http://www.archives.gov/publications/prologue/2004/summer/civil-rights-act-2.html.

Goethals, George. 2005. "Presidential Leadership." *Annual Review of Psychology* Vol. 56: 545–570.

Goodwin, Doris Kearns. 2006. *Team of Rivals: The Political Genius of Abraham Lincoln*. New York: Simon and Schuster.

Goldstein, Joel. 1982. *The Modern American Vice Presidency: The Transformation of a Political Institution*. Princeton, NJ: Princeton University Press.

Gould, Lewis L. 2008. "1912 Republican Convention: The Return of the Rough Rider." *Smithsonian Magazine*. Retrieved on July 14th, 2010, from http://www.smithsonianmag.com/history-archaeology/1912-republican-convention.html.

Graham, Katharine. 1997. "The Watergate Watershed: A Turning Point for a Nation and a Newspaper," online excerpt from *Personal History*. New York: Knopf Doubleday Publishing Group. Retrieved on June 11th, 2012, from http://www.washingtonpost.com/wp-srv/national/longterm/watergate/stories/graham.htm.

Green, Donald, and Ian Shapiro. 1994. *Pathologies of Rational Choice Theory: A Critique of Applications in Political Science*. New Haven, CT: Yale University Press.

Greenfield, Jeff. 1996. *The People's Choice*. New York: Plume.

Greenstein, Fred. 1969. *Personality and Politics*. Chicago: Markham Publishing Company.

———. 2000. "Fred Greenstein: Reagan's Style of Politics and Governing." History News Network, George Mason University. Retrieved on June 7th, 2011, from http://hnn.us/roundup/entries/5590.html.

Gronke, Paul, and Brian Newman. 2003. "FDR to Clinton, Mueller to ?: A Field Essay on Presidential Approval." *Political Research Quarterly* Vol. 56, No. 4 (December 2003): 501–512.

Halberstam, David. 1972. *The Best and the Brightest*. New York: Random House.

Haldeman, H. R. 1978. *The Ends of Power*. New York: Times Books.

Hamdan v. Rumsfeld, 548 U.S. 557 (2006).

Hamdi v. Rumsfeld, 542 U.S. 507 (2004).

Hamill, Pete. 1964. "When the Client Is a Candidate: Five TV Commercials for the Democrats." *The New York Times*, October 25th.

Hamilton, Alexander. 1788. "The Federalist #68." March 14th. Retrieved on October 20th, 2012, from http://thomas.loc.gov/home/histdox/fed_68.html.

Hargrove, Erwin. 1966. *Presidential Leadership: Personality and Political Style*. New York: The Macmillan Company.

———. 1973. "Presidential Personality and Revisionist Views of the Presidency." *American Journal of Political Science* Vol. 17, No. 4 (November 1973): 819–835.

———. 1974. *The Power of the Modern Presidency*. Philadelphia, PA: Temple University Press.

———. 1993. "Presidential Personality and Leadership Style." In George Edwards, John Kessel, and Bert Rockman, eds., *Researching the Presidency: Vital Questions, New Approaches*. Pittsburg, PS: University of Pittsburg Press, pp. 69–110.

Hargrove, Erwin, and Michael Nelson. 1984. *Presidents, Politics, and Policy*. New York: Alfred A. Knopf.

Harvard Crimson, The. 1952. "The Eyes of Texas." June 3rd. Retrieved on July 14th, 2010, from http://www.thecrimson.com/article/1952/6/3/the-eyes-of-texas-psenator-tafts/.

Harvard Law Review Association. 2001. "Rethinking the Electoral College Debate: The Framers, Federalism, and One Person, One Vote." *Harvard Law Review* Vol. 114, No. 8 (June 2001): 2526–2549. Retrieved on July 21st, 2010, from http://www.jstor.org/stable/pdfplus/1342519.pdf.

Heclo, Hugh. 1975. "OMB and the Presidency—The Problem of Neutral Competence." *The Public Interest* No. 38 (Winter): 80–98.

Heilemann, John, and Mark Halperin. 2010. *Game Change: Obama and the Clintons, McCain and Palin, and the Race of a Lifetime*. New York: Harper Collins.

Hermann, Margaret. 1995. "Advice and Advisers in the Clinton Presidency: The Impact of Leadership Style." In Stanley Renshon, ed., *The Clinton Presidency: Campaigning, Governing, and the Psychology of Leadership*. Boulder, CO: Westview Press, pp. 149–166.

Herring, George. 1979. *America's Longest War: The United States and Vietnam—1950–1975*. New York: Alfred A. Knopf.

Hess, Stephen. 2002. *Organizing the Presidency*, 3rd Edn. (with Jamis Pfiffner). Washington, DC: Brookings Institution Press.

Hill, Larry. 1989. "Reconsidering American Bureaucratic Power in the Light of Recent Political Change." Paper presented at the annual meeting of the American Political Science Association, Atlanta, GA.

Hillary: The Movie. Retrieved on July 7th, 2010, from http://hillarythemovie.com.

Hinckley, Barbara. 1985. *The Problems of the Presidency: A Text with Readings*. Glenview, IL: Scott, Foresman and Company.

Howes, John, and Jim Twombly. 1995. "Speeches and Popularity: A Time Series Treatment." Paper presented at the American Political Science Association annual meeting, Chicago, IL, August–September.

Hylton v. U.S., 3 Dall. 171 (1796).

Ingraham, Patricia. 1991. "Political Direction and Policy Change in Three Federal Departments." In James Pfiffner, ed., *The Managerial Presidency*. Pacific Grove, CA: Brooks/Cole, pp. 180–194.

INS v. Chadha. Immigration and Naturalization Services v. Chadha, 462 U.S. 919 (1983).
Jackson, John, and William Crotty. 2001. "The Presidency and the Press: The Paradox of the White House Communications War." *The Politics of Presidential Selection*, 7th Edn. New York: Longman.
Jacobs, Lawrence R. 2003. "The Presidency and the Press: The Paradox of the White House Communications War." In Michael Nelson, ed., *The Presidency and the Political System*, 7th Edn. Washington, DC: Congressional Quarterly Press, pp. 305–328.
Janis, Irving. 1972. *Victims of Groupthink: A Psychological Study of Foreign Policy Decisions and Fiascos*. Boston, MA: Houghton Mifflin.
Jay, John. 1788. "The Federalist #64." Retrieved on October 20th, 2012, from http://thomas.loc.gov/home/histdox/fed_64.html.
Johnson, Lyndon. 1968. "Address to the Nation Announcing Steps to Limit the War in Vietnam and Reporting His Decision Not to Seek Reelection." Johnson Presidential Library. Retrieved on July 27th, 2010, from http://www.lbjlib.utexas.edu/johnson/archives.hom/speeches.hom/680331.asp.
Jones, Charles O. 1997. "From Campaigning to Governing: Perspectives on the Second Clinton Transition." Washington, DC: Brookings Institution. Retrieved on June 3rd, 2011, from http://www.brookings.edu/articles/1997/winter_politics_jones.aspx.
Jones, Jeffrey. 2007. "Americans Continue to Rate NASA Positively: Little Change in Ratings Over the Last Few Years." October 31st. Retrieved on June 22nd, 2011, from http://www.gallup.com/poll/102466/Americans-Continue-Rate-NASA-Positively.aspx.
———. 2012a. "Record-High 40% of Americans Identify as Independents in '11 More Americans Identify as Democrats Than as Republicans, 31% to 27%." Gallup.com, January 9th. Retrieved on July 2nd, 2012, from http://www.gallup.com/poll/151943/Record-High-Americans-Identify-Independents.aspx.
———. 2012b. "Atheists, Muslims See Most Bias as Presidential Candidates: Two-thirds Would Vote Gay or Lesbian." Gallup.com, June 21st. Retrieved on June 26th, 2012, from http://www.gallup.com/poll/155285/Atheists-Muslims-Bias-Presidential-Candidates.aspx.
Kagan, Elena. 2001. "Presidential Administration." *Harvard Law Review* Vol. 114, No. 8 (June 2001): 2245–2385.
Kagan, Jerome, Nancy Snidman, Vali Kahn, and Sara Towsley. 2007. "The Preservation of Two Infant Temperaments into Adolescence." *Monographs of the Society for Research in Child Development*, Vol. 72, No. 2, pp. 1–75.
Karabell, Zachary. 1998. "The Rise and Fall of the Televised Political Convention." The Joan Shorenstein Center on the Press, Politics, and Public Policy. The John F. Kennedy School of Government, Harvard University. Discussion Paper D-33, October 1998.
Karnow, Stanley. 1983. *Vietnam: A History*. New York: Viking Press.
Kaufman, Herbert 1981. "Fear of Bureaucracy: A Raging Pandemic." *Public Administration Review* Vol. 41, No. 1 (January–February 1981): 1–9.
Kennedy, Robert. 1969. *Thirteen Days: A Memoir of the Cuban Missile Crisis*. New York: W. W. Norton & Company.
Kernell, Samuel. 1978. "Explaining Presidential Popularity." *American Political Science Review* Vol. 72, No. 2 (June): 506–522.
———. 1997. *Going Public: New Strategies of Presidential Leadership*, 3rd Edn. Washington, DC: Congressional Quarterly, Inc.
Kessel, John. 2001. *Presidents, the Presidency, and the Political Environment*. Washington, DC: CQ Press.
Keynes, John Maynard. 1936. *The General Theory of Employment, Interest, and Money*. New York: Harcourt, Brace, and Company.
Kornblut, Ann. 2009. *Notes from the Cracked Ceiling*. New York: Crown Publishing Group.

Kramer, Stanley (Producer) ; Dmytryk, Edward (Director) ; Roberts, Stanley and Michael Blankfort (Writers). 1954. *The Caine Mutiny*. [Motion Picture] United States: Columbia Pictures. Based on the novel by Herman Wouk.

Kravitz, Walter. 1993. *Congressional Quarterly's American Congressional Dictionary*. Washington, DC: Congressional Quarterly, Inc.

Kurtz, Howard. 1992. "Perpetual Punditry: Analysis unto Death; Why don't the Talking Heads Shut up and Cover the News?" *The Washington Post*, July 19th, p. C7. Retrieved on July 28th, 2010, from http://www.lexisnexis.com/us/lnacademic/search/homesubmit Form.do.

———. 2010. "Howard Kurtz—Clinton and Echoes of 1995." *The Washington Post*, Tuesday, April 20th, 7:57 a.m. Retrieved on June 20th, 2012, from http://www.washingtonpost.com/wp-dyn/content/article/2010/04/20/AR2010042001456.html.

Kusch, Frank. 2004. *Battleground Chicago: The Police and the 1968 Democratic National Convention*. Chicago, IL: University of Chicago Press.

LA Times. 1996. "McGeorge Bundy; Advisor to Two Presidents in 1960s." September 17th. Retrieved on February 28th, 2012, from http://articles.latimes.com/1996-09-17/news/mn-44663_1_mcgeorge-bundy.

Laffer, Arthur. 2004. "The Laffer Curve: Past, Present, and Future." Retrieved on June 25th, 2012, from http://www.heritage.org/research/reports/2004/06/the-laffer-curve-past-present-and-future.

Lamb, Charles, and Jim Twombly. 2001. "Presidential Influence and Centralization: The Case of Nixon and Romney." *Politics and Policy* Vol. 29, No. 1 (March): 91–120.

Lasswell, Harold. 1930. *Psychopathology and Politics*. Chicago, IL: University of Chicago Press.

———. 1948. *Personality and Politics*. New York: W. W. Norton Press.

Lauter, David, and Melissa Healey. 1987. "Ginsburg Admits Smoking Marijuana in '60s and '70s." *The Los Angeles Times*, November 6th. Retrieved on June 19th, 2012, from http://articles.latimes.com/1987-11-06/news/mn-12868_1_judge-ginsburg.

Lee, Jong. 1975. "Presidential Vetoes from Washington to Nixon." *The Journal of Politics* Vol. 37, No. 2 (May 1975): 522–546.

LeLoup, Lance, and Steven Shull. 2003. *The President and Congress: Collaboration and Combat in National Policymaking*, 2nd Edn. New York: Longman.

Lewis, David. 2004. "The Adverse Consequences of the Politics of Agency Design for Presidential Management in the United States: The Relative Durability of Insulated Agencies." *British Journal of Political Science*, Vol. 34, No. 3 (July): 377–404.

Lincoln, Abraham. 1864. Letter to A. G. Hodges, April 4th, 1864. Source: John Nicolay and John Hay, eds., 1905. *The Complete Works of Abraham Lincoln*, Vol. 10. New York: Francis D. Tandy Co.

Lipset, Seymour M. 1986. "Beyond 1984: The Anomalies of American Politics." *PS* Vol. 19, No. 2 (Spring 1986): 222–236.

Liptak, Adam. 2010. "A Rare Rebuke, in Front of a Nation." *New York Times*, January 29th. Retrieved on May 3rd, 2011, from LexisNexis.

Longley, Lawrence D., and Neal R. Peirce. 1996. *The Electoral College Primer*. New Haven, CT: Yale University Press.

Lublin, David. 2008. "Electoral College Reform? Not So Easy." America.gov. *eJournal USA*, September 5th. Retrieved on July 21st, 2010, from http://www.america.gov/st/elections08-english/2008/september/20080905122842ebyessedo0.3771936.html.

Lyons, Michael. 1997. "Presidential Character Revisited." *Political Psychology* Vol. 18, No. 4 (December 1997): 791–811.

MacKuen, Michael. 1983. "Political Drama, Economic Conditions, and the Dynamics of Presidential Popularity." *American Journal of Political Science* Vol. 27: 165–192.

Madison, James. 1787. "Notes of the Debates in the Federal Conventions of 1787," Debate: Monday, June 4th, 1787.

———. 1788. "The Federalist #51." February 6th. Retrieved on October 20th, 2012, from http://www.ourdocuments.gov/doc.php?flash=true&doc=10&page=transcript.

Marbury v. Madison, 1 Cranch 137 (1803).

March, James G. 1962. "The Business Firm as a Political Coalition." *The Journal of Politics* Vol. 24, No. 4, pp. 662–678.

Marvick, Dwaine. 1980. "The Work of Harold D. Lasswell: His Approach, Concerns, and Influence." *Political Behavior* Vol. 2, No. 3 (1980): 219–229.

Matalin, Mary, and James Carville (with Peter Knobler). 1994. *All's Fair: Love, War, and Running for President*. New York: Random House.

Matthews, Christopher. 2011. "Reagan and O'Neill: A Political Friendship Worth Recalling." *Atlanta Journal Constitution*, January 25th. Retrieved on June 14th, 2012, from http://www.ajc.com/opinion/reagan-and-oneill-a-815721.html.

Mayhew, David. 1974. *Congress: The Electoral Connection*. New Haven, CT: Yale University Press.

McCullough, David. 2001. *John Adams*. New York: Simon and Schuster.

McClure, Robert, and Thomas Patterson. 1976. *The Unseeing Eye: The Myth of Television Power in National Elections*. New York: G. P. Putnam's Sons.

McDonald, Forrest. 1974. *The Presidency of George Washington*. Lawrence, KS: University Press of Kansas.

———. 1994. *The American Presidency: An Intellectual History*. Lawrence, KS: University Press of Kansas.

McKenna, Marian C. 2002. *Franklin Roosevelt and the Great Constitutional War: The Court-packing Crisis of 1937*. New York, NY: Fordham University Press.

Meier, Kenneth. 1993. *Politics and the Bureaucracy: Policymaking in the Fourth Branch of Government*. 3rd Edn. Pacific Grove, CA: Brooks/Cole.

Mieczkowski, Yanek. 2004. "The Secrets of Gerald Ford's Success...30 Years after He Became President It's Time to Consider What Made Him Tick." History News Network, George Mason University. Retrieved on June 7th, 2011, from http://www.hnn.us/articles/6501.html.

Milakovich, Michael, and George Gordon. 2001. *Public Administration in America*, 7th Edn. New York: Bedford/St Martin's.

Milkis, Sidney, and Michael Nelson. 1994. *The American Presidency: Origins and Development (1776–1993)*, 2nd Edn. Washington, DC: CQ Press.

———. 1999. *The American Presidency: Origins and Development, 1776–1998*, 3rd Edn. Washington, DC: CQ Press.

———. 2012. *The American Presidency: Origins and Development, 1776–2011*, 6th Edn. Washington, DC: CQ Press.

Miller Center. 2012. "American President: Gerald Ford (1913–2006). Domestic Affairs." Miller Center, University of Virginia. Retrieved on June 25th, 2012, from http://millercenter.org/president/ford/essays/biography/4.

Moe, Terry. 1985. "The Politicized Presidency." In John E. Chubb and Paul E. Peterson eds., *The New Direction in American Politics*. Washington, DC: Brookings Institution, pp. 235–271.

Montgomery, Bruce. 2009. *Richard B. Cheney and the Rise of the Imperial Vice Presidency*. Westport, CT: Praeger.

Morgan, Robert. 1974. *A Whig Embattled: The Presidency under John Tyler*. Hamden, CT: Archon Books.

Morgan, Ruth. 1975. "Review of: The Presidential Character: Predicting Performance in the White House. by James DavidBarber." *The Journal of Politics* Vol. 37, No. 1 (February 1975): 305–307.

Morris, Irwin. 2010. *The American Presidency: An Analytical Approach.* New York: Cambridge University Press.

Mueller, John. 1970. "Presidential Popularity from Truman to Johnson." *The American Political Science Review* Vol. 64, No. 1 (March): 18–34.

———. 1973. *War, Presidents, and Public Opinion.* Lanham, MD: University Press of America.

Murray, Shailagh, and Paul Kane. 2010. *The Washington Post*, April 13th. Retrieved on June 19th, 2012, from http://www.washingtonpost.com/wp-dyn/content/article/2010/04/13/AR2010041303678.html.

Museum of the Moving Image. 2008. "The Living Room Candidate." Retrieved on July 23rd, 2010, from http://www.livingroomcandidate.org/.

National Council of State Legislatures (NCSL). 2011. "National Popular Vote." Updated April 19th, 2011. Retrieved on May 22nd, 2011, from http://www.ncsl.org/default.aspx?tabid=20944.

National Federation of Independent Business v. Sebelius, 132 S. Ct. 2566 (2012).

National Park Service. n.d. *The American Revolution: Date in History: 1783.* Retrieved on February 29th, 2012, from http://www.nps.gov/revwar/revolution_day_by_day/1783_main.html.

Nelson, Michael. 2003. "The Psychological Presidency." In Michael Nelson, ed., *The Presidency and the Political System*, 7th Edn. Washington, DC: CQ Press, pp. 190–214.

Neustadt, Richard. 1990. *Presidential Power and the Modern Presidents: The Politics of Leadership from Roosevelt to Reagan*, 5th Edn. New York: Free Press.

New York Times Magazine. 1987. "On Language; Running the Traps RUNNING ON EMPTY." December 6th. Retrieved on April 30th, 2011, from http://www.nytimes.com/1987/12/06/magazine/on-language-running-the-traps-running-on-empty.html.

Nixon v. Fitzgerald, 457 U.S. 731 (1982).

Norpoth, Helmut. 1987. "Guns and Butter and Government Popularity in Britain." *The American Political Science Review* Vol. 81, No. 3 (September 1987): 949–959.

O'Brien, Meredith. 2004. "Counting the Costs: Convention Boosters Promise a Windfall that Rarely Materializes." The Center for Public Integrity, Investigative Journalism in the Public Interest, August 24th. Retrieved on July 27th, 2010, from http://www.publicintegrity.org/articles/entry/501.

Obama, Barack. 1995. *Dreams from My Father: A Story of Race and Inheritance.* New York: Three Rivers Press.

———. 2006. *The Audacity of Hope: Thoughts on Reclaiming the American Dream.* New York: Crown Publishing/Random House.

Office of the Press Secretary. 2009. "President Obama Launches Office of Public Engagement: A New Name, Mission for White House Liaison Office." Press Release, May 11th. Washington, DC: The White House. Retrieved on May 19th, 2011, from http://www.whitehouse.gov/the_press_office/President-Obama-Launches-Office-of-Public-Engagement/.

Onwuachi-Willig, Angela. 2005. "Using the Master's 'Tool' to Dismantle His House: Why Justice Clarence Thomas Makes the Case for Affirmative Action." *Arizona Law Review* Vol. 47: 113.

OPS-Alaska and Fairvote. n.d. "American Plan Presidential Primary Reform: The Best of Both Worlds." Retrieved on July 15th, 2010, from http://pweb.jps.net/-md-r/ps/AmPlan_ES_Comparison.pdf.

Ostrom, Charles W., Jr., and Dennis M. Simon. 1985. "Promise and Performance: A Dynamic Model of Presidential Popularity." *American Political Science Review* Vol. 79: 334–358.

Paine, Thomas. 2003. *Common Sense and Other Writings*. New York: Random House.
Patterson, James, 1973. "Review: Politics, Personality, and Psychohistory." *Reviews in American History* Vol. 1, No. 1 (March): 59–65.
Patterson, Thomas. 2009. "Voter Participation: Records Galore This Time, but What about Next Time." In Smith, Steven S. and Melanie J. Springer, eds., *Reforming the Presidential Nomination Process*. Washington, DC: Brookings Institute Press, pp. 44–63.
PBS. 2008 (DVD Release). "American Experience: The Presidents." Clips viewable at http://www.pbs.org/wgbh/amex/presidents/video/lbj_24_qt.html#v249.
PBS. n.d. "The Election of 1980." *The American Experience*. Public Broadcasting. Retrieved on May 5th, 2011, from http://www.pbs.org/wgbh/americanexperience/features/general-article/carter-election1980/.
Perrow, Charles. 2006. "The Disaster after 9/11: The Department of Homeland Security and the Intelligence Reorganization." *Homeland Security Affairs: The Journal of the Naval Postgraduate School Center for Homeland Defense and Security*. Retrieved on February 21st, 2012, from http://www.hsaj.org/?fullarticle=2.1.3.
Pew Research Center. 2010. "Independents Oppose Party in Power…Again More Conservative, More Critical of National Conditions." Released September 23rd. Retrieved on May 5th, 2011, from http://people-press.org/2010/09/23/section-3-trends-in-party-affiliation/.
Pfiffner, James. 1998. "Sexual Probity and Presidential Character." *Presidential Studies Quarterly* Vol. 28, No. 4 (Fall): 881–886.
Pika, Joseph A., and John Anthony Maltese. 2010. *The Politics of the Presidency*, rev. 7th Edn. Washington, DC: CQ Press.
Polsby, Nelson, and Aaron Wildavsky. 2000. *Presidential Elections: Strategies and Structures of American Politics*, 10th Edn. New York: Chatham House.
Ragsdale, Lyn. 1993. *Presidential Politics*. Boston, MA: Houghton Mifflin Company.
Rasul v. Bush, 542 U.S. 466 (2004).
Reaves, Jessica. 2001. "The Marc Rich Case: A Primer," Time.com. February 13th. Retrieved on July 27th, 2010, from http://www.time.com/time/nation/article/0,8599,99302,00.html.
Rennert, Leo. 1991. "President Back on the Job, Medication Gets Heart on Track, Averts Need for Quayle to Fill In." *Modesto Bee*, May 7th. Retrieved on September 1st, 2011, from LexisNexis Academic at http://www.lexisnexis.com.
Ridout, Travis, and Glen Smith. 2008. "Free Advertising: How the Media Amplify Campaign Messages." *Political Research Quarterly* Vol. 61, No. 4 (December 2008): 598–608.
Roche, John. 1961. "The Founding Fathers: A Reform Caucus in Action." *American Political Science Review* Vol. 55 (December 1961): 799–816.
Rogers, Will. n.d. BrainyQuote.com. Retrieved on May 9th, 2011, from BrainyQuote.com Web site: http://www.brainyquote.com/quotes/authors/w/will_rogers_5.html.
Rogow, Arnold. 1976. "Review: Untitled." *The American Political Science Review* Vol. 70, No. 4 (December 1976): 1299–1301.
Rohde, David, and Dennis Simon. 1985. "Presidential Vetoes and Congressional Response: A Study of Institutional Conflict." *American Journal of Political Science* Vol. 29, No. 3 (August 1985): 397–427.
Roosevelt, Theodore. 1913. *The Autobiography of Theodore Roosevelt*. Centennial Edn. New York: Charles Scribner's Sons.
Rose, Richard. 1991. *The Postmodern President*. Chatham, NJ: Chatham House Publishers.
Rothschild, K. W. 1946. "The Meaning of Rationality." *Review of Economic Studies* Vol. 14: 50–52.
Safire, William. 1977. "The Carter Touch." *The New York Times*, February 7th. Retrieved on June 12th, 2012, from http://select.nytimes.com/gst/abstract.html?res=F70A12F83B5F167493C5A91789D85F438785F9.

Safire, William. 2003. "The Way We Live Now: 1–26–03: On Language; Smoking Gun." *New York Times Magazine*, January 26th. Retrieved on October 21st, 2012, from http://www.nytimes.com/2003/01/26/magazine/the-way-we-live-now-1-26-03-on-language-smoking-gun.html.

Santa Clara County v. Southern Pacific Railroad Co.; California v. Central Pacific Railroad Co.; California v. Southern Pacific Railroad Co., 118 U.S. 394 (1886).

Savva, N. 1991. "U.S. Sweats on Quayle—Bush May Need Shock Treatment." *Herald Sun*, May 7th. Retrieved on September 1st, 2011, from LexisNexis Academic at http://www.lexisnexis.com.

Schlesinger, Arthur. 1965. *A Thousand Days: John F. Kennedy in the White House*. New York: Greenwich House.

———. 1973. *The Imperial Presidency*. Boston: Houghton Mifflin.

———. 1978. *Robert Kennedy and His Times, Vol. II*. New York: Houghton Mifflin.

Schneider, Bill. 2008. "It Could All be Over after Super Duper Tuesday." CNN.com. Retrieved on July 2nd, 2012, from http://articles.cnn.com/2007-02-05/politics/schneider.superduper.tuesday_1_new-hampshire-south-carolina-democrats-diverse-states?_s=PM:POLITICS.

Schwartz, John. 2011. "For Obama, a Record on Diversity but Delays on Judicial Confirmations." *The New York Times*, August 6th. Retrieved on June 19th, 2012, from http://www.nytimes.com/2011/08/07/us/politics/07courts.html?pagewanted=all.

Segal, Jeffrey, Richard Timpone, and Robert Howard. 2000. "Buyer Beware? Presidential Success through Supreme Court Appointments." *Political Research Quarterly* Vol. 53, No. 3 (September 2000): 557–573.

Seidman, Harold, and Robert Gilmour. 1986. *Politics, Position, and Power: From the Positive to the Regulatory State*, 4th Edn. New York: Oxford University Press.

Shear, Michael. 2008. "Conservatives Ready to Battle McCain on Convention Platform." *Washington Post*, July 7th. Retrieved on July 14th, 2010, from http://www.washingtonpost.com/wp-dyn/content/article/2008/07/06/AR2008070602322.html.

Shoemaker, Anthony. 2010. "Cleveland Is Finalist to Host 2012 Democratic Convention." *Dayton Daily News*, Ohio Politics Blog, July 1st. Retrieved on July 27th, 2010, from http://www.daytondailynews.com/blogs/content/shared-gen/blogs/dayton/ohiopolitics/entries/2010/07/01/cleveland_is_finalist_to_host.html.

Shogan, Colleen J. 2006. *The Moral Rhetoric of American Presidents*, 1st Edn. College Station, TX: Texas A & M University Press.

Simon, Herbert. 1957. *Models of Man: Social and Rational—Mathematical Essays on Rational Human Behavior in a Social Setting*. New York: Wiley.

———. 1985. "Human Nature in Politics: The Dialogue of Psychology with Political Science." *The American Political Science Review* Vol. 79, No. 2 (June 1985): 293–304.

Simon, Scott. 2000. "Convention Dispatch, August 3rd, 2000, Scott Simon's Convention Notebook." National Public Radio. Retrieved on July 15th, 2010, from http://www.npr.org/news/national/election2000/conventions/simon.html.

Simonton, Dean Keith. 1987. *Why Presidents Succeed: A Political Psychology of Leadership*. New Haven, CT: Yale University Press.

Slonim, Shlomo. 1986. "The Electoral College at Philadelphia: The Evolution of an Ad Hoc Congress for the Selection of a President." *The Journal of American History* Vol. 73, No. 1 (June 1986): 35–58.

Smith, Adam. 2008. "Florida Finally Counts in Democratic Race." *St. Petersburg Times*, June 1st. Retrieved on May 4th, 2011, from LexisNexis.

Smith, J. Allen. 1907. *The Spirit of American Government: A Study of the Constitution: Its Origin, Influence, and Relation to Democracy*. New York: The MacMillan Company.

Smith, Stephanie. 2008. "Former Presidents: Federal Pension and Retirement Benefits." CRS Reports. Retrieved on July 9th, 2010, from http://www.senate.gov/reference/resources/pdf/98-249.pdf.

Smith, Steven S., and Melanie J. Springer. 2009. "Choosing Presidential Candidates." In Steven S. Smith and Melanie J. Springer, eds., *Reforming the Presidential Nomination Process*. Washington, DC: Brookings Institute Press, pp. 1–22.

Smithsonian.com. 2008. "Conventional Facts." *Smithsonian Magazine*, August 1st. Retrieved on July 23rd, 2010, from http://www.smithsonianmag.com/history-archaeology/conventional-facts.html.

Snyder, Glenn, and Paul Diesing. 1977. *Conflict among Nations: Bargaining, Decision-Making and System Structure in International Crises*. Princeton, NJ: Princeton University Press.

Sollenberger, Mitchell. 2008. *The President Shall Nominate: How Congress Trumps Executive Power*. Lawrence, KS: University of Kansas Press.

Spoehr, Luther. 2007. "Review of Jules Witcover's *Very Strange Bedfellows: The Short and Unhappy Marriage of Richard Nixon & Spiro Agnew* (Public Affairs, 2007) and Elizabeth Drew's *Richard M. Nixon, 1969–1974* (Times Books, The American Presidents Series, 2007)." On History News Network. Retrieved on April 26th, 2011, from http://hnn.us/roundup/entries/40675.html.

Stanley, Harold, and Charles Hadley. 1987. "The Southern Presidential Primary: Regional Intentions with National Implications." *Publius* Vol. 17, No. 3, pp. 83–100.

Stanley, Harold, and Richard Niemi. 1988. *Vital Statistics on American Politics*. Washington, DC: CQ Press.

———. 2000. *Vital Statistics on American Politics—1999–2000*. Washington, DC: CQ Press.

Stephanopoulos, George. 1999. *All Too Human: A Political Education*. New York: Little, Brown and Company.

Stephens, Mitchell. n.d. *History of Newspapers*. New York University. Retrieved on February 29th, 2012, from http://www.nyu.edu/classes/stephens/Collier%27s%20page.htm.

Stricherz, Mark. 2003. "Primary Colors: How a Little-Known Task Force Helped Create Red State/Blue State America." *Boston Globe*, November 23rd. Retrieved on February 21st, 2011, from http://www.boston.com/news/globe/ideas/articles/2003/11/23/primary_colors/.

Stuart, Reginald. 1986. "Adjusting the Speed Limit to Match Reality." *The New York Times*, October 26th.

Sussman, Barry. 1974. *The Great Coverup: Nixon and the Scandal of Watergate*. New York: Penguin Group (US), Signet Special.

Taft, William Howard. 1916. *Our Chief Magistrate and His Powers*. New York: Columbia University Press.

Tashjian, Secretary of State of Connecticut v. Republican Party of Connecticut et al., U.S. 1043 (1986).

Teachout, Zephyr, and Tom Streeter et al. 2008. *Mousepads, Shoe Leather, and Hope*. Boulder, CO: Paradigm Publishers.

Time. 1974. "POLITICS: Getting Up to Date in Kansas City." December 9th. Retrieved on April 30th, 2011, from http://www.time.com/time/magazine/article/0,9171,908954,00.html#ixzz1L4IFHQ31.

Toobin, Jeffrey. 2008. *The Nine: Inside the Secret World of the Supreme Court*. New York: Anchor Books.

———. 2009. "Diverse Opinions." *The New Yorker*, June 8th. Retrieved on June 19th, 2012, from http://www.newyorker.com/talk/comment/2009/06/08/090608taco_talk_toobin.

Traister, Rebecca. 2010. *Big Girls Don't Cry*. New York: Simon and Schuster Adult Publishing Group.

Tufte, Edward. 1978. *Political Control of the Economy*. Princeton, NJ: Princeton University Press.
United States v. Nixon, 418 U.S. 683 (1974).
United States Constitution.
United States Code, Title 3, Chapter 2, § 102.
———, Title 18, § 3056.
United States Forest Service. n.d. "Story of Smokey Bear." Lincoln National Forest webpage. United States Department of Agriculture. Retrieved on June 9th, 2012, from http://www.fs.usda.gov/wps/portal/fsinternet/!ut/p/c5/04_SB8K8xLLM9MSSzPy8xBz9CP0os3gjAwhwtDDw9_AI8zPwhQoY6IeDdGCqCPOBqwDLG-AAjgb6fh75uan6BdnZaY6OiooA1tkqlQ!!/dl3/d3/L2dJQSEvUUt3QS9ZQnZ3LzZfME80MEkxVkFCOTBFMktTNVVJNDAwMDAwMDA!/?navtype=BROWSEBYSUBJECT&cid=stelprdb5190286&navid=091000000000000&pnavid=null&ss=110308&position=Not%20Yet%20Determined.Html&ttype=detailfull&pname=Lincoln%20National%20Forest%20-%20Home/.
US DOD. 2011. *Overview, United States Department of Defense Budget Request FY 2012*. Retrieved on February 20th, 2011, from http://comptroller.defense.gov/defbudget/fy2012/FY2012_Budget_Request_Overview_Book.pdf.
US Term Limits v. Thornton, 514 U.S. 779 (1995).
Vennocchi, Joan. 2008. "Obama and McCain—flip-flop, flip-flop." *The Boston Globe*, June 22nd. Retrieved on May 5th, 2011, from http://www.boston.com/bostonglobe/editorial_opinion/oped/articles/2008/06/22/obama_and_mccain___flip_flop_flip_flop/.
Vitta, Matthew, and Helen Dewar. 2000. "Congress Debates Election Reform; Members' Proposals Range from Modest Changes to Abolition of Electoral College." *The Washington Post*, Final Edn., November 17th. Retrieved on July 21st, 2010, from http://www.lexisnexis.com/us/lnacademic/results/docview/docview.do?
Warshaw, Shirley Anne. 1996. *Powersharing: The White House-Cabinet Relationship in the Modern Presidency*. Albany, NY: SUNY Press.
———. 1997. *The Domestic Presidency: Policy Making in the White House*. Boston: Allyn and Bacon.
———. 2000. *The Keys to Power: Managing the Presidency*. New York: Longman.
Wayne, Stephen. 1978. *The Legislative Presidency*. New York: Harper Collins Publishers.
———. 2009. *The Road to the White House 2012*, 9th Edn. Boston, MA: Wadsworth—Cengage.
———. 2011. *Personality and Politics: Obama for and against Himself*. Washington, DC: Sage / CQ Press.
Weber, Max. 1997. *The Theory of Social and Economic Organization*. New York: Free Press.
West Coast Hotel v. Parrish, 300 U.S. 379 (1937).
Westen, Drew. 2007. *The Political Brain: The Role of Emotion in Deciding the Fate of the Nation*. New York: Public Affairs.
Whicker, Marcia Lynn, and Raymond Moore. 1988. *When Presidents Are Great*. Englewood Cliffs, NJ: Prentice Hall.
Whitaker, L. Paige. 2004. "Campaign Finance: Constitutional and Legal Issues of Soft Money." A *CRS Issue Brief for Congress*. Washington, DC: Congressional Research Service, Library of Congress.
White House Historical Association. n.d. *PRIMARY DOCUMENTS: The President and the Press / FDR's First Press Conference: March 1933*. Retrieved on March 1st, 2012, from http://www.whitehousehistory.org/whha_classroom/classroom_documents-1933.html.
White, Theodore. 1961. *The Making of the President—1960*. New York: Atheneum Publishers.
———. 1969. *The Making of the President—1968*. New York: Atheneum Publishers.

———. 1973. *The Making of the President—1972*. New York: Atheneum Publishers.
———. 1982. *American in Search of Itself: The Making of the President—1956–1980*. New York: Harper & Row.
WhiteHouse.gov. n.d. "About CEA." Retrieved on September 8th, 2011, from http://www.whitehouse.gov/administration/eop/cea/about.
———. n.d. "Executive Office of the President, Fiscal Year 2011, Congressional Budget Submission." Retrieved on July 2nd, 2012, from http://www.whitehouse.gov/sites/default/files/2011-eop-budget.pdf.
———. n.d. "National Security Council." Retrieved on September 6th, 2011, from http://www.whitehouse.gov/administration/eop/nsc.
Whitford, Andrew, and Jeff Yates. 2003. "Policy Signals and Executive Governance: Presidential Rhetoric in the 'War on Drugs.'" *The Journal of Politics* Vol. 65, No. 4 (November): 995–1012.
Wildavsky, Aaron. 1966. "The Two Presidencies." *Trans-Action* Vol. 4: 7–14.
Will, George F. 2002. "The Framers' Electoral Wisdom." *The Washington Post*, November 2nd, Final Edn. Retrieved on July 21st, 2010, from http://search.proquest.com/docview/409043675/139F52D91C225BFF53D/1?accountid=10728.
Wilson, James. 1966. *The Amateur Democrat: Club Politics in Three Cities*. Chicago, IL: University of Chicago Press.
Wilson, Woodrow. 1887. "The Study of Administration." Reprinted in *Political Science Quarterly* Vol. 56, No. 4 (December 1941): 481–506.
———. 1908. *Constitutional Government in the United States*. New York: Columbia University Press.
Witcover, Jules. 1977. *Marathon: The Pursuit of the Presidency, 1972–1976*. New York: Viking Press.
Woodward, Bob, and Scott Armstrong. 1979. *The Brethren: Inside the Supreme Court*. New York: Simon and Schuster.
Woolley, John. 1991. "Institutions, the Election Cycle, and the Presidential Veto." *American Journal of Political Science* Vol. 35, No. 2 (May 1991): 279–304.
Worcester v. Georgia, 31 U.S. (6 Pet.) 515 (1832).
Wright, Gerald C. 2009. "Rules and the Ideological Character of Primary Electorates." In Steven S. Smith and Melanie J. Springer, eds., *Reforming the Presidential Nomination Process*. Washington, DC: Brookings Institute Press, pp. 23–42.
Yates, Brock. 1988. "In New York, They Throw Money at It and Hope It Slows Down." *The Washington Post*, July 31st.
Youngstown Sheet and Tube Co. v. Sawyer, 343 U.S. 579 (1952).
Zeleny, Jeff. 2009. "It's Never Too Soon to Think about 2012." *New York Times*, The Caucus Blog, March 23rd. Retrieved on July 12th, 2010, from http://thecaucus.blogs.nytimes.com/2009/03/23/its-never-to-soon-to-think-about-2012/.

Index

Adams, John
   active-negative 96
   Marbury v. Madison 174
   rational 100
   as vice president 84, 85
Air Force One 10
Amar, Akil Reed 9
Ambassadors 11
American Israeli Political Action
      Committee (AIPAC) 193
The American Presidency (McDonald
      Forrest) 4
Anti-Mason Party 30
Articles of Confederation 3–4, 105
Audacity of Hope (Barack Obama) 206
Authorization for Use of Military Force
      (AUMF) 178

Barber, James David
   Nixon's psychology 91, 92, 97
   presidential character 92, 94–97
Bay of Pigs invasion 126, 127–129
Brownlow, Louis 106
Brownlow Commission 16, 106, 212n2
Brzezinski, Mika 108
Bureau of the Budget (BOB) 17, 18,
   184–185
Bureaucracy 117–118, 153
   government agencies 119–120
   politics/administration
      dichotomy 118–119
   presidential control 120–122, 184
      appointments 121
      budget 121
      centralization 122
      creation of new agencies 121
      reorganization 121
Burr, Aaron 15, 29, 70
   1800 election 29

Bush, George H. W.
   approval ratings 20
   imperial/imperiled presidency 21
   interpersonal relations 101
   Iran Contra Scandal 149
   judicial appointments 169–170, 171, 173
   Persian Gulf War 150, 195
   as vice president 83–84, 87, 90, 195
   vice president selection 59
   weakened presidency 202
Bush, George W.
   2002 midterm elections 155
   approval ratings 149, 150, 155
   Bush v. Gore 203
   Congress & foreign policy 195
   conventions 61, 63
   creation of Department of Homeland
      Security 121
   expansion of presidential power 13, 178,
      207–208
   Hamdi v. Rumsfeld 178–179
   imperiled presidency 20–21
   Iraq & Afghanistan wars 150, 178
   judicial appointments 169
   Persian Gulf foreign policy 195
   Rasul v. Bush 178
   relationship with Cheney 84, 207
   response to 9/11 21, 121, 122, 143, 190
   scandal accusation 20
   State of the Union Address 146
   strengthened presidency 203
   style 103

Camp David Accords 151
The Campaign 73–75
campaign finance
   about 45–46
   Bipartisan Campaign Reform Act
      (BCRA) 47–49

campaign finance—*Continued*
  Buckley et al. v. Valeo 45, 47, 48
  Citizens United v. FEC 45, 49–50, 175
    Obama's State of the Union
      Address 45, 175
  Congress regulations 45–47
  Federal Election Campaign Act 45
  Federal Election Commission v. Wisconsin Right to Life 48
  history 46–47
  invisible primary 45
  political action committees 47
  reform 50–51
  soft money 47
  spending as speech
  Tillman Act 45
Carter, Jimmy
  1980 party nomination 36
  approval ratings 151
  Camp David Accords 195
  Camp David negotiations 11
  domestic policy 185, 186
  Fireside Chat 143, 144
  imperiled presidency 20
  interpersonal relations 102
  Iran Hostage Crisis 151
  judicial appointment reform 169
  Mondale vice president selection 59–60, 84, 90
  Rose Garden Strategy 76
  weakened presidency 202
  working with legislature 8
Central Intelligence Agency (CIA) 19, 127, 177, 195, 202
Checks and balances 5–6, 8, 161, 194
Cheney, Richard 84, 207
Civil War 14, 16, 163
Clinton, Hillary
  2008 national nominating campaign 55, 201
  2008 nomination 25
  Democratic Convention 60
  scandal accusations 20, 49
Clinton, William
  1998 midterm elections 155
  ability in office 102
  approval rating 148, 149, 150–151, 203
  balanced budget 192
  Clinton v. Jones 178
  economic agenda 107, 221n4

  impeachment trial 164, 178
  imperiled presidency 18
  judicial appointments 168, 170
  Lewinski scandal 143, 150
  library & museum 11
  National Economic Council 107
  North American Free Trade Agreement (NAFTA) 160
  popular vote 72
  presidency 20, 202–203
  scandal accusations 20, 152, 167
  speech 57
  style 102
  vice president selection 59
  weakened presidency 202–203
  working with Congress 8
Cold War 17, 108, 131, 195, 197
Commerce Department 196
Commission on Delegate Selection and Party Structure 35–36
The Commission on Democratic Participation *see* Fowler Commission
Commission on Presidential Nomination and Party Structure 36–37
Committee on Administrative Management *see* Brownlow Commission
Common Sense (Thomas Paine) 140
Congress
  advise and consent power 193
  agencies created 105
  behavior 156–165
    advertising 156, 157
    constituency cultivation 157
    credit claiming 156, 157
    position taking 156, 157
  checks on the president 7, 8, 19, 179, 193
  committees 157–158
  elastic clause, necessary & proper clause 8
  elections 154–155
    house 155–156
    single member, single plurality system (SMSP) 158
  Obama health care reform 205
  oversight of Federal Reserve System 188
  party system 158
  powers 8, 88, 177
    impeachment 164–165
    overriding a veto patterns 161–162

Index

overturning a veto 161–162
power of the purse 8, 193
relationship with president 154–166, 182, 183, 186, 196
role in presidential foreign policy 193
role in strong executive model 5
role in weak executive model 4
shared powers with president 159, 179
The Tenure of Office Act 163
term limits 154
timeframes 159
War Powers Act 194, 195
Constitution
14th Amendment, Rights of Political Parties 39–42
22nd Amendment 154
25th Amendment 87, 88
applications to impaired presidency 15
applications to prerogative presidency 14
applications to strict constructionist presidency 14
Article XI 163
Article 2 5, 105, 207
commerce clause 183
constitutional basis for initiative 183–184
Constitutional Convention 3–4, 15, 69, 84, 207
constitutional law 175
crisis 163, 176
Electoral College 67–68, 73
First Amendment Protection of Press 142
manner for choosing the president 29
minimum qualifications for the presidency 9, 204
age requirements 9
minimum qualifications to fill presidential vacancy 88–89
necessary compromises 69
president as chief diplomat 11
president as Commander-in-Chief 5, 193
president's role in foreign policy 192–194
rights of the accused 177–179
role of Senate 159
two term limit 9
The Council of Economic Advisors 107, 181, 190
Cuban Missile Crisis 119, 125, 130, 131–136

De Lolme, Jean-Louis 4
Democracy 67–68, 79, 93, 205
Democratic National Convention (DNC)
1968 31–32, 34, 35
1972 35
2008 60
2008 Commission 38
Winograd Commission 36
Democratic Party 74, 190
2006 midterm elections 156
Domestic Policy 182–186
attempts to organize domestic advice 185–186
changes in the political system 183–185
Dreams from My Father (Barack Obama) 204
Dwight, Eisenhower
Spot Ads 76–77

Eagleton, Tom 35, 54, 59
Economic policy 186–192
Federal Reserve System 188–189
Keynesian economics 188, 190, 192
management
direct wage and price controls 189
fiscal policy 187–188
Jawboning 189–190
monetary policy 187–188
monetarist 190–191, 192
Milton Friedman 190–191
president's role 187, 191–192
Ayn Rand 191
supply side economics 191
Arthur Laffer 191
tricke-down economics 191
Eisenhower, Dwight
approval rating 148
balanced budget 192
enforcing Supreme Court decision 176
Fair Play proposal 58
judicial appointments 171
Elections
midterm 154–155, 164
surge and decline 154
term limits 154, 225n1
Electoral College
2000 election 68, 73
about 67–71
critiques 71–73
electors 70–71

Electoral College—*Continued*
  reform proposals 73
    automatic plan 72
    direct popular vote 72
    district plan 72
    National Popular Vote Compact 73
    proportional plan 72
  tie with Jefferson & Burr 15, 29, 70
Executive model
  strong 4–5
  weak 4–5
Executive Office of the President
    (EOP) 17, 106, 181, 184
Executive Power, limitations 8
Executive privilege 177

Federal Reserve Board (the Fed) 187, 188
Federal Reserve System 188–189, 191
Federalism 4, 69, 217n11
Federalist #68 72, 85
Federalist Papers #64 9
Filibuster 157, 159
Ford, Gerald
  imperiled presidency 20
  interpersonal relations 101
  judicial appointments 168
  pardon of Richard Nixon 8, 149, 167
  weakened presidency 202
  Whip Inflation Now campaign 190
Foreign Policy 192
  executive agreements 194
  president's advisors 198
  support structure 196, 197–198
Fowler Commission 37
Framers
  establishment of Electoral College
    68–69, 70
  feared tyranny 15–16, 69

Gallup 147
Going public 142–144
Gore, Al 59, 68, 84, 203
Gramm, Phil 159
Great Depression 14, 106, 155, 181,
    221n3
Groupthink 104, 126–127, 129–130

Hamilton, Alexander 70, 72, 110
  cabinet approach 110
Harrison, Henry 86

Historical periods 15–21
  impaired presidency 15–16
  imperial presidency 16–18
  imperiled presidency 18–21
  modern presidency, *see* Imperial
    presidency
  postmodern presidency *see* Imperiled
    presidency
  premodern presidency *see* Impaired
    presidency
The History of the Washington Presidency
    (McDonald Forrest) 110
Hoover, Herbert 16, 100, 183
Humphrey, Hubert 19, 31–32, 43, 58

Impeachment 162–165
Incumbent advantage 75–76
  Rose Garden Strategy 76
Interest Group 109, 110
International Law 8, 132, 196
Iran Hostage Crisis 151
Iran-Contra Scandal 149–150, 151

Jackson, Andrew
  grassroots campaign 29
  remarks about judiciary 176
  vetoes 15
Janis, Irving
  Bay of Pigs invasion 127–128
    what went wrong 128–129
  on groupthink 125–127, 129
  preventing groupthink 129–130
Jay, John 9
Jefferson, Thomas
  1800 election 29
  active-positive 96
  Louisiana Purchase 182
  presidency 15
  tie with Burr 15, 29, 70
Johnson, Andrew 5, 161, 163–164
  impeachment trial 162–164
Johnson, Lyndon
  balanced budget 192
  "The Little Girl with the
    Daisy" ad 77–78
  race against Bobby Kennedy 31
  taking office after assassination 10
  as vice president 88
  vice presidential nomination 59
  Vietnam Tet Offensive 30

INDEX

Judicial appointments 168–173
Judicial review 8, 174
Justice Department 169, 170, 172, 196

Kennedy, Bobby 19
   assassination 31
   race against Lyndon Johnson, Eugene McCarthy 31
Kennedy, John
   1972 election debate 77
   as active positive 135
   assassination investigation 174
   Bay of Pigs invasion 126, 127–129, 131, 151
   cabinet 112
   collegial advisor style 104
   Cuban Missile Crisis 119, 130, 131–132, 134–135, 151
   enforcing Supreme Court decision 176
   first Catholic president 202
   imperiled presidency 18
   judicial appointments 171
   Lyndon Johnson as vice president nominee 59
   TV ads 77
Kennedy, Ted 36, 54, 58
   nomination rule motion 54
Kerry, John 103
King, Martin Luther 31
Kissinger, Henry 89, 108, 196
Korean War 176

Lame Duck period 154
Lincoln, Abraham
   cabinet 112, 182
   impaired presidency 16
   prerogative presidency 14
Locke, John 4
Lower Court – appointments 169–170
Lyndon, Johnson
   Great Society programs 19
   Vietnam involvement 19, 148–149, 150

Madison, James 5, 96, 100, 174
   passive-positive 96
McCain, John
   2008 nomination 25, 201
   vice president selection 54
   waffling 75

McCain-Feingold *see* Campaign finance Bipartisan Campaign Reform Act (BCRA)
McCarthy, Eugene 19, 31, 42, 214n4
McGovern, George 34–35, 54, 59
Merriam, Charles 93, 94, 106
Mikulski Commission *see* Commission on Delegate Selection and Party Structure
Mondale, Walter 59, 84, 90
Montesquieu, Baron de 4
Mr. Smith Goes to Washington 44
My Life (Bill Clinton) 57

National Aeronautics and Space Administration 120, 196, 222n7
National Archives and Records Administration (NARA) 10
National Economic Council 107, 181, 190
National nominating convention 53–65
   Brokered Convention 60–62
   fall campaign launch 55
   functions of 53–55
   key issues 62–63
   party platform 54
   platform disputes 58
   security 55
   TV coverage 55–56, 57, 58
   party rules & regulations 53–54
   president & vice president selection 54
   reforms & proposals 62–65
   Republican Convention 2000 61
National Security Council 108, 132, 182, 196
Natural Born Citizen 9
Nixon, Richard
   1972 presidential debate 77
   active-negative 95, 97, 103
   reorganization plan 112
   Bay of Pigs invasion 127
   budgetary limitations 121
   China relations 151, 195, 196
   conflict with George Romney 110, 122
   cooperative-unsuccessful veto pattern 161
   creation of office of domestic policy 181
   Domestic Council 185
   HUD 122
   impeachment trial 164
   imperial presidency 16, 18, 19

Nixon, Richard—*Continued*
  Iron Triangle 110
  judicial appointments 174
  Nixon v. Fitzgerald 177
  presidency 18, 112, 185
  reelection 32
  United States v. Nixon 164, 177
  wage and price controls 189
  War Powers Act 194
  Watergate Scandal 19–20, 91–92, 150–151, 164, 177
  weakened presidency 202
Nixon Administration
  Plumbers Squad 141

Obama, Barack
  2008 democratic convention 60
  2008 midterm elections 154
  2008 national nominating campaign 55, 201
  active negative 206
  appeal to voters 26, 201, 203
  Barber analysis 205–206
  bipartisanship 204–205
    critics 205
  Birther critics 9, 204
  congressional approval in Libya 194
  first black president 202
  grassroots campaign 43
  healthcare reform 183, 184, 205
  hope and change 201, 203
  imperiled presidency 21
  judicial appointments 168, 169
  keynote speaker at 2004 DNC 56, 206
  lack of experience 195, 204
  maintaining presidential power 208
  presidency 206–208
  presidential campaign 184, 203–204
  qualifications for president 204
  religious beliefs 204
  waffling 75
Obama on the Couch: Inside the Mind of the President (Justin Frank) 204
Office of Legislative Affairs 160
Office of Management and Budget (OMB) 17, 18, 184–185
Order of succession 88–89
  1947 Act of Succession 88
Organization of Petroleum Exporting Countries (OPEC) 192

Palin, Sarah 54, 59
Parliamentary systems 8
Party Identification (PID) 74–75, 79
Pitt, William 9
Political parties
  as associations 39–40
  rights protected 40
    Cousins et al. v. Wigoda el al. 40–41
    Democratic Party of the United States el al. v. Wisconsin et al. 41
    Tashjian, Secretary of State of Connecticut v. Republican Party of Connecticut et al. 41
Presidency, future 201, 210
President
  compensation 10–11
  control of economy 191–192
  domestic policy 182–186
  economic policy 186–192
    management – direct wage and price controls 189
    management – fiscal policy 187–188
    management – Jawboning 189–190
    president's role 187, 191–192
  foreign policy 192–197
    advisors 198
    executive agreements 194
    support structure 196, 197–198
  future of the presidency 201, 210
  honeymoon period 165
  inaugural address 184
  judicial powers
    clemency 167–168
    grant of amnesty 167
    pardon 167–168
  media
    adversarial relationship 140–142
    constitutional freedom 141
    direct address 143
    formal press conference 143
    going public 142–144
    history 140
    leak 141
    planned leaks 141
    presidential rhetoric 144–146
    press conference 140–141
    traveling 144
  pension & retirement package 10
  personal bureaucracy 106
  policy making 181–198

position in power 210
power of persuasion 208–210
powers – judicial appointments 168–173
  factors in making nominations 170–172
proposing legislation 6, 112, 158–160, 182, 185–186, 210
relationship with bureaucracy 181
relationship with congress 154–166, 182, 183, 186, 196
  honeymoon period 165, 186
  how to achieve successful 165–166, 186
  structural characteristics 154–159
    midterm elections 154–155
    term limits 154
  tools for president 160–162
    media & public 160
    Office of Legislative Affairs 160
    partisanship 160
    work with Congress 160
  two presidencies theory 165, 194–195
  veto 160–162, 185
relationship with judiciary 167–174, 176–179, 181
  nominations 170–174
  other roles for justices 173–174
relationship with media 139–142
salary 10
shared powers with Congress 159
State of the Union Address 184
war with media 109
Presidential advisory system
  cabinet
    decline in role 109–112
    who gets appointed 112–113
  early history 105–106
  evolution of the contemporary system 106–107
  growth 107–109
  National Security Advisor 108, 196
Presidential approval
  congratulation/rationalization effect 149, 187
  decline 148–151
  defined 147–148
  institution of the presidency 148
  job performance 147–148
  likeability 148
  maintaining 151–152
  military involvements 149–152
  performance of economy 149, 155, 187

Presidential character
  James David Barber
    personality matrix 95–97
      active-negative 95–97
      active-positive 95–97, 135
      passive-negative 95–97
      passive-positive 95–97
    presidential character 94–97
    presidential style 101–102
    presidential worldview 102–103
  critiques of Barber 97–101
  importance of 93–94
  interactive styles to advisors 103–104
  social scientists
    James David Barber 92, 94–97
    Choiniere & Keirsey 99–100
    Edwine Hargrove 92, 93, 94, 98–99, 101
    Harrold Lasswell 92, 93
    Michael Lyons 92, 99
    Michael Nelson 98–99, 101
Presidential decision making 125
  flawed 125–127
  Graham Allison's analysis 132–135
Presidential libraries 10–11
  Carter Library 11
  Clinton Library 11
  Ford Library 11
  Kennedy Library 11
  Reagan Library 11
Presidential powers
  appointments 7–8, 110, 121, 167–173, 174–175, 188, 192–193, 198
  within bureaucracy 121–122
  foreign policy 6–7, 125, 181–182, 186–187, 192–198
  in the late twentieth century 201–203
  public policy 6–7, 181–197
  reprieves and pardons 7–8, 167–168, 224n5
  special sessions 6
  use of 13
  veto – patterns 161–162
  veto power 6, 15, 153, 158, 160–162, 185, 194, 211n2
Presidential rhetoric 144–146
Presidential roles
  chief diplomat 11
  commander-in-chief 5–6, 11, 121, 131, 177

Presidential roles—*Continued*
   head of government (bureaucracy) 11–12
   head of state 11, 92
   legislative leader 6, 11
   party leader 12
Presidential selection
   968 democratic nomination 30
   caucus 28, 29, 37–38, 41
   closed primary 27, 63
   crossover primary 27
   evolution 26
   general election 27, 67
   general process 25–26
   going viral 78
   historical periods 29–32
      Brokered Convention period (1836–1968) 29, 30
      legislative caucus period (1800–1832) 29–30
      popular Choice period (1972–present) 29
   Hunt Commission 36–37
   hybrid contests 28
   Iowa & New Hampshire 34, 37–38, 42–43, 64
   loophole primary 36, 37
   McGovern-Fraser Commission 32, 33–34, 36, 213n1
   media influence 43, 44
   minimum threshold 37
   national nominating convention 28, 30
   nomination stage 27–28
   open primary 27, 63
   political scandal 150
   primary 27, 37–38, 40, 41
   Republican reforms 39
   role of the Internet 79–80
      bloggers 79
   semiclosed primary 27, 63
   super delegates 36–37, 38, 39
   Super Duper Tuesday 38, 42
   system changes 34–35, 35–39
   TV influence 30, 31–32, 76–80
      earned media 76–77, 78
      "Little Girl with the Daisy" 77–78
      negative advertising 78
      news networks 79
      paid media 76–77
   unit rule 34
Public policy 181–198

Rally Round the Flag Effect 150–151, 203
Reagan, Ronald
   approval rating 147
   Cold War 195
   Great Communicator 102
   Grenada 149
   honeymoon period 165
   imperiled presidency 18, 20
   Iran Contra Scandal 149
   judicial appointments 169–170, 171, 172–173
   nomination rule motion 54
   press refusal 143
   process of domestic policy 185
   strengthened presidency 202
   televised addresses 160
   trickle-down economics 191
Red & Blue States 68
Reelection of Congress 155–159
Reelection of president 155, 159
Reorganization Act of 1939 106
Republican Party 74, 190
   contract with America 156
Rice, Condeleezza 108, 196
Romney, George 110, 122
Roosevelt, Franklin
   1934 midterm elections 155
   attempted judicial appointments 168–169
   Brownlow Commission 16–17
   competitive advisor style 104
   creation of EOP 181
   evolution of the presidential advisory system 106–107
   four electoral victories 9
   imperial presidency 16–17
   pack the court scheme 14, 17, 179, 212n3
      Adkins v. Children's Hospital 17
      Justice Owen Roberts 17
      West Coast Hotel v. Parrish 17
   press conferences 140
   public works 16
   response to Great Depression 183
   revenue & expenditure decisions 187
   Stewardship Presidency 14
Roosevelt, Theodore
   1912 convention 57
   Bully Pulpit 189
   campaign finance reform 46
   stewardship presidency 14

Index

Secret Service protection 10
Senate
  checks on the president 7, 8
  executive appointments 88, 188
  investigative power 5
  judicial appointments – confirmation process 172–173
Shay's Rebellion 4
Special envoys 11
Stanton, Edwin 163–164
Stare decisis 171–172
State Department 105, 108, 130, 182, 196
Supreme Court
  appointments 168–169
  Brown v. Board of Education 176
  Bush v. Gore 203
  checks on the president 20, 177
  confirmation process 172–173
  defining presidential boundaries 176, 177
  factors in making nominations 170–172
  Hamdan v. Rumsfield 179
  Hylton v. U.S. 174
  independent judiciary 175
  INS v. Chadha 194
  Marbury v. Madison 174
  other roles for justices 173–174
  powers 5
    impeachment 164
  presidential appointments 7, 168
  relationship with Congress 175–176
  relationship with president 175–176
  Roosevelt's packing the Court *see* Roosevelt, Franklin, pack the court scheme
  setting own agenda 174
  writ of certiorari 174

Taft, Robert
  1952 Republican convention 58
Taft, William Howard
  1912 election 57
  passive-positive 95, 97
  strict constructionist 14, 21
Term limits 9
Thatcher, Margaret 150
A Thousand Days (Arthur Schlesinger) 125–126
Thurmond, Strom 58
Treasury department 105, 184, 189, 196

Truman, Harry 6, 17, 97, 99–100, 177, 183
  domestic policy making 183
  steel mill strike 177
Tyler, John 86–87

Unitary executive 207–208

Veto patterns 161–162
Vice president 83–90
  animosity in the office 85–86
  constitutional duties 86–87
  constitutional duties 86–87
  creation of office 84–85
  extraconstitutional duties 87–88
  order of succession 86–87, 88–89
  positives of the office 89–90
Views of the presidency 13–14
  prerogative presidency 14, 17, 21
  public presidency 14
  stewardship presidency 14
  strict constructionist presidency 14

Wallace, George 32
War Powers Act 8, 194–195, 229n20
Warren Commission 174
Warren, Earl 171, 174
Washington, George
  passive-negative 96
  precedents established 15
  role of Supreme Court in presidency 173
  two term limit precedent 9
Weber, Max 117–118
Whig Party 86–87
White House 10
  Office of Public Engagement 109
White House Press Secretary 139
Wigoda, Paul 40
William, Clinton
  honeymoon period 165
  national health insurance reform 156, 160
Wilson, James 4, 69
Wilson, Woodrow
  Federal Reserve Act of 1913 188–189
  formal press conference 143, 144
  public presidency 14
Winograd Commission *see* Commission on Presidential Nomination and Party Structure
World War II 14, 17, 108, 197

Printed in the United States of America